CHALLENGES FOR EDUCATIONAL RESEARCH

New BERA Dialogues

The BERA Dialogues series was created by the British Educational Research Association in order to facilitate the publication of collections of high quality educational research papers on particular themes. Paul Chapman Publishing took over publication of the series – New BERA Dialogues – for BERA in 1995. To be included in the series, collections should normally meet the criteria of

(a) being internally coherent, with all the papers addressing a clearly identified theme;

(b) consisting of scholarly papers, with at least most of those in any collection being of a standard that would make them acceptable to leading journals such as the *British Educational Research Journal*;

(c) being of interest to the international educational research community.

Among appropriate starting points for editions of Dialogues can be collections of papers delivered at a BERA Day Conference or in a symposium at the BERA Annual Conference. While most collections in the series have been of papers reporting research, not all editions need be of that kind. For example, collections of papers debating methodological, political or ethical issues in educational research could be highly appropriate for the series.

Paul Chapman Publishing meet annually with the series editor, currently Donald McIntyre, to agree on a set of new editions which will meet the above criteria and which will be commercially viable. Donald McIntyre (School of Education, University of Cambridge) or Marianne Lagrange of PCP welcome suggestions for additions to the series from potential editors.

CHALLENGES FOR EDUCATIONAL RESEARCH

edited by
Jean Rudduck
and
Donald McIntyre

New BERA Dialogues

Paul Chapman
Publishing Ltd

Selection and editorial material © Copyright 1998
Jean Rudduck and Donald McIntyre.
Chapter 1 © Copyright 1998 Jean Rudduck
Chapter 2 © Copyright 1998 John Gray
Chapter 3 © Copyright 1998 Stewart Ranson
Chapter 4 © Copyright 1998 Caroline Gipps
Chapter 5 © Copyright 1998 David Hamilton
Chapter 6 © Copyright 1998 David Bridges
Chapter 7 © Copyright 1998 Michael Bassey
Chapter 8 © Copyright 1998 Michael Beveridge
Chapter 9 © Copyright 1998 David Hargreaves
Chapter 10 © Copyright 1998 Seamus Hegarty
Chapter 11 © Copyright 1998 Roger Murphy
Chapter 12 © Copyright 1998 Peter Hannon
Chapter 13 © Copyright 1998 Sally Brown and Wynne Harlen
Chapter 14 © Copyright 1998 Rosemary Deem
Chapter 15 © Copyright 1998 Donald McIntyre

First published 1998

Paul Chapman Publishing Ltd
A SAGE Publications Company
6 Bonhill Street
London EC2A 4PU

SAGE Publications Inc
2455 Teller Road
Thousand Oaks, California 91320

SAGE Publications India Pvt Ltd
32, M-Block Market
Greater Kailash - I
New Delhi 110 048

British Library Cataloguing in Publication data

A catalogue record for this book is available from the British Library

ISBN 1 85396-441-7
ISBN 1 85396-442-5 (pbk)

Printed and bound in Great Britain

CONTENTS

Section 2

Responses to Section 2

Overviews

THE CONTRIBUTORS

Michael Bassey, Professor of Education (Emeritus), University of Nottingham Trent, and Academic Secretary, British Educational Research Association

Michael Beveridge, Professor of Education, University of Bristol

David Bridges, Professor, School of Education and Professional Development, and Pro-Vice-Chancellor, University of East Anglia

Sally Brown, Professor of Education and Deputy Principal, University of Stirling

Rosemary Deem, Professor of Educational Research and Dean of Social Science, University of Lancaster

Caroline Gipps, Professor and Dean of Research, Institute of Education, University of London

John Gray, Professor and Director of Research at Homerton College, Cambridge

David Hamilton, Professor of Education, University of Umea, Sweden (until recently, Professor of Education, University of Liverpool)

Peter Hannon, Professor in the Division of Educational Studies, University of Sheffield

David Hargreaves, Professor of Education, University of Cambridge

Seamus Hegarty, Director of the National Foundation for Educational Research

Wynne Harlen, Director of the Scottish Council for Educational Research

Donald McIntyre, Professor and Head of the School of Education, University of Cambridge

Roger Murphy, Professor and Dean of Education, University of Nottingham

Stewart Ranson, Professor of Education, University of Birmingham

Jean Rudduck, Professor and Director of Research at Homerton College, Cambridge

GENERAL EDITOR'S PREFACE

This is an especially appropriate book for the New BERA Dialogues series. It reflects and pursues a very serious and sharp debate among British educational researchers about the state of their profession and about the future which should be sought. The early stages of the debate focus primarily on the difficult question of what we should be doing educational research on: what should be the priority themes? what have we been neglecting? This leads on however to a range of other questions, among the most important of which are questions about the usefulness of educational research: is it useful enough? is it worth the money spent on it? and, if not, why not? And, in order to answer these evaluative questions, the more fundamental question is necessarily raised of how we should expect educational research to be useful; and it is around that fundamental question that the debate tends to be fiercest.

Important and helpful parts of the debate relate too to the relationship between educational research and research in other areas. Should educational research be useful in the same ways as medical or engineering research, and how in fact does it compare with research in these areas? Should educational research not be making use of the most penetrating new developments in the various social sciences, and if it should but isn't, why not?

However, the debate is not limited to the academic plane, because it directly concerns matters of great political importance for educational research: who should decide what research is to be done and who should do it? how should these decisions be made? how should research be funded? The political context is that the organisation and funding of educational research in Britain may well change quite substantially, for better or for worse, because of positions taken on the matters debated in this book.

The political debate, like the academic one, is far from over; but the questions that will continue to be debated are those that are raised in this book.

Donald McIntyre

Introduction

1

EDUCATIONAL RESEARCH: THE PROSPECT OF CHANGE. . .

Jean Rudduck

. . . the prospect of change now seems to be perpetually present, as both promise and threat . . . What is now necessary is 'neither a return to the alleged virtues of the past nor a simple revival of the approaches of the present, . . . but a change in perspective, in the frame of mind with which we approach things.
(Smart, 1992, p. 1, quoting Dahrendorf, 1975)

Educational researchers seem to be prone to bouts of collective uncertainty about the status and identity of educational research. But at the moment what may look like a recurrence of nagging self-doubt is in fact a justifiable and potentially constructive attempt, across countries and continents, to re-examine structures, directions and relationships in the light of fundamental changes in aspirations for education and in its system of governance.

EDUCATIONAL RESEARCH: SOME COMMON CONCERNS

Reports of two major reviews of educational research, completed in the early 1990s, were fairly widely discussed in the UK. *Educational Research in Australia* was initiated by the Australian Research Council (ARC) which had encouraged pivotal reviews of research in several key areas; this, the second in the series, was published in 1992. *Educational Research and Development* was commissioned by the Council for CERI (Centre for Educational Research and Innovation) which has a long-term commitment to looking at the means and ends of improving the knowledge base for educational practice and policy-making. The report, published in 1995, marks the end of the first phase of the CERI inquiry. The two reports are discussed briefly here to provide a broader context for the debate in the UK. There are clearly some common concerns.

The CERI report

The CERI report, *Educational Research and Development*, with its edgy, wide-open subtitle, *Trends, Issues and Challenges*, was prompted in part by the recognition that the contribution of educational R & D to the improvement of practice had been somewhat disappointing. When educational research is driven by a commitment to improvement, policy-makers and consumers want to know whether the investment was well judged. As James Calderhead said in his address to the European Conference on Educational Research (1996, p. 4), 'With such large sums of public funding being devoted to education, one might reasonably argue that we need evidence of what is happening in education'. But the CERI report also noted that investment in R & D tends to be 'far lower' in education 'than in any other sector of comparable size' (1995, p. 9).

The report reflects the view that confidence in educational research weakened after the 1970s. The return on investment was judged to be disappointing but also researchers were thought by policy-makers to be preoccupied with their own internecine academic feuds – although these may have been the attacks and counterattacks that accompany any fundamental shift of ground in an established field, for at this time researchers were struggling with the emergence of new, and often more democratic, modes of inquiry. The battles were a necessary part of moving forward but they made educational research look, to the outside world, 'fragmented and politicised'. The CERI report (*ibid.*, p. 20) comments: 'This state of instability and disarray, which lasted for several years, did little to keep consumers' faith in the trustworthiness and applicability of the knowledge and insights produced by the various camps of educational researchers'.

But if there was a loss of confidence in research, it could be argued that the problems were as much – if not more – about the *organisation* and *funding* of educational research as about the practices of researchers. We have seen in recent years how the convenience of a 'blame culture' has been taken up by politicians. Researchers can easily be used as the fall guys for the failures of policy and the CERI report (*ibid.*, p. 15) is cautious in its interpretation of the causes of the 'crisis of confidence': 'It is an open question whether or not this critical perspective on the nature and value of educational research is fully justified.' Indeed, a contributory factor to the shortfall in achievement may well have been the intractability of educational institutions – the tenacity of their regimes in the face of even the most substantial and challenging initiatives for change.

However in the 1990s, says the CERI report, there was a revival of interest throughout the OECD and in individual countries, and a 'renewed faith in the power [of research and development] to advance social and educational ends' (*ibid.*, p. 21). Thus, the report urges, the 'crisis of confidence' in educational research should not be seen as a destructive force but as having served a useful purpose in bringing about change. It provoked self-evaluation and critical reflection in the research community. It stimulated governments to examine ways to channel funds and to make the research systems 'more efficient and effective in contributing to the knowledge base for policy-making and practice' (*ibid.*, p. 26). And it helped to focus attention on the 'future directions of the research agenda'.

The ARC review

The starting point for the Australian review was the feeling that 'educational research had lost focus and impetus' (1992, p. iii). Educational researchers in Australia (as in Europe) 'were frustrated by a perceived lack of support' (from both government agencies and higher education); indeed, the review team judged that the funds available for education research were low 'relative to the size of the education sector and relative to other fields' (*ibid.*, p. x) – a comment echoed in the CERI report. Researchers, policy-makers and practitioners, from their different perspectives, thought that insufficient attention had been given to the dissemination of research findings (policy-makers and practitioners also claimed that much research was irrelevant to their interests); there was general agreement that, for a host of complex and inter-related reasons, research tended to be poorly co-ordinated and thinly spread.

Like the CERI document, this report emphasises the importance of constructing a common agenda for research, of ensuring continuity in developing the knowledge base, and of facilitating collaboration at all stages of the research effort. For example, recognising the 'increasing scope and complexity of educational issues' it suggests that teams of researchers should 'work together in a sustained way upon larger issues' (*ibid.*) and should show 'a mix of skills, disciplinary perspectives and collaboration with education practitioners' (*ibid.*, p. xv).

The report is constructive in its desire to develop 'a picture of where research in the discipline should be in ten to fifteen years time' (*ibid.*, p. iii) and it offers two sets of criteria to guide practice in determining the priorities. The criteria make clear that 'the focus in setting priorities should be on key issues and questions in education and not on the disciplines on which the research might draw' (*ibid.*, p. xi). Three criteria relate to the *application, use* and *benefits* of research:

- social and economic needs;
- equity and social justice; and
- the needs of professional practice.

The other criteria relate to the *needs* of educational research:

- the need to preserve and capitalise on existing research strengths;

- the need to contribute to and capitalise on advances in research; and
- the need to remedy important gaps and weaknesses in research (*ibid.*).

The report argues the case for a set of priorities that would guide 'the national educational research effort' and that would hold for a minimum period of three years and then be reviewed 'on a rolling triennial basis' (*ibid.*). It also recommended that the procedures by which such priorities are established should be 'as broadly based as possible and be subject to periodic review' (*ibid.*, p. xv). The priorities identified in 1992, when the review was published, were these (and it is interesting to compare them with the priorities identified by the working party set up in the UK by the Economic and Social Research Council (ESRC) which reported at about the same time):

- Fundamental research on areas of continuing importance to education and the improvement of professional practice:
  - teaching of thinking skills;
  - learning in the preschool and adult years; and
  - assessment of student learning.

- Research on the organisation and management of educational structures, programmes and personnel, and the inter-relationship between education and the wider society:
  - leadership and management in devolved education systems;
  - education, training and work; and
  - teachers' work.

- Research directed towards the revision and improvement of specific areas of the curriculum:
  - mathematics education;
  - science education; and
  - language and literacy education.

In short, the review, *Educational Research in Australia*, sought to identify, to use its own words, 'new, clear and widespread agreement on directions for the future' (*ibid.*, p. iii).

PROGRESS IN EDUCATIONAL RESEARCH

Both reports point to evidence of the 'considerable strengthening' of public perceptions of educational research in recent years and they identify achievements in particular areas that have helped to restore its standing: for example, research into influences on student participation in education; research into issues of education and inequality; research into the history, management and organisation of education. But where the reports mainly emphasise *substantive* achievements, it is important to acknowledge also the *procedural* and *epistemological* achievements of the period. The skirmishes within the research community may have irritated policy-makers but they encouraged a new flexibility for educational research that allowed it to tackle complex problems in different and often more appropriate ways – and they also paved the way for a dramatic broadening of the constituency of educational research.

Educational research has come a long way in a short time. The British Educational Research Association (BERA) was launched in 1974 and its first president, Professor John Nisbet, said that only in the last ten years had educational research established itself as an area in its own right. He recalled that when he started to teach educational research the textbooks he inherited were Burt's *Mental and Scholastic Tests*, Whipple's *Manual of Mental and Physical Tests* and Vernon's *The Measurement of Abilities*: indeed, psychometrics *was* educational research. BERA grew out of an informal interest group launched by Edgar Stones and others which was joined by an increasing number of people who wanted something different: 'to reach across established boundaries and find new ways of thinking about and conducting research in education' (Simon, 1978, p. 2).

The curriculum development movement, which flourished in the 1970s and early 1980s, contributed in a direct way to the necessary destabilisation of dominant ways of thinking about purposes and practices in research. A number of us, myself included, have careers that, as Barry MacDonald said, 'were carved out of the opportunity structure that opened up as the innovation industry recast the credentials of personal advance' (1991, p. 5). We were 'plucked from nowhere by an unsystematic trawling procedure' (*ibid.*) which used long nets to catch its aspiring recruits, and we 'hooked ourselves', like William Morris a hundred years before, 'on to the practical movement' (Briggs, 1962, p. 36). When the curriculum development movement came to an end, the expectation was that we would be put back into the sea and swim back to our old spawning grounds in primary and secondary schools, but instead many of us turned tail and established what Barry calls 'beachheads of an unfamiliar kind' in departments of education in colleges and universities, under the banner of curriculum studies, school and classroom studies and, of course, evaluation. This group of aliens, he said, with characteristic self-deprecation, had to invent a research they could do – and they indulged in 'unholy methodological improvisation' of a mainly qualitative nature (with such labels as 'illuminative evaluation'). But in fact qualitative researchers took strength from the traditions of historical research and social anthropology, and they steadily gained ground while trying to evade total capture by what Philip Jackson (1990, p. 154) calls 'the ancient bugaboos' of research.

So, paradigms have shifted over the past thirty years and, as Huberman said, 'When the paradigm shifts, one of our roles as researchers is to chase after it' (1996, p. 127). Interpretive approaches challenged assumptions about the construction of knowledge and opened up a path for action research, for case-study research, for holistic and democratic forms of evaluation, and for feminist research. The pursuit of criteria for recognising quality across the different landscapes of educational research continues, and rightly so. Audiences have also shifted. Consumer/user groups now have a more prominent position in the research enterprise – and teachers have a dual nationality passport: they can be both practitioners of teaching and practitioners of research. Indeed, applied researchers who, fifteen years ago, were uncomfortable about acknowledging their interest in research which improved practice are now not only out of the closet but also finding their commitment nationally endorsed.

Similar developments are recorded in other countries. Huberman (like Nisbet, earlier) reminds us how far we have come over the last thirty-odd years. In the early days of educational research, he says, 'researchers' paradigms [were] deliberately designed to perpetuate the sense of powerlessness of those in the teaching profession and thereby extend researchers' hegemony on the conduct of "scientific" studies of teaching, learning and policy' (1996, p. 126). But, he goes on, 'the teacher-research movement in the US now has enough momentum to qualify as a mainstream perspective, a genuine contender for widespread epistemological and methodological acceptance'. And one of the benefits of teacher research is that it 'sometimes acts as a sort of "shadow" opposition party, a salutary role in restoring the balance of power' between researchers and user communities (*ibid.*, p. 129).

THE ORIGINS AND CONTEXT OF THE BOOK

The book grew out of a one-day conference organised by BERA to provide a forum for discussion of some recent relatively small-scale reviews of educational research in the UK. The ESRC had initiated two linked inquiries. First, it set up a working party in 1991, chaired by Professor John Gray, which was asked 'to review the position of research into education in the United Kingdom with a view to increasing the Council's knowledge of the particular problems facing educational research and its development over the next decade'. The draft report (*Frameworks and Priorities for Research in Education: Towards a Strategy for the ESRC*) was completed and circulated for comment in 1992 and a final version was presented to the Council of the ESRC in 1993.

Appended to the report was a paper on the organisation and management of educational research which the working party had commissioned. The author, Professor Stewart Ranson, was subsequently invited by the ESRC to take some of the issues further by organising a wider consultative debate. His report, *The Future of Education Research: Learning at the Centre*, was submitted to the ESRC in June 1995.

A further inquiry, a 'strategic review of educational research' commissioned by the Leverhulme Foundation, was conducted in 1995 by Professor David Hargreaves and Professor Michael Beveridge. Their remit was a wide one which included questions about the educational problems on which research was most needed, about the quality and use of educational research in the UK, and about its location, its users and its funding. Also included in this remit were questions about what educational research in the UK could learn from other countries, from research in other professional fields and from the social sciences.

In May 1996, these four – Gray, Ranson, Beveridge and Hargreaves – were invited to present a summary of their observations at a conference on 'The Future of Educational Research' which was organised by BERA and held at Birkbeck College in London. The conference was attended by about 100 people, mainly from higher education. The presentations provoked strong reactions among those who were there (not least because all the speakers – a reflection of the pattern of sponsorship of the inquiries – were men). But whereas the waspish mood of the research community in the 1970s reflected its internal struggles over research methods, the unease of the mid-1990s was much more a concern about external threats.

There was a lot at stake, for the issues that were now being highlighted nationally included the funding of research in education, selectivity in the distribution of funds and procedures for establishing priorities for the research agenda – all issues that had been prefigured in the ARC and CERI reports.

There was a feeling that governments had, when it was politically expedient to do so, sought to side-step the guidance on education policy that the education research community could provide. Then there was the issue, highlighted in the CERI and ARC reports, of the process by which, and the arena in which, priorities for the national education research agenda could be identified and agreed – an issue that is also addressed in the reviews of educational research supported by the ESRC and the Leverhulme Foundation.

There was also some unease about the criticism of educational research (expressed also in the ARC and CERI reports) on grounds of fragmentation and lack of cumulation. James Calderhead (1996, p. 5), in his presidential address to the European Educational Research Association conference, takes up this issue: 'Much educational research is being pursued by individuals or small groups, sometimes unaware of similar research being pursued elsewhere. The research lacks co-ordination, and because much research is relatively small-scale and pursued in a variety of different contexts, its conclusions are often contradictory.' In the UK researchers felt that the situation had been made worse by the pressures of the centrally imposed Research Assessment Exercise (RAE) which had led departments of education to prioritise research that has short-term goals rather than research that builds longer-term, cumulative understandings. It had also, to some extent, created a climate of competitive individualism rather than easy collaboration. And it had led to a proliferation of outlets for publication as though publication itself rather than the impact of ideas on structures of thinking and practice is what matters. The RAE casts a long shadow but its virtue is that it has put research firmly on the agenda.

The issues of selectivity – whether, to avoid fragmentation and to ensure work of a consistently high quality, funding for research should be given to a small number of highly rated departments – were undoubtedly sharpened by the operation of the RAE. This issue was particularly sensitive given the fairly recent translation into 'universities' of other HE institutions whose research record was less strong than that of most universities where research had traditionally been given more emphasis and support.

There was also some parochial and sharply focused irritation with the ambitions of the fairly recently established Teacher Training Agency (TTA) which had endorsed the view that educational researchers were out of touch with and negligent of the needs and interests of practitioners – a position that could less easily have been challenged some years back but that was now to a large extent out of date (see Murphy, 1996; Slavin, 1997). The TTA seemed to be using the technique perfected by Margaret Thatcher of giving a pseudo-democratic, commonsense appeal to policy proposals and in this way justifying stronger central intervention – a technique that Michael Apple (1993, p. 20) calls 'the restoration politics of authoritarian populism'. Its accusations about the higher education research community legitimised its policy to highlight *teacher* research. Research with and by teachers is something that many researchers in higher education have been supporting for a very long time (see Stenhouse, 1983; Huberman, 1996); it remains to be seen whether the TTA's 'version' of teacher research is robust enough both to empower teachers and to build new insight and understanding in significant areas of practice.

This then was the context in which the BERA conference took place. The research community was restless and had its usual problem of finding a public voice to respond to the issues that were in the air. What Huberman (1996, p. 124) had said of teacher researchers is in fact true of the research community as a whole: 'They evoke in my mind the bar scene in Star Wars, in which there is an unlikely assemblage of inhabitants from different planets who, as it happens, all like to drink.' The diversity of educational research is a source of strength and the last thing it needs is to be becalmed in a state of serene consensus but there are occasions when the 'community' needs to offer clear and definitive guidance about issues of organisation, funding and agenda-setting.

This book is an attempt to record, disseminate and extend the debate. The issues are still being explored and some strategy is still being sought that would enable the different constituencies (members of the research community, the various practitioner and user groups, and policy-makers) to move forward together and produce a plan for education research that would command a fair degree of support. As Seamus Hegarty (1996, p. 16) put it in his address later that year to mark the 50th anniversary of the NFER:

> The challenges facing us are to capitalise on our diversity while reducing the incoherence of present organisational arrangements, to invest in professional development despite the pressures on research budgets and deadlines, to insist on the public dimension of the work we carry out and, if these were not challenges enough, to find ways of working collaboratively within a competitive climate.

THE STRUCTURE OF THE BOOK

As editors, Donald and I decided to reproduce versions of the summary reports outlined at the conference and to invite some members of the research community (seven who were present at the conference and one who was not) to offer a personal commentary. In the interests of balance we asked four people to comment on the presentations of the ESRC-commissioned reports given by John Gray and Stewart Ranson, and four to comment on the presentations of the Leverhulme-commissioned report given by David Hargreaves and Mike Beveridge. (Each commentator was asked to limit him or herself to about 2,000 words.) We tried to ensure that each group of commentators would include people who seemed in sympathy and people who seemed to be more sceptical of the analysis and/or the proposals for moving forward. Because the four people who convened the inquiries were all men, and because we felt that an all-male view of the issues under scrutiny might be thought to be limited (acknowledging, however, that the consultations, discussions and working parties had included or canvassed the views of women as well as men) we asked Professor Rosemary Deem to look at and comment on the four presentations from a feminist perspective.

The relationship of the versions published here to the formal reports varies. None of them was published as such: the first was widely circulated but the other three were used mainly to inform the sponsoring bodies. John Gray, who was responsible for drafting the earliest of the four reports, offers a shortened verbatim version of the actual report, preceded by a commentary on its context and outcomes. Stewart Ranson also offers a shortened version of the actual report. The pieces by Mike Beveridge and David Hargreaves are elaborations of the presentations they made at the conference in May: written for this book – rather than being taken verbatim from their reports to their sponsors – they are more personally reflective in style.

Reflecting the logic of chronology, the summaries of the two ESRC reports are presented first, followed by the four commentaries – from Michael Bassey, David Bridges, Caroline Gipps and David Hamilton. Then come the two parts of the Leverhulme report, followed by the four commentaries – from Sally Brown and Wynne Harlen (writing jointly), Peter Hannon, Seamus Hegarty and Roger Murphy. Rosemary Deem's commentary follows. Donald McIntyre agreed to write the concluding section.

REFERENCES

Apple, M. W. (1993) *Official Knowledge: Democratic Education in a Conservative Age*, New York and London, Routledge.

Australian Research Council (1992) *Educational Research in Australia*, Canberra, Australian Government Publishing Service. (The report was written by the members of the Review Panel: Barry McGaw, David Boud, Millicent Poole, Richard Warry and Phillip McKenzie.)

Calderhead, J. (1996) Europeanisation of educational research, *EERA Bulletin*, Vol. 2, no. 3, pp. 3–8.

CERI (1995) *Educational Research and Development: Trends, Issues and Challenges*, Paris, OECD. (The report was 'prepared principally' by Maurice Kogan and Albert Tuijnam.)

Hegarty, S. (1996) Educational research in context. Opening address to the conference to mark the 50th anniversary of the National Foundation for Educational Research.

Huberman, M. (1996) Moving mainstream: taking a closer look at teacher research, *Language Arts*, Vol. 73, February, pp. 124–40.

Jackson, P. W. (1990) Looking for trouble: the place of the ordinary in educational studies, in E. W. Eisner and A. Peshkin (eds.) *Qualitative Inquiry in Education: The Continuing Debate*, New York and London, Teachers' College Press, Columbia University.

MacDonald, B. (1991) Critical introduction: from innovation to reform – a framework for analysing change, in J. Rudduck (ed.) *Innovation and Change*, Milton Keynes, Open University Press.

McGaw, B., Kogan, M. and Tuijnman, A. (1996) Educational R & D in OECD countries, *EERA Bulletin*, Vol. 2, no. 1, pp. 3–12.

Morris, W. (1894) How I became a socialist, *Justice*, 16 June. (Reprinted in A. Briggs (ed.) (1962) *William Morris: Selected Writings and Designs*, London, Penguin Books, p. 36.)

Murphy, R. (1996) Our agenda is firmly rooted in classrooms, *The Times Educational Supplement*, 28 June, p. 15.

Nisbet, J. (1974) Educational research: the state of the art, *Proceedings of the Inaugural Meeting of the British Educational Research Association*, pp. 1–13.

Simon, B. (1978) Educational research: which way?, *British Educational Research Journal*, Vol. 4, no. 1, pp. 2–7. (Presidential address to the annual conference of the British Educational Research Association, 1977.)

Slavin, R. E. (1997) Design competitions: a proposal for a new federal role in educational research and development, *Educational Researcher*, Vol. 26, no. 1, pp. 22–8.

Smart, B. (1992) *Modern Conditions, Postmodern Controversies*, London, Routledge.

Stenhouse, L. A. (1983) Research as a basis for teaching, in *Authority, Education and Emancipation*, London, Heinemann Educational Books. (The chapter reproduces the text of Lawrence Stenhouse's inaugural lecture at the University of East Anglia in 1979.)

Stones, E. (1985) The development of the British Educational Research Association, *British Educational Research Journal*, Vol. 11, no. 2, pp. 85–90.

Teacher Training Agency (1996) *Teaching as a Research-Based Profession*, London, TTA Information Section.

Section
One

2

AN EPISODE IN THE DEVELOPMENT OF EDUCATIONAL RESEARCH

John Gray

Editor's note: A slightly shortened version of the ESRC working party's report (which was completed in 1993) follows this introductory note by the chair of the working party. In it he outlines its origins and comments on some of the outcomes.

In 1991 I found myself chairing a working party for the ESRC with a brief to review research in education. In the background was a feeling amongst some senior decision-makers at the ESRC that, before they could commit more resources to initiatives in education, they needed to have a clearer sense of where the field was heading and what it had been achieving. As someone put it, 'Ideally you will come up with *a couple of ideas* which have the *full support* of the educational community'. There was also a vague sense, never properly articulated, that educational research was not delivering and might need treatment.

The working party was given some formal terms of reference but the central challenges were clear enough. The potential rewards were also fairly obvious: the ESRC's backing for initiatives started at around one million pounds.

THE WORKING PARTY'S APPROACH

The working party had twelve members (seven men and five women). The ESRC assumed that its members would be familiar with how it worked, which meant, in practice, that they would mostly have to be drawn from across its various committees. I was anxious, however, that at least a few 'users' of research should be recruited: a chief education officer, an HMI from the Scottish Office and another from the (then) DES. Everyone recognised, however, that our efforts would be judged primarily by researchers in other social science disciplines – not by policy-makers and practitioners.

From an early stage rumours abounded about what the group was *really* up to. I took some comfort from the discovery that similar reviews had been going on in Australia and the USA. However, I also remember feeling that the task of boiling down the entire educational research agenda to just 'a couple of areas' which demanded initiatives was going to be problematic. It was going to be even less easy to persuade other social scientists that these ideas were sufficiently at the 'cutting-edge' to be given priority over their own concerns.

There were many respects in which the frequently repeated suggestion that educational research was somehow a poor relation at the ESRC's table simply didn't add up. The amounts of funding educational researchers were securing were fairly modest but one could scarcely argue that they were being starved. There were several research initiatives. There was a designated research centre, although this was fairly small by the ESRC's standards. And crucially, in the single arena (the Research Grants Board) where all the social sciences were treated on an equal and competitive footing, educational researchers were undoubtedly holding their own. In short, on most counts educational research was getting its dues. There was one respect, however, in which the whole picture was skewed. Most of the initiatives in education had been relatively small scale; a new and well funded one would make a sizeable difference.

Reaching consensus within the working party proved difficult. Consultations with a range of other groups increased the number of potential initiatives to some thirty. Eventually the working party winnowed the thirty areas down to eleven. The challenge of reducing them still further, however, proved too much. The group decided that it was not its job to determine which particular one(s) should be put forward for funding. They merely expressed the hope that, by one means or another, the ESRC would take steps to support substantial parts of their agenda.

THE EMERGING ARENA

The working party submitted its draft report. Not surprisingly, the ESRC decided that the next step should be to put the draft out for consultation to the educational community. This took somewhat longer to arrange than I had imagined and the initial list had some rather odd omissions; neither of the two major headteachers' unions, for example, was originally included.[1] Eventually, however, the exercise was completed satisfactorily and over 100 replies were received, an unexpectedly large response.

I read all the replies. Some 'users' of educational research expressed surprise that the ESRC had bothered to consult them but most were undoubtedly pleased that they had done so. Naturally, some respondents regretted that the working party had lacked the wisdom or foresight to prioritise their favoured neck of the woods and others were not particularly complimentary about some of the details. Quite a few had missed the point that the proposals were primarily directed at areas in which new initiatives were required with the result that arguments for topics which were, in the working party's view, already well researched were repeated.[2] Two leading researchers penned separate critiques questioning, in one case, whether the proposals were sufficiently novel and, in the other, whether different starting points and orientations would have resulted in different conclusions. Overall, however, the general consensus was that the working party had got it about right.

Meanwhile events had been moving on at the ESRC. The committee which had commissioned the review (and which consequently best understood the nature of its remit) would soon be having its last meeting; there seemed little point in putting the report on their final agenda. The new super-committee which was replacing it seemed a better bet (although they would not be as familiar with the context). Other social science disciplines were also wondering, sometimes out loud, why educational research was so special that it required its own review. There were other changes afoot at the ESRC as well. The ESRC's Council had initiated a programme of strategic reviews of some of the disciplines it funded. Did they have a prototype in the working party's report?

One of the reasons for such strategic reviews was to facilitate communication with potential users of research. In one of those twists which are difficult to anticipate the 'users of educational research' who were actually consulted were not those in the mainstream of education such as teachers and LEA officers. The ESRC branch responsible for business liaison had some funds available and volunteered them to probe the *business* community's reactions to the working party's report. Not altogether surprisingly, this group of users liked some of the proposals rather more than others. In particular, they warmed to the suggestion that there should be an initiative on 'Lifelong Education and Training'.

SOME OUTCOMES

So what happened as a result of the working party and what, if anything, was achieved?

First, I think a much stronger sense was developed amongst a number of important constituencies, at the ESRC and elsewhere, that educational researchers did have a sizeable agenda which was capable of commanding considerable support.

Secondly, there was clear evidence (probably for the first time) that educational research should *not* be considered as 'a suitable case for treatment'. Unlike management studies, which lagged behind at that time on most of the ESRC's indicators of research performance, it was achieving at the same levels as many other social science disciplines.

Thirdly, the case was accepted that there should be further initiatives in education. About a year after the working party had reported, the groundwork for 'The Learning Society' initiative commenced. By the standards of some earlier initiatives in education it was quite handsomely funded.

Fourthly, even though ten of the eleven areas had not benefited directly from initiative funding, some three years later it was clear that educational researchers had succeeded in securing ESRC support, albeit on a more modest scale, in almost all of them.

There were some other areas where the working party also recommended action. In relation to educational policy-makers it proposed, for example, that the ESRC should 'take the initiative in establishing better liaison with other major funding bodies' including the DES. Progress on this front was, however, relatively slow until the recent amalgamation of the Departments of Employment and Education into the DfEE. A specific and related recommendation, drawing on developments in Scotland, was the suggestion that several 'policy forums' should be created to facilitate closer dialogues between researchers and potential users.[3] Developments on this front have to date been rather patchier although several groups of researchers have taken deliberate steps to involve practitioners in their discussions. Meanwhile other recommendations have met with varying fates which it has not always been possible to predict.[4]

Finally, the working party learnt that planning research is a difficult business. It solves some problems but creates others in its wake. Those who believe in the benefits of planning ignore this particular message at their peril.

NOTES

1. This is by no means the first occasion on which this sort of difficulty has emerged in relation to educational research. When the Universities Funding Council circulated the list of organisations it intended to consult about the criteria for assessing educational research in the second of its Research Assessment Exercises it included the British Psychological Association and the National Foundation for Educational Research but not the British Educational Research Association.

2. The teaching of reading and work on assessment came into this category.

3. The working party considered the proposal of the review group operating in Australia that a single national board could take on this function but preferred a more devolved approach.

4. Recently, for example, ESRC took up the suggestion that more attention should be given to summarising bodies of research rather than single studies; see Wallace and Weindling (1997).

THE REPORT:
Frameworks and Priorities for Research in Education: Towards a Strategy for the ESRC

John Gray, Paul Black, Sally Brown, Robert Burgess, Hilary Constable, Rosemary Deem, Rosalind Driver, Alan Gibson, Paul Light, Peter Mortimore, Roger Murphy, Andrew Pollard, Ann Phoenix, Ernest Spencer and Peter de Vries

Editor's note: The version of the working party's report presented here has been cut by John Gray, at the request of the editors, to around two-thirds of its original length. Cuts are marked by the symbol (. . .)

1 THE NEED FOR REVIEW

The study of education and educational institutions has been a longstanding concern of British social scientists. Nonetheless, there are several important reasons for taking stock at this time. First, we are living through a period of major educational reforms which will have significant effects over the coming decade; all sectors of the educational system are affected. Second, there have been substantial developments among some of the contributory disciplines, particularly with respect to increasing levels of conceptual and methodological sophistication. And third, there is heightened public interest in what and how well people of all ages are learning as well as the ways in which they are being educated and trained. (. . .)

The educational agenda is one of change and many educational systems are currently being restructured. Several OECD countries have been worried about the 'performance' of their educational systems. Such concerns have related not only to periods of formal schooling but to the post-compulsory sectors and the provision for training made by industrial companies. In Britain the debates have been particularly intense as the country has found itself in the lower half of various tables comparing national performances as well as achievements in certain subject areas. Given that the United Kingdom currently spends annually some £27 billion this concern is scarcely surprising. (. . .)

Defining the field

(. . .) Researchers carrying out work in education come from a wide variety of disciplinary backgrounds. Those with some previous experience of psychology and sociology have been especially prominent. Consequently they have frequently adopted the methods and paradigms used in these areas. Over the last thirty years, however, there has been an increasing tendency for research addressing educational issues to be seen as a specialist endeavour. This development is reflected in the extent to which significant numbers of academics now define themselves primarily as *educational* researchers. There are few characteristics of their modes of enquiry, however, that differ in any substance from the more general field of social science. Far from being a weakness, we believe this diversity of approach contributes strengths which enable researchers to match their perspectives, paradigms and theories to the nature of the problems they are studying.

Some areas of strength

We have not attempted to undertake a sustained review of all the important contributions researchers in education have made in recent years; our time and resources were too limited. There are several areas, however, in which British research has had demonstrable world-wide influence. These include (in no particular order) research on: Assessment, Science Education, the Development of Thinking and Learning, Special Educational Needs and School Effectiveness. These are all areas in which the ESRC and other sponsors have made sizeable investments over the past decade. The link between investment and influence is not coincidental. There are several other areas in which British studies have also been highly influential. If they currently fall short of world-wide influence it is probably because the investment has been too limited. Work on pre-school development, for example, falls into this category.

There are at least two methodological areas where the British contribution to the international research effort has been substantial. The first is in the development of qualitative approaches to data-gathering and analysis. The ESRC has indirectly supported this development through its willingness to fund a variety of projects using qualitative methodologies. British researchers have also been prominent in a second area variously described as 'teacher' or 'practitioner' research. This has involved different forms of action research in which practitioners have been collaborating partners. The direct contributions of research sponsors (including the ESRC) to this form of research have been rather limited. Most of the more recent work has stemmed from the efforts of lecturers in HE institutions, using their own research time, and from collaborative projects with local education authorities.

Improving the qualities of research

There are three key requirements for an area of research in the social sciences to sustain its vigour. It needs to develop strategies for promoting theoretical advancement; it needs to initiate ways of further improving its methodological contributions; and it needs to demonstrate some practical significance to the wider world. No single piece of research could, of course, be expected to fulfil all three requirements in equal measure. Taking a whole field of research, however, its general health is likely to depend on getting these various elements in balance.

The practical significance of much research in education is considerable; indeed, at the current time, this may well be the field's particular strength. Ideas drawn from research have, for example, informed much curriculum development and some aspects of assessment. In the areas of methodological improvement, however, there is more room for debate about the current contribution. There is growing awareness, for instance, of the need to improve the major methodologies being employed. A few examples will have to suffice. Many of the most interesting phenomena are best studied in 'real time'; longitudinal research designs (even of relatively short duration) are generally more powerful than cross-sectional ones. There is an important 'middle-level' of generalisations that can be informed by a combination of qualitatively and quantitatively-oriented strategies. Efforts to experiment with and implement change programmes offer fertile grounds for research. Such developments are, of course, costly. Furthermore, some methodological ingenuity is required to compress the time it takes children and young people to pass through the major educational institutions into the confines and constraints imposed by short-term funding.

There have been times in recent years when the development of theory has either been seen as unfashionable or been pushed off many researchers' agendas by the pressures of short-term, narrowly focused studies. Researchers in education need to keep abreast of developments elsewhere if they are to sustain the theoretical vigour of their enquiries and to impact, more generally, on the collective social science endeavour. As with all forms of science, if this aspect of the research process is neglected, empirical findings (no matter how important in themselves) will remain unconnected.

For the foreseeable future the greater preponderance of non-ESRC funding for research on education is likely to be for studies of an essentially applied and short-term nature. Ways must therefore be found for ensuring that as much theoretical benefit as possible can be gained from such work. (. . .)

Developing the infra-structure

How theoretically and methodologically sophisticated a field of enquiry can become depends, in substantial measure, on the way it is organised and the kinds of researchers it attracts and retains. Researchers in education have hitherto given relatively little systematic consideration to such questions, at least at the national level. We are, in fact, reluctant to recommend a particular structure for the whole field of educational enquiry in this country. Its eventual shape will be determined in large part by the various decisions of HE institutions rather than the ESRC and the plans that are currently being made to locate more initial teacher training in schools. We would anticipate, however, that a fairly broad base is needed, with several centres of excellence and a considerably larger number of groupings pursuing significant research agendas. For new ideas to flourish good inter-disciplinary and international links are required. Structures must also be created to ensure that new recruits are encouraged and enabled to develop high levels of theoretical and methodological expertise.

The current research capability in education is widely (some would say thinly) spread, a position that is shared in common with many other disciplines supported by the ESRC. The Australian review group mentioned earlier argued that, in order to make maximum use of the limited opportunities available, the national research effort needed to be 'guided by a set of priorities' which would be subject to periodic three-year review (ACER, 1991). (. . .) What we took from the lengthy Australian discussion was the point that attempts to inject a measure of coherence into the research effort can contribute to the efficiency and effectiveness with which resources are deployed.

Resources for research in education are in short supply. Indeed, given the scale of expenditure on education the resources currently committed to researching it are, by comparison, minute. The Australian report quoted an officially calculated figure of 0.35% of total expenditure and suggested that it should be doubled. We followed similar procedures in making estimates. We used up-to-date-evidence on the size of research grants and contracts and made generous assumptions about the size of the resources currently being committed (the 'research time' of all those in the education sectors of HE institutions being by far the biggest component). Nonetheless, we had some difficulty in producing estimates as high as 0.25% of total educational expenditure. By any yardstick the overall levels of support for research seem low, both in absolute and relative terms.

A role for the ESRC

Responsibility for ensuring the continuing development of research does not currently rest with any one organisation – nor could it. There are many partners to the process beyond those represented in the current and proposed funding arrangements for higher education. The ESRC's direct contribution to funding for research in education is comparatively modest. Through its policies and strategies, however, it is probably better placed than any other body to enhance the overall quality of the research being conducted. It is to some of the opportunities that this strategic role affords that the rest of this review is addressed.

2 THE ESRC's PORTFOLIO IN EDUCATION: BREADTH AND QUALITY

What kinds of topics are researchers in education currently pursuing with ESRC support? There is, of course, no specific allocation of funds for education or any other particular area of the social sciences; ideas and topics have been identified and supported on a competitive basis. Nonetheless, a broad range of concerns has emerged. Consequently the United Kingdom has a stake in many of the areas currently of international concern although the extent of that commitment is sometimes small.

Research grants

Over the period 1988–90 the Research Grants Board funded some fifty proposals relating to the area of education. These were selected from just under 190 that were submitted for consideration. The Board is entirely responsive – it funds what it (and its referees) deem to be the best proposals from those put forward in each round (. . .). There were numbers of projects in the fields of Instruction and Learning, Educational Governance/ Management, Educational Policy and Institutional Effectiveness. These groupings are, of course, rather broad ones. The full range of interests can only be grasped by reading a list of the full titles of individual projects.

Research initiatives

The Human Behaviour and Development Group has recently supported four initiatives of direct interest to researchers in education. Each has been multi-disciplinary, bringing together a variety of research interests. The 'National 16–19 Initiative', for example, involved psychologists, sociologists and educationists as well as researchers of both quantitative and qualitative persuasions. It looked at some of the ways in which young people's careers were structured and their identities shaped by the changing contexts of training and employment opportunities. A wide range of interests has also been represented in the initiative on 'Information Technology in Education' (InTER) in which a number of researchers already prominent in science education and cognitive science have been involved. (. . .)

Two other initiatives (on 'Multi-Cultural Education' and 'Adult Education & Training') have been more narrowly targeted, reflecting their smaller-scale funding. Each of these initiatives ended fairly recently or is currently in the process of doing so. Researchers in education are also prominently involved in carrying out research for the Training Board's current initiative on 'Postgraduate Training'. They have also had modest involvements in one or two other current ESRC-sponsored initiatives.

The 1988 Education Reform Act stimulated a considerable amount of research activity. The ESRC's main response was to launch an initiative on 'Innovation and Change: The Quality of Teaching and Learning'. The sustained focus of this initiative on 'quality' in a changing educational system is probably unique. Competition amongst researchers to participate was intense; only ten projects could be funded from amongst the 250 proposals which were originally submitted.

Research Centres

The ESRC is a partner, along with government departments, in supporting research in the Centre for Educational Sociology (CES) at Edinburgh University. The Centre has studied a wide range of issues including the transition from education to the youth labour market and aspects of school effectiveness. After a successful mid-term review, it has embarked upon its second period of funding. A new Centre focusing on Instruction, Training and Learning is about to begin at Nottingham University. These two centres are based, respectively, in departments of sociology and psychology, although at least in the case of the CES the range of interests involved is considerably wider than the institutional location might suggest.

We argued earlier that research in education is often multi-disciplinary in character and organisation. This seems to be borne out by the evidence from the ESRC's education portfolio (. . .) over two-thirds have been based in departments which are recognisably departments of education; the remainder have been undertaken by researchers from a variety of disciplinary backgrounds including psychologists, sociologists and economists. A number of these latter projects have involved collaboration with other departments including those in education. We envisage a similar pattern of contributions continuing for the foreseeable future.

The quality of proposals submitted to the Research Grants Board

It is clear from this review that there is no shortage of interest on the part of researchers in education in securing ESRC funding; indeed, competition for funds has clearly been intense and is likely to grow as polytechnics join the bidding process for research funds on a more routine basis (PCFC, 1990).

Substantial numbers of proposals from researchers in education are regularly put forward to the Research Grants Board. In each of the past three years there have been 60 or more. The best have stood comparison with those from virtually every area of the social sciences. Some others, however, have been highly speculative; methodologically imprecise; or simply duplicated work already being carried out elsewhere. At best these have indicated circumstances in which the applicants have been poorly informed about their prospects of research council funding. This is an issue which the research community must address. There has been a larger group of projects, however, which have presented different problems. These proposals have been deemed worthy of funding but have not received any (the so-called 'unfunded alphas'). Typically such proposals have scored highly in terms of their practical significance but only modestly in relation to the two other criteria which are used to judge proposals, namely their contributions to 'theoretical advancement' and to 'methodological improvement'.

Has the success of education proposals actually differed from that in other areas? Analysis for the last three years for which detailed information is available [shows that] the general position seems to have been broadly similar to the ESRC averages [table not shown]. The overall success rate was a little lower (at 27% compared with 30%) but the average financial value of projects funded was somewhat higher (£53k compared with £44k). Proposals from researchers in education made up 10% of all those submitted, 9% of those which were funded but around 11% in terms of total funds granted. The aggregate figures also mask some interesting trends. In 1988/89 the success rate of all proposals in Education fell to below two out of ten; in both 1989/90 and 1990/91 it rose to around three out of ten. Part of the reason for the improvement may have been that the total number of applications from researchers in education fell slightly in the second two years. However, even taking this into account, the overall success rate improved somewhat whilst the total overall sums allocated also increased considerably. Overall, the experience of the Research Grants Board would appear in recent years to suggest that proposals for research in education are broadly similar in quality to those received from across the whole gamut of social sciences.

Other forms of ESRC funding

Other forms of ESRC funding make a contribution to the portfolio of research in education although the Research Grants Board probably makes the major contribution. Several seminars on educational topics are being supported and small numbers of students receive ESRC studentships for research training, both at Masters and doctoral level [table not shown]. It has to be acknowledged, however, that with respect to one major source of ESRC funding (research centres) no proposal to date from a department of education has excited sufficient interest to secure funding. Since the ESRC plans to invest more of its resources in research centres over the next few years this is an issue to which the research community needs to address itself and to which we return in a later section.

3 STRENGTHENING THE FUNDING BASE

Who funds research in education? What sorts of sums are involved? And what kinds of general topics have been getting funded? An analysis was recently commissioned by the ESRC from the Centre for Higher Education Studies (CHES) at the London Institute of Education. It looked at all the various sources of external funding for social science (CHES, 1991). Some caution must be exercised in interpreting the results, because they are confined to one year only (1988/89), but the findings are nonetheless instructive. Preliminary figures for another year suggest broadly similar patterns.

The survey estimated that around £16m was spent on research in education during 1988/89 [table not shown]. In interpreting this sizeable total, the fairly broad view of what was counted as 'research' needs to be recognised; some monitoring and evaluation activities as well as aspects of curriculum development were included. Of the total the ESRC, through its various activities, contributed £1.15m (around 7% of the total).

How did these figures compare with other areas? The CHES study provides some general indications of the orders of magnitude although we suspect the precise figures should not be interpreted too literally. The ESRC's contribution was at the lower end, when compared with the various other areas of social science it supports, but not markedly so. The significance of these sums cannot be properly gauged, however, without placing the ESRC's resources within the broader context of the overall levels of resources being devoted to the different subject areas under its remit.

The nature of the research receiving funding

The CHES survey tried to allocate all the projects it considered to one of three main categories according to whether the research was judged to be of a fundamentally 'basic', 'strategic' or 'applied' nature. Around a third (34%) of all funding for research in education was categorised as being for Basic/Strategic purposes. Within this, the proportion of ESRC funds judged to be for research of a Basic/Strategic nature was around two-thirds (63%).

How do these figures compare with other areas of the social sciences? One way of gaining some purchase on this question is to compare research on Education with research on Health and Welfare. In terms of the sheer volume of research funds both Education, at around £16m, and Health and Welfare, at around £11.5m, outstripped the other areas under ESRC's auspices [table not shown]. The total funding currently secured from the ESRC was fairly similar for the two areas, with Education at £1.15m compared with £1.36m for Health and Welfare. Both areas also spent roughly similar proportions of ESRC funds on Basic/Strategic research. The major difference between the two areas emerged in relation to the proportions of the total research effort devoted to Basic/Strategic research; Health and Welfare spent double the proportion in Education. Even acknowledging the difficulties underlying attempts to characterise research as being of one kind or another, it is difficult to avoid the conclusion that the effort in Education devoted to research of a Basic/Strategic kind has been on the low side.

The main areas being funded

The CHES survey attempted to classify the general areas within which research on education was being conducted; eleven categories were used. These were: Pre-School, Primary Education, Learning Processes & Methods, Teaching Methods, Curriculum, Exams & Assessment, Humanities, Science Education, Further & Higher Education, Organisation & Resources, and Education & Training for the Disabled. The somewhat rough-and-ready nature of this classification needs to be recognised. Of the areas listed, however, just two accounted for around two-thirds of the total funding – Exams & Assessment and Further & Higher Education. Both these areas have, of course, been especially prominent amongst recent government reforms.

The total amounts of funding recorded for the other areas of research on education were modest, both in absolute and relative terms. None received as much as 10% of the total. For example, Science Education, which is an area in which Britain's international research strengths are widely recognised, received a total of around £860k during the year; this represented about 8% of the total. Primary Education as a whole, by comparison, was underpinned by around £250k or just over two per cent. The general messages are clear. Overall funding for research on education has been highly concentrated in a small number of research areas and has been a good deal more modest in most of them than the figures for total spending might suggest.

The major funding bodies

A variety of groups currently fund research on education. By far the most prominent are the Department of Education & Science, the Scottish Office Education Department and the Department of Employment Group (including the former Training Agency). The Welsh Office, the Northern Ireland Office, the Department of Trade & Industry and the Department of Health have made smaller contributions.

There are a number of other nationally-funded bodies which direct part of their funds towards research on education including: the National Curriculum Council and the Schools Examinations & Assessment Council; the Further Education Unit and the National Council for Vocational Qualifications who operate in the post-schools sector; the Health Education Authority and, on a much smaller scale, the Equal Opportunities Commission and the Commission for Racial Equality. Funds from bodies such as the Council of Europe, the European Science Foundation and OECD have to date been very modest and researchers in education have yet to participate in their activities on any scale. Funding from (and joint initiatives with) other research councils has been negligible.

Major national and international energy companies such as BP, Esso, Shell and British Gas have made fairly sizeable grants. Charitable bodies (amongst whom some of the most prominent have been Leverhulme, Nuffield and the Sainsbury Trust) have put in equivalent amounts. Several local authorities and examination boards have also made contributions, either through their own units or through contributions to the National Foundation for Educational Research, which is at the same time, a major and direct recipient of government funds.

Some continuing problems

The distinctive nature of the ESRC's funding needs to be recognised alongside the contributions of these various other bodies; none of them devoted as much as a third of their funds to research of a Basic/Strategic nature and their projects were often dominated by relatively short-term, practical concerns. Significantly, some of them have also differed in their attitudes towards the publication of research findings. Several researchers have, in recent years, reported finding themselves severely constrained by their sponsors.

Contractual restrictions on publication are also likely to inhibit the development of rigorous research.

With one or two exceptions we have not been able to establish the exact nature of the plans these various funding bodies have for supporting further research on education. In several cases their agendas can probably be guessed at with a fair degree of success. The Scottish Office Education Department, for example, has an annual competition for projects in which it is interested. But such developments are still relatively unusual. In England and Wales decisions concerning government-funded research in education have been taken discretely by separate policy branches within the DES and by other bodies outside it (such as the NCC, SEAC and the FEU). In these circumstances the research community has found it difficult to discern the intended priorities and interests and to make proposals in relation to them. We are left with a sense of a national research effort that is incoherent and unplanned.

There are a number of modest but constructive steps which the ESRC could usefully take to improve the current situation in relation to what is being planned and funded; some are, of course, already being undertaken on an *ad hoc* basis. Any or all of the following would be worthwhile: maintaining and circulating an up-to-date account of its own education portfolio along with a commentary on some of its likely interests; commissioning overviews of research in areas of contemporary public interest and concern; liaising regularly with other funding bodies; continuing discussions with other sponsors about the possibilities for co-funding; opening up and encouraging more international links, notably with respect to Europe; and developing frameworks for further dialogue between researchers, policy-makers and practitioners with a view to identifying areas for further research.

4 IDENTIFYING SOME PRIORITIES FOR RESEARCH

What areas of research should the ESRC be supporting over the next five-to-seven year planning period? In distilling some priorities we took account of a variety of factors whilst bearing in mind the need for advances on a relatively broad front. Our criteria included: existing research strengths and investments (by the ESRC and others), the potential for development in particular research areas and the nature of the gaps in the general coverage of the British research effort. We were guided by wider considerations at the same time. What kinds of questions might parents, teachers and politicians reasonably expect researchers in education to be addressing as part of their contribution to national efforts to improve educational outcomes, processes and practices?

We were aided in the process of establishing priorities by the outcomes of similar deliberations recently concluded in the USA and Australia (see Sroufe, 1991 and ACER, 1991). We also made some effort to pool information about the intentions of our counterparts in European countries although, inevitably, lacking evidence from comparable and recent reviews, our efforts were more patchy.

In drawing up our suggestions for future activity we particularly kept in mind the broad contours of the ESRC's most recent Corporate Plan. All four areas for potential development identified and outlined in the sections that follow will undoubtedly contribute to the ESRC's major goal of 'increasing understanding of social and economic change'. In seeking ways forward, however, we were mindful of the need to operate on several fronts and in several different ways. We were also particularly concerned to enhance the commitments of British researchers in education to certain kinds of developments over the next few years. First, to research which is likely to be of international significance and which incorporates some explicit international dimensions. Second, to research which is likely to be of direct interest to the various partners to the educational process. And third, to research which not only takes note of methodological advances but contributes to them.

Strengthening methodologies

We have noted the importance of upgrading the methodological foundations on which British research in education is currently based. Where methodologies are explicitly chosen on the grounds of cost, or highly constrained by such considerations, there is relatively little that can be done. Nor are we proposing that a major initiative be launched which is guided largely or exclusively by methodological considerations. Our concern is that such issues will be built more routinely into the ESRC's portfolio of projects in education. Given the history of efforts to date, however, some deliberate steps will probably need to be taken.

The list of methodological casualties is depressingly predictable when resources come under pressure. It is headed by longitudinal studies. Whilst the consequences of any single decision to forgo a longitudinal component are likely to be comparatively modest, the cumulative effects are considerable. With the recent demise of some key sponsors of such approaches, there is a danger that Britain's internationally-recognised contributions will be severely diminished. At the same time some attention needs to be devoted to ensuring that such investments as have already been made in high-quality longitudinal research are retained and developed; fairly modest resources, for example, could ensure that key data-sets were suitably archived for subsequent exploitation through secondary analysis.

One or two other areas of methodological importance need to be enhanced in the next few years. Our expertise in comparative and experimental approaches, for example, is distinctly limited. Worryingly, our capacity to undertake sophisticated analyses of largely qualitative data is in danger of lagging behind because of the rapid developments being made in this area. To date no British centre has developed the capacity to maintain and develop enough technical expertise in this area to match the efforts being mounted in North America and Australia. At the same time more attention needs to be paid to the problems of integrating qualitative and quantitative approaches. All of these issues are of general concern to researchers across the social sciences. They are also likely to be shared by those who plan to direct their research energies to the main areas of work we are proposing.

Four areas for research to focus on

We have organised our specific proposals for further research into four focus areas. Each incorporates two or three themes that would lend themselves to more immediate development. The focuses are:

    I: Learning in Educational Settings;
    II: Management and Organisation in Educational Institutions;
    III: Enhancing Professional Training & Development; and
    IV: Informing Policy Development.

Focus I: Learning in educational settings

Understanding more about learning in its various guises is central to the agenda for research on education. There are new pressures on educational institutions brought about by changing national priorities. The National Curriculum is one such source; the need for new skills in the work-place another. Several strands in recent work are of particular importance and require further support. The assumption that what is taught is what is learnt has been challenged by empirical evidence in a range of teaching contexts; what teachers take to be self evident is often problematic for the learner. This has led to a new emphasis on understanding learners' perspectives on the learning process at both a general and a specific level. Recent theoretical developments in anthropology, sociology and the cognitive sciences are indicating how learning is socially mediated and situated in specific contexts. These developments have very significant implications for the design of effective learning environments. An initiative in 'Communication and Learning' would enable some of these fruitful theoretical advances to inform and impact upon educational practices.

In some subjects which draw on structured and hierarchical knowledge-bases (such as the sciences, mathematics and modem languages) levels of student attainment and motivation are a cause of national concern and warrant particular attention. Whilst theoretical advances are being made in understanding the processes of 'Learning in Specific Subject Domains' further research, which focused on the implications of these theoretical advances for instructional practices, would be timely.

Technological advances are permeating many aspects of modern life. Until recently expenditure considerations have largely kept such developments out of educational settings. Rather simplistic assumptions about learning sequences have also tended to prevail when new technologies have been introduced. The last two or three years, however, have witnessed major transformations in the practical possibilities as the costs of pieces of equipment have fallen, the assumptions and commitments underpinning their use have shifted and the expertise to handle more educationally worthwhile approaches has begun to develop. British research is distinctive in the extent of its commitment to exploring the social factors and environments that underpin and influence learning outcomes. The ESRC has already backed some work in this area. A new initiative around the theme of '*New Technologies in Learning*' would permit the continuing pursuit of lines of enquiry that have already been fostered and which have important applications in primary, secondary and tertiary settings.

The influence of family backgrounds on children's intellectual development has long been recognised. Such influences, however, have often been characterised in negative and stigmatising ways. More recent work has begun to explore the potency of '*The Family Setting as a Learning Environment*' and the extent to which it is susceptible to direct educational intervention by teachers and para-professionals. In the process the energies of both parents and their offspring have been successfully harnessed. A number of groups would be well-placed to contribute to a research initiative. Pre-school researchers have had interests in this area for some time. The introduction of attainment targets for seven year-olds has, moreover, injected a new sense of urgency, notably in relation to the development of pre- and early language and literacy skills. Other researchers have also undertaken promising exploratory work in relation to a broader range of social and intellectual outcomes with older age-groups, with the socially disadvantaged and amongst those with special educational needs. It is, perhaps, worth noting at the same time that work in this general area is of interest to at least two government departments.

Focus II: Management and organisation in educational institutions

Major programmes of managerial and organisational change have been introduced into educational institutions in recent years. We envisage three separate areas of work in order to explore aspects of their consequences.

The first would focus on '*Performance and Accountability in Educational Institutions*' and would consider the extent to which the various reforms had been bringing about improvements in the efficiency and effectiveness with which educational services were being delivered. All levels of the system have been affected. Several researchers have begun to make headway in this area. They are drawn from a variety of theoretical and disciplinary backgrounds. Further fundamental work of both a conceptual and empirical nature is now required on these developments to match that which has taken place in other areas of the public sector. A concerted push would be timely, given that many of the reforms are now rather more firmly established. How far have they become integrated into managerial and institutional thinking and practice? What kinds of factors contribute to 'high performance'? And what kinds of benefits and opportunities can be shown to flow from their implementation?

A second strand of reforms have concentrated on restructuring the relationships between the various participants in educational institutions. New kinds of educational organisation have been introduced. Particular prominence has been given to the claims of parents who have been given extended opportunities to choose amongst the schools on offer in their localities and to become more fully informed about (and involved in) their governance. The various reforms have influenced the relationships between educational institutions and their communities in other ways as well. Employers, for example, have been given a greater voice in the organisation and provision of local opportunities through Training and Enterprise Councils; and young people themselves are being given Training Credits with which to 'purchase' further education and training opportunities. An initiative on '*New Organisational Forms, Democracy and Participation*' would enable the consequences of these potentially far-reaching strategies to be explored and compared with attempts to open up other public sector institutions where similar reforms have been introduced or attempted. At the same time there is considerable scope for comparisons with other European systems.

Interest in issues relating to '*Cost-Effectiveness, Finance and Productivity in Education*' has been slow to emerge in this country. There are several reasons for this. Definitions of some central concepts (such as 'cost-effectiveness') have been considered unusually problematic; appropriate data have not been readily available to social scientists or easily collected; and interest, until recently, amongst practitioners has been sporadic. The British research effort has consequently been negligible, not least in comparison with that in North America. There have been considerable shifts in attitudes over the past two or three years, however, as educational institutions have faced the implications of declining units of resource and newly devolved responsibilities for their management. New sources of data are also becoming available. The group of researchers with specific expertise in the analysis of these economic and financial issues in education is currently rather small; there are signs, however, that other researchers are interested. Developments in this area would be timely.

Focus III: Enhancing professional training and development

The nineties are witnessing a restructuring of the major routes into professional positions. Training opportunities in medicine and health, the law and
social work have all been affected along with education and new approaches
to training have emerged (or are in the process of doing so). With particular respect to education there is widespread agreement that the quality of the
teaching force may need to be reviewed; that some of the particular functions it undertakes need to be re-examined; and that several routes into the
profession need to be developed. The government has consequently introduced a series of reforms. Some of them are modest, others are more ambitious. All, in one way or other, impact upon the ways teachers are initially
educated and trained, their subsequent professional development, the nature
of their work and its appraisal.

There have been parallel developments in other professions. Consequently
we believe there is considerable scope for an initiative which focuses on '*The
Education and Training of Enabling Professionals*' and explores some common themes across professions in an inter-disciplinary way. Such an initiative would explore the variety of routes to professional status which have
recently been established and the various polices and practices that currently
underpin the professional development of teachers and other groups. It would
give particular attention to competing conceptions of what skills and com-
petencies are required in different professional environments.

Focus IV: Informing policy development

There is a long-standing tradition in social research of researchers and policy-makers working alongside each other to facilitate the development of
strategy and policy. This style of research has shorter time-scales and is sometimes more eclectic. It is an approach that has been less frequently adopted
in education. However, we believe there are at least three areas in which
work which could contribute both to theory and to practice would be timely.

Between one in six and one in seven young people are educated in 'inner
city' schools. A raft of recent government initiatives, prompted in part by
continuing evidence of low standards and under-achievement, have refocused
attention on this area. Explanations and theories which merely take school
processes as their starting points, however, are of limited utility. A variety of
social factors which structure and underpin educational provision are clearly
influential. It seems difficult for formal educational provision to function
effectively in 'communities' which lack social cohesion. Yet what is perhaps
most striking about the research evidence currently available is the extent to
which there is variation amongst individuals and across institutions in inner
city contexts in terms both of experiences and outcomes. There are consequently considerable opportunities to take advantage of various 'natural

experiments' in researching the likely consequences of policy development whilst, simultaneously, extending their range and diversity by supporting further explicitly-designed interventions in inner-city areas. There is a powerful tradition of such interventions from North America and other OECD countries (especially in relation to the younger age-groups) on which an initiative on '*Education in the Inner City*' could draw.

The recent expansion of provision in higher education has been dramatic; at the same time there is evidence that post-16 participation rates have begun to climb steadily. Both developments have considerable consequences for the ways in which higher education institutions will be developing over the coming decade. An initiative on '*The Changing Face of Higher Education*' would aim both to take advantage of, and to feed into, these changes. There is considerable speculation about the likely shape of the emerging system. Comparative analyses, which sought to develop a firmer understanding of the alternative options and evidence relating to their effects, would be especially helpful in the short to medium-term. What are the distinctive strengths (and weaknesses) of the British approach? In the longer term a series of studies which revisit the basic propositions on which strategies for teaching and learning in higher education are premised is required. A small cadre of researchers is currently engaged in this area but their efforts would need to be supplemented by researchers working on younger age-groups redeploying some of their energies.

There is undoubtedly a visionary element to current proposals for 'systems' of '*Lifelong Education and Training*'. This reflects, in part, the relatively low base from which British practice is starting and, in particular, the ingrained habit of treating post-adolescent learning as largely occurring during periods of full-time participation in formal educational institutions. The UFC, by way of redressing this imbalance, has recently supported some promising projects. The Nottingham research centre will also be looking at certain aspects of the effectiveness of training and instruction. The challenges to be met, however, extend considerably beyond such concerns as policy-makers strive to reform and develop current practices and to install the rudiments of a lifelong system. There is an urgent need to ensure that such efforts are premised upon realistic accounts of adults' 'learning careers' and opportunities. Such limited research as we have available to date in this country indicates that our understanding of how and when adults learn is both conceptually and empirically at the early stages of its development.

5 ORGANISING FOR CHANGE

In the last five years there have been significant changes in the ways in which research in education has come to be organised. More developments can be anticipated as HE institutions come to terms with the full implications of changing funding patterns. The ESRC's Corporate Plan outlines some of the ways ahead in terms of enhanced opportunities for research training and further funding for research centres. (. . .)

Researchers in education share a number of organisational and strategic problems in common with other social scientists. They are, for example, concerned about the ways in which individual projects fit into the broader scheme of theoretical advance; about the difficulties for research workers in pursuing research careers; about the need for improved forms of postgraduate research training; and about the circumstances within which new ideas are generated. Furthermore, they generally appear to recognise the need for further steps to be taken to strengthen the infra-structures currently supporting research.

In order to understand more about recent trends and about some of the particular problems to be faced, we commissioned Professor Stewart Ranson of Birmingham University to undertake a synthesis of the recent experiences of some leading researchers (Ranson, 1992). It is clear from his account both that considerable progress has been made and that more remains to be done.

Building a research-focused culture

The conviction that a strong commitment to research was crucial to their survival was rather slow to emerge in many university departments of education, where the bulk of the British research effort in education has been located. Most had historically been concerned with the training of teachers; many had tended to see research as an optional activity. As Ranson's account shows, the past decade has witnessed a significant transformation in attitudes as departments have attempted to build what he terms 'cultures of research'; in the past few years the pace of change has quickened still further.

The strategies Ranson describes range from the mundane to the innovative. That some of these 'strategies' now appear obvious seems to us no bad thing. In our experience, few departments across the social sciences have managed to sustain the 'basics' of a research infra-structure without re-committing themselves periodically to them. (. . .)

One important step that leading departments have taken has been to facilitate the emergence and support of departmental research programmes. Such strategies have helped to identify issues requiring theoretical development whilst offering frameworks for establishing which particular opportunities for external funding to pursue. Programmes of research are most convincing, of course, when they emerge from and build upon established track records of relevant research endeavour. There are echoes here of the proposals a high-level review group recently made for the emergence of research excellence in the 'hard' sciences (Ziman, 1991).

A second step in many leading departments has been to create the conditions within which teams of researchers could be established and maintained. They have had high-level leadership, often at professorial level. (. . .) Such research teams have generally been on the small side in education, ranging from perhaps three to six members, with established staff making up half or less of these numbers. The more successful teams have managed to stay together for a number of years. (. . .)

Since funding for the maintenance of such teams has tended to come from a number of sources (of which the ESRC has usually only been one), they have had to devote considerable energy to the problems of securing continuity. Few teams in education have been in a position to rely on funds from single sources for more than relatively short periods of time; fewer still have been in a position to rely on continuity of funding from the ESRC. What is both surprising and welcome is the extent to which these research teams have continued to look to the ESRC for support. Indeed, most saw it as crucial, enabling them to pursue research of 'cutting-edge' importance against a background of more bread-and-butter activities. (. . .)

Creating the conditions for research careers

The most pressing problem to be faced by those running research programmes and teams continues to be to secure continuity for those who seek 'careers' in research. We commissioned a small survey of researchers from Dr Michael Youngman of Nottingham University to explore these issues (Youngman, 1992). It covered all those who were employed as research workers in the field of education during the Autumn term of 1991 on projects funded by the ESRC. Interest in the survey amongst researchers was high and an 80 per cent response rate was achieved, despite the tight time constraints under which it was conducted.

The study confirmed many of the general findings of a 1987 survey conducted for the ABRC by the Institute of Manpower Studies (Varlaam, 1987). It had the advantage, however, of providing a sufficiently sizeable sample to describe the particular attitudes and circumstances of those in education. The survey emphasised the precarious position of this group of researchers. Four out of ten were on contracts of less than two years' duration and almost half said that their current contracts had less than a year to run. Fewer than half wanted to stay on in full-time research after their present post and almost all were of the view that there were 'few career opportunities in research'. Many of those intending to leave full-time research hoped to take up employment teaching in higher education institutions but only a minority of the group were confident that they would be successful in realising this ambition.

There are few aspects of the evidence on researchers in education which set them apart from research workers in other social sciences. One or two points are, however, of particular note. Researchers in education tended to be somewhat older, fewer than half had previously held research posts, and only four out of ten held doctorates. Not only did the survey indicate a relatively high turnover of research staff but it suggested that many acquired their expertise 'on the job'.

Given the difficulties of doing research in education, why did these research workers take on the challenge? A recent account by Stronach and MacDonald (1991) of the experiences of research workers on the InTER initiative provides some clues. There is intellectual excitement to be found at the 'cutting edge'. 'The project' they report 'is a remarkably motivating vehicle for individual commitment and communal loyalty'. But there was also a downside. 'Research workers exhibited self-sacrificing behaviour in relation to their careers and were prone to self-exploitation' (p. 70). We would add, on the basis of the survey evidence, that in most cases such workers did not appear to be prepared to engage in this self-denying behaviour for very long; more pragmatic concerns quickly surfaced.

Responsibility for the employment of research workers lies with HE institutions rather than the ESRC. As Youngman indicates the issues to be faced are considerable. Stronach and Macdonald go further. They maintain that 'the recruitment, training and employment of educational researchers is unplanned, ineffective and often unfair' (Stronach and Macdonald, 1991, p. 71 and Norris, 1991). Ranson's report reveals some instances of good practice within a generally bleak picture. (. . .) Many research leaders accepted that a measure of instability was likely to be a continuing feature of research life; they wondered, however, whether the levels of turnover currently being encountered might not be counter-productive. A trained and experienced cadre of researchers was essential for the future.

Whilst acknowledging the pressures on and limits to ESRC's role, many of the researchers Ranson interviewed were of the opinion that the ESRC could help by creating strategies for medium-term funding which reflected more closely the opportunities and constraints facing researchers in education. Strategies for securing continuity of staffing and research expertise were urgently required. Several ideas were put forward. A competition for 'centres' that were a good deal smaller in terms of funding and duration than those maintained under current arrangements was one idea that received support. To upgrade the research effort advances were required on several fronts at any one time; several 'small' centres, possibly with funding from other sources, would enable this goal to be achieved more readily within existing resource constraints. Another suggestion was that the ESRC, in order to provide greater stability, might try to find ways of providing small amounts of funding for research teams over relatively extended periods of time. The bulk of funding would come from other sources. A third idea was that a small number of senior research fellowships, for especially talented individuals working on priority topics, might be supported. (. . .) Some of these steps could, of course, be accommodated within existing ESRC practices.

Restructuring the provision of training opportunities

The ESRC has been undertaking a major review of the arrangements through which it supports research training. Research in education shares many concerns in common with other areas of the social sciences. There are, however, some particular problems which are specific to those areas (such as health, management and social work) where there is an expectation that future researchers will also have obtained experience as practitioners. In the case of education this means that potential employers (usually in HE institutions) are typically looking for a period spent as a teacher alongside research skills. Given the collapse in full-time secondments for teachers several years ago, it is now comparatively rare for someone in their late twenties to have secured both experiences. (. . .)

The ESRC plays a central role in research training in education. Over the past few years, however, there have only been about six full-time ESRC awards a year to doctoral students in education at a time when other sources of full-time student support have become very limited. The exact number of awards to education is determined, of course, by the strength of competition for awards across the social sciences. There are indications, however, that the scheme has not proved attractive to many of the most able prospective entrants to research careers, many of whom have already successfully completed a number of years in teaching.

The ESRC has begun to respond to some of these problems through its decision to explore support for part-time modes of doctoral study. Such approaches could ensure that those already involved in education and interested in applying for research posts could build up relevant research-based qualifications. The field of education would also benefit considerably from any proposals to provide opportunities for fellowships which allowed experienced mid-career professionals to develop or enhance their research skills, and from the continuation of training workshops, focusing on particular issues such as methodology. (. . .) There was widespread agreement amongst research leaders that, at the current time, several routes into research needed to be maintained. (. . .)

The issue of 'critical mass'

The challenge facing researchers in education is a major one. A considerable proportion of the research effort will continue to be undertaken by individual researchers. It is clear, however, that much energy has recently been devoted to reviewing and restructuring the arrangements for supporting research in the belief that this investment will achieve greater pay-offs over the next few years.

Our review indicates that whilst only a relatively small number of groups have, to date, achieved international status a number of others are well-placed to do so. For a significant number to take this important step, however, ways of creating greater concentrations of expertise will probably need to be explored. The question of 'critical mass' is a discussion that has only just begun amongst researchers in education. Strategies for enhancing cross-institutional collaboration merit exploration in the short term and may make some contribution. In the longer term, however, more radical steps, possibly involving some restructuring of current organisational arrangements, may well be required.

6 UTILISING RESEARCH

It has often been said that social scientists – including educationists – could do a good deal more to ensure the effective communication of their research. We are sceptical, however, of the extent to which dissemination can safely be left in the hands of energetic individuals and would want to argue for some reorientation of current approaches. Not all research, for example, lends itself to the processes of newspaper publicity; there are sometimes dangers in dissemination before preliminary peer review has taken place; and single projects can easily be dismissed unless care is taken to locate them within a broader context. In particular, the idea that dissemination invariably takes place after the research project has been 'completed' needs to be re-examined. This is not, however, to deny the importance of making research results available in summary and digestible forms. Most projects could usefully produce a readable summary of their work written with non-academic audiences in mind alongside the more formal, end-of-award reports currently demanded of them.

Over the past few years researchers in education have been struggling with some of these problems with a view to increasing the impact of their research. One response has been the development of research networks which have begun to flourish in several areas; indeed, one or two have been maintained over fairly lengthy periods of time. Such groupings serve multiple purposes. They facilitate the generation and exchange of new ideas; they provide a critical forum for the review of new findings; they offer perspectives on the broader context within which any particular piece of research may be located; and they have the capacity to distil the cumulative messages from a particular field of research. At their best they can also improve dialogue across a number of boundaries (disciplinary, institutional, national and linguistic). We should like to see two or three such networks being initiated each year. The seminars competition offers one funding route but more extensive arrangements, in which the ESRC is possibly a co-sponsor, are required.

Another initiative which we should like to see is the development of policy forums. Policy-makers and practitioners often complain that research in education is irrelevant to their concerns. Some of it may be but more could be done to bring the various parties together. If the energies of these groups could be enlisted in the tasks of establishing research priorities then they would be less likely to dismiss the outcomes. In the Health Service quite extensive arrangements for developing such priorities are already taking shape (see Peckham, 1991). Research in education would benefit from the development of parallel, albeit more informal strategies.

A third possibility has already been given shape by the ESRC. Research is a cumulative process. Only a handful of studies in any one year are of sufficient importance to stand on their own. Reviews of Current Knowledge, commissioned by the ESRC, provide a useful strategy for identifying and shaping research agendas. We should like to see two or three small-scale consultancies supported each year on topics in education that are of public interest; these would be written up for wide dissemination in an accessible style. (. . .)

7 SUMMARY OF OUR RECOMMENDATIONS

The Working Party is keen to see the ESRC retaining its commitment to funding high-quality research of theoretical and methodological significance on a range of contemporary issues in education. There are a number of ways in which we believe this goal could be facilitated and our main recommendations are outlined below.

On funding and collaboration

The Working Party recognises the importance of securing more opportunities for joint funding and of increasing current levels of international collaboration. It therefore recommends:

(1) The ESRC to take the initiative in establishing better channels for liaison with other major funding bodies (including the DES) in order to clarify their research priorities and to seek opportunities, where appropriate, for co-funding of projects with the potential for medium and long-term development. The creation of policy forums would help in this respect.
(2) To create specific opportunities for participation in European educational research programmes over the next three years.

On priorities for research

The Working Party has identified a number of areas within which it would particularly like to see research initiated over the next five years. Clearly, given the scale of activities envisaged, these proposals would need to compete for support under several of the ESRC's current mechanisms for funding: initiatives, research centres and major projects. A total of eleven themes in four focus areas have been selected.

(3a) **Focus I: Learning in educational settings**

    (i)   Communication and Learning
    (ii) Learning in Specific Subject Domains
    (iii) New Technologies in Learning
    (iv) The Family Setting as a Learning Environment

(3b) **Focus II: Management and organisation in educational institutions**

    (v)   Performance and Accountability in Educational Institutions
    (vi) New Organisational Forms, Democracy and Participation
    (vii) Cost-Effectiveness, Finance and Productivity in Education

(3c) **Focus III: Enhancing professional training and development**

    (viii) The Education and Training of 'Enabling' Professionals

(3d) **Focus IV: Informing policy development**

    (ix) Education in the Inner City
    (x)   The Changing Face of Higher Education
    (xi) Lifelong Education and Training

(4) **Strengthening methodologies**

Attention needs to be given to methodological issues which have particular relevance for research in education. These include: supporting longitudinally-based research, underwriting advances in the analysis of qualitative data, developing and maintaining expertise in the analysis of large data-sets, and finding ways of integrating different methodologies.

On research organisation

(5) To explore ways of supporting several small research centres in education in order to promote advances on the range of research fronts in which the UK has international standing.

(6) To encourage further cross-institutional collaboration where this offers a real prospect of more rapid progress towards international excellence.

(7) To provide a small number of longer-term fellowships for experienced

researchers linked to the individuals in order to maintain expertise in educational research.

On research training

(8) To increase the overall numbers of full and part-time Master and doctoral level awards, as the quality of candidates permits, with a view to maintaining several routes into research positions, giving particular attention to the need to create a cadre of young researchers who have combined their research training with a period of practical experience.

(9) To develop opportunities for mid-career entrants to HE institutions to upgrade their research skills through short-term fellowships and short programmes of intensive research training.

On dissemination

A number of strategies are already in place but would benefit from increases in the current levels of activity. In addition the ESRC should take steps:

(10) To facilitate liaison between the various learned societies interested in research in education with a view to establishing a collaborative mechanism for reviewing and updating the overall agenda for research in education.

REFERENCES

ACER (Australian Council for Educational Research) (1991) *Education Research in Australia: Interim Report of the Review Panel: Strategic Review of Research in Education*, Canberra, Australian Government Publishing Service.

Centre for Higher Education Studies (1991) *Review of UK Social Science Resources*, London, Institute of Education, University of London.

Norris, N. (1991) *A Survey of the Terms and Conditions of Contract Research Workers in UK Universities*, Norwich, Centre for Applied Research in Education, University of East Anglia.

PCFC (1990) *Research in the PCFC Sector*, report of the Committee of Enquiry Appointed by Council, The Polytechnics and Colleges Funding Council.

Peckham, M. (1991) Research and development for the National Health Service, *The Lancet*, Vol. 338, pp. 367–71.

Ranson, S. (1992) *The Management and Organisation of Educational Research*, Birmingham, Centre for Education Management and Policy Studies, School of Education, University of Birmingham.

Sroufe, G. E. (1991) Education enterprise zones: the new national research centers, *Educational Researchers*, Vol. 20, no. 4, pp. 24–9.

Stronach, I. and MacDonald, B. (1991) *Faces and Futures: An Inquiry into the Jobs, Lives and Careers of Educational Researchers in an ESRC Initiative*, Norwich, Centre for Applied Research in Education, University of East Anglia.

Varlaam, C. (1987) *Contract Researchers in Universities: A Study for the ABRC*, Brighton, Institute of Manpower Studies, University of Sussex.

Wallace, M. and Weinding, D. (eds.) (1997) *Managing Schools in the Post-Reform Era: Messages of Recent Research*, Cardiff, University of Wales for the Economic and Social Research Council.

Youngman, M. (1992) *Careers of Contract Researchers in Education: Situations and Perceptions*, Nottingham, School of Education, University of Nottingham.

Ziman, J. (1991) *Restructuring Academic Science: A New Framework for UK Policy*, London, Science Policy Support Group, Concept Paper 8.

3

THE FUTURE OF EDUCATIONAL RESEARCH: LEARNING AT THE CENTRE

Stewart Ranson

Editor's note: The working party chaired by John Gray commissioned Stewart Ranson to write a paper on 'The organisation and management of education research'. The paper was appended to the first ESRC report. It was constructed from evidence gathered in a series of conversations between Stewart Ranson and a range of researchers, administrators and policy-makers. The themes explored in this paper can be briefly summarised: it suggested that departments of education in higher education institutions were responding well to a more competitive climate for education research, seizing opportunities where they arose, but also planning strategically in support of defined research priorities and promoting appropriate staff development. However, it also argued that since the pressures for economic regeneration and cultural renewal were pointing to the need for a wider analysis of learning in different contexts, then the field as a whole might need a broader conception of education.

The ESRC decided to invite Stewart Ranson to develop these issues and to present a further report. This further report, with a few minor modifications and some cuts, is presented in this chapter.

In drafting the report, Stewart Ranson drew on a number of sources: the deliberations of a discussion group convened by Peter De Vries, a discussion held at the BERA annual conference at Oxford in September 1994, and contributions (written and spoken) to a seminar held at the East London University in autumn 1994 and to two invitational one-day seminars held at the University of Birmingham in December 1994 and March 1995.

The report was submitted to the ESRC in June 1995. Stewart Ranson also prepared an article, published in the British Educational Research Journal *in December 1996 (Vol. 22, no. 5), which summarises the themes of his report and quotes passages from the written and spoken contributions to the seminars.*

I PREDICAMENTS

In periods of social transition, education becomes central to our future well-being. Only if learning is placed at the centre of our experience can individuals continue to develop their capacities and institutions be enabled to respond openly and imaginatively to a period of change. Learning, and the institutions which support it, become indispensable to the purposes of cultural renewal and economic regeneration. Interpreting the significance of learning in this way suggests the importance of educational research for the future of our society. Only by improving our understanding of the processes and institutions of learning can society understand how to support individuals, organisations and communities through the transition.

Can Departments of Education (DEs) bear such expectations placed upon them? DEs, like others in higher education, have experienced the pressures of change. The restructuring of HE funding, accelerating competition for research grants, and the critical significance of the HEFCE Research Assessment Exercise have created a context of market competition and a culture of contract and income generation. In addition, DEs have had to respond to a sea change in initial teacher training and in-service provision, while the education service itself has been the focus of massive legislative reform.

DEs have often fared well in this competitive climate.[1] A mixture of proactive strategies and a willingness to respond to new opportunities has supported and maintained the vitality of educational studies. There have been beneficial effects including increased collaboration between academics and practitioners and a growing sensitivity to policy issues. However, these changes have brought anxieties. Questions are being asked about the scope of research in the field, about the value of its contribution to the social sciences, about its status as a discipline, and about the trend of grants allocated to educational researchers:

- Is education research becoming too specialised, too preoccupied with narrow, short-term, 'results oriented', policy evaluation projects?
- Is there less 'fundamental' research concerning long-term and broader issues which do not arise out of current policy concerns and paradigms?
- Is education research neglecting the theoretical knowledge and discoveries occurring in the various academic disciplines?
- Is the written output of research tending towards shorter works (i.e., articles and edited collections) rather than authored books?

The quality and relevance of educational research has become the subject of vigorous debate. This debate has been enjoined as much by those within the field of educational studies as by the critical gaze of observers from outside (including Lord Skidelsky in a 1993 House of Lords debate on the Education Bill[2].) Some wonder whether it is wise for the field to respond to this emerging critique. For others debate is inescapable and can only strengthen the field.

The aim of this report is to describe and analyse the debate. It begins with the controversies, clarifies a strategy for redirection and concludes with a discussion of the future for education research.

Controversies

Intellectual controversy and uncertainty is the chronic condition of the post-modern world. The meta-narratives which have provided secure purposes and boundaries for inquiry since the Enlightenment have appeared to dissolve in the face of the shifting and kaleidoscopic differentiations which characterise late modernity. Discovering shared meanings, identities and purposes has become increasingly problematic. Differences appear incommensurable. Yet facing the spectre of a relativism that erodes all points of connection, the post-modern conversation has begun to shift its understanding of how to conceive the contemporary predicament: to explore what can be reconciled in the relationship between difference and universality.[3]

Educational studies, no less than other academic disciplines, has in recent years been influenced by this wider discourse and the epistemological uncertainties it has produced. There has been a lively and sometimes agitated debate between the traditions within educational studies about its status and forms of inquiry. The lack of any dominant traditional paradigm may have accentuated the lack of accord. Nevertheless, it can be argued that controversy is inescapable during a period of great social, economic and cultural upheaval. Indeed, any discipline which is not critically re-evaluating the very foundations of its work – and asking whether 'foundations' are any longer possible – is vulnerable to the charge of intellectual closure and ossification. That educational studies has engaged in a public debate about its research must be considered a considerable virtue.

This report wishes to argue that, despite evident differences of perspective amongst colleagues within the field, an emergent meta-frame can be identified which could create not only the possibility of cohesion but more significantly a robust discipline which can bear the practical and intellectual demands being placed upon it during a period of social transformation. The fissures which beset educational studies are discussed in turn.

Defining values and purpose

While some colleagues define their vocation in terms of understanding and supporting the professional practice of teachers, others are committed to furthering knowledge of education within the social sciences. The field, it appears, is 'split between those wanting research to be relevant directly to practice and those wanting to make a theoretical and empirical contribution to knowledge'. This is an accurate account of the division which runs through many university departments of education. It is, however, as a number are recognising, not only a false distinction but one which serves to undermine one of the distinctive contributions which education can make to the social sciences. Knowledge and practice cannot be opposed but only mutually reinforcing. Practice without understanding of the enduring forms of knowledge is blind, while knowledge detached from the world of practice remains impotent and pointless. The learning process is not a 'technical competence' and cannot unfold without a recognition that knowledge is explored through, but also created in, reflective practice.

The scope of inquiry

If much educational research has in recent years become overly narrow and specialised around descriptive and evaluative studies, there is growing recognition of the need both to strengthen cross-fertilisation within educational studies and, more importantly, to recognise the much broader contribution which educational research can make to the key issues of our time. The preoccupation with the statutory sector has caused neglect of pre-five education, post-16 education and training, and higher and continuing education. Yet many are beginning to consider the reach of educational studies beyond the boundaries of educational institutions conventionally understood. Issues of learning can be seen to lie at the centre of concerns surrounding human aggression, community health, environmental pollution, dissolving prejudice and discrimination and supporting a more active citizenship in civil society. By placing learning at the centre of educational studies, exploring its processes and institutional conditions in different learning contexts, educational studies can begin to address the central issues of our time.

Theory and the social sciences

Although disputed by some, it is increasingly acknowledged that educational studies has become too isolated from the key theoretical debates of the period. This neglect of theory has impoverished its research. Only theory can provide the capacity to explain the issues – practical as well as policy – by constructing the propositions which analyse why such and such is the case. But theory contributes much more than this formal analysis implies: it introduces the ideas and concepts that locate the interpretive space for the analysis, and theory provides the critical challenge to practice by revealing the structures of power that underlie it. Theory is the indispensable intellectual capital that connects the particular to its context while analysing, explaining and challenging the relationship between them. Theory, moreover, secures the lineages of action: 'savoir pour prevoir, prevoir pour pouvoir': a plausible interpretation of the past can more adequately guide the future. Theory tests the imagination, exposes the analytical rigour, ties idea to practice.

The status of the discipline in question

What kind of knowledge, however, does educational studies constitute? Can it be said to form a discipline at all? The community is divided on the issue of whether education is itself 'a topic', or 'a discipline' or whether it is 'a site' for disciplinary/multi-disciplinary inquiry. There is a consensus that the issues which constitute educational studies can only be addressed through multi-disciplinary inquiry. The skills of the social sciences are indispensable to analysis of educational issues. It is this characteristic which leads some to emphasise 'the importance of education as a place where significant social science disciplines intersect (where they meet) and as an arena that offers opportunities to study the development of the relationships that follow'. This is consistent with Colin McCabe's account of cultural studies which he would deny is a discipline because 'it's more an area in which the disciplines get reconfigured and where the relations between academic knowledge and the world get restated'.[4]

Yet this powerful conception of the role of the disciplines within a field does itself – and here I wish to argue against McCabe – constitute a distinctive discipline of knowledge. The task of exploring the relationship between disciplines and between theory and practice to develop understanding of the purposes, tasks and conditions of learning is, arguably, properly understood as a distinctive discipline of knowing, one that will require its own theories and methodologies. The uniqueness of this epistemology of education lies in the special kind of knowledge that can only be formed of learning by occupying and analysing *the space between* 'subjects' and *between* subjects and practice. This way of understanding the distinctive 'discipline' of knowing learning suggests a field that is not only a space within which the disciplines separately explore their ideas, but one that offers forms of knowing that can contribute significantly to the traditional academic disciplines of social science.

Despite differences between traditions of enquiry within educational studies, this discussion suggests the possibility of discovering common purpose in the face of the transformations facing the field generally. MacIntyre's recent work[5] argues that the crises which confront traditions of enquiry can lead them not only to interrogate their standards of rationality internally but also in relation to those expressed within rival traditions such that discourse and intellectual progress become possible between them.

II REDISCOVERING DIRECTION

The challenge for educational studies is the need to develop a new paradigm that moves the field from its perceived position at the periphery to the centre of analysis and purpose within the social sciences and in relation to the key issues facing society. The new paradigm would comprise five interdependent dimensions:

(a) Reconceptualising the problematic: from education in school to learning in society

The dominant culture within DEs emphasises teacher training and development with the accompanying research tasks focusing upon practice in the classroom. Schools, teachers, children and classrooms are the typical preoccupation. The first cultural shift to a new paradigm is to broaden the conception of the role and purpose of DEs so as to embrace the education of all members of society, encouraging research and analysis of pre-five learning as much as post-sixteen education and training. The post-compulsory sector is likely to become the dynamic centre of policy in education for the remainder of the century as the country struggles not only to regenerate the economy but also to accommodate society to a period of change.

This understanding can place education at the centre of the issues of our time. The processes and conditions of learning in the workplace, in the home and in the community become as important as those within the classroom or lecture hall. Understanding the processes of learning, moreover, can inform knowledge of creativity in the arts, discovery in the sciences, and innovation in the world of practice. Thus the intellectual challenge for research and teaching in DEs is to focus upon developing analysis of, and enabling the conditions for, learning throughout society.

(b) Towards a theory of learning

If one of the central tasks of our time is to transform the way people think of themselves and what they are capable of, then it is only by changing the sense students have of themselves as learners that they will begin to develop their capacities and realise their potential. It requires a comparative theory of learning which can embrace what is unchanging and what varies with the contexts of learning.

Learning itself begins with a sense of discovery of new knowledge or skills. But the deeper significance of learning lies, through its forming of our powers and capacities, in our unfolding agency, in our understanding of who we are and what we can do as a person. Such learning depends upon motivation – and the motivation young people need to sustain this self-development can only grow out of an understanding that the struggle to develop as a person has some point.

A theory of learning will need to recognise the complexity of learning in different contexts. Education research, many are increasingly willing to argue, has been too preoccupied with learning within the statutory sector and within institutionalised settings within that sector. There is a need for research into how people learn in different contexts of the home, community and work as well as within the formal boundaries of school, college and university. Such enquiry is likely to lead to a more complex theory of learning that acknowledges the domain specificity of much learning. The tools for a theory of learning will need to be sensitive to the topic being learned, and they will be sensitive to the setting of the context in which the learning is taking place.

(c) Redefining professional practice: from pedagogy as teaching to learning through action research

It seems clear that the best practice of teacher training, and especially the in-service professional development of teachers, is already being reformed from a training model based on transmission to one which increasingly encourages a learning model based upon action research for teachers in support of the reflective development of their practice within schools. The major task, however, is to broaden this conception of pedagogic practice. A new paradigm for DEs would seek not only to reinforce this emergent model of learning within their traditional client group of teachers but to extend its principles to work with the wider audience of those involved in enabling learning: trainers, managers, health workers as well as community developers.

(d) A distinctive discipline at the centre of the social sciences

Issues of learning are implicated in the structural transformations of our time which must, it has been argued,[6] become the central focus for the work of the social sciences. The economic, social and political changes are altering the structure of experience: the capacities each person needs to flourish, what it is to live in society, the nature of work and the form taken by the polity. In this context learning what it is to be a person in a post-modern world, how to live with and value difference within the community, and to participate more actively in a changing democracy not only place educational issues at the centre of the work of the social sciences individually but also create a distinctive disciplinary space for the intrinsic educational issue of learning itself. Only by 'reconfiguring' the frames of psychology, sociology, economics, for example, can we begin to explain and develop interpretive analysis of the domains of learning within personal, communal and political development. The understanding of the discipline of learning that emerges in turn feeds back into knowledge of 'leadership', or 'civil society' or 'a democratic polity'.

(e) Learning at the centre of public policy

The distinctive disciplinary knowledge of learning necessarily explores a space between theory and practice which places it inescapably within and, it is argued, at the centre of public policy. Because the task of theory is not only to explain why forms of learning are as they are within society but also to theorise the conditions for different forms, it is essentially normative, driven by 'strong evaluation' of the social, moral and political order. Educational studies on learning can describe, explain and propose public values of learning which locate education at the centre of the issues facing the public domain.

These values, it is argued, are the need to regenerate a democratic public domain for the learning society. The education policy literature lacks a framework of values about the public domain which it brings to its analysis. The appropriate values for public policy and its analysis are those of democracy and citizenship for the learning society. The transformations of the time require a renewed valuing of and commitment to learning: as the boundaries between languages and cultures begin to dissolve, as new skills and knowledge are expected within the world of work so, most significantly, new generations, rejecting passivity in favour of more active participation, require to be encouraged to exercise such qualities of discourse in the public domain. A learning society, therefore, needs to celebrate the qualities of being open to new ideas, listening to as well as expressing perspectives, reflecting on and inquiring into solutions to new dilemmas, cooperating in the practice of change and critically reviewing it.

III AN AGENDA FOR THE FUTURE OF EDUCATION RESEARCH

The task of shaping the future agenda of educational research could be supported by an audit of current research. Rosalind Driver proposed that it would be helpful to have a survey of the scope of current educational research in the UK summarising the research being supported by ESRC, DfEE, the Charitable Trusts etc. 'This could be an important state of the art review'.

Whatever such a review revealed, there was an important need at this moment, David Halpin and Barry Troyna argued, for educational researchers to forge more clearly *their* research agendas rather than give the impression of being uncritically captured by fashionable trends or issues of the moment. Examples of this, they suggest, might include the preoccupation with 'school effectiveness', 'reading recovery' and studies of 'value added performance'.

> Whilst not wishing to dismiss these and other related subjects as worthy topics of educational research, we need to ask ourselves sometimes if our work on any or all of them is guided too much by the needs of practitioners and policy makers at the expense of certain enduring concerns such as those to do with equality of opportunity which brought many of us into the business in the first place.

What would such an agenda look like? It would be an agenda which would be characterised as much by 'modes' of research and 'focus' as by substantive 'themes' or issues for research.

Modes

A paradigm which places the discipline of learning at the centre of public policy and the social sciences' analysis of and prescriptions for the transformations of our time suggests the appropriateness of distinctive modes of research in educational studies:

Praxis

Grounded in practice yet sophisticated as theory and directed to informing the key policy issues of our time.

Comparative

There is a need to break down the narrow compartmentalisation of research and to bring out the inter-connections across education studies and thus to develop the field of knowledge. This suggests the need for comparative studies of the tasks and conditions of learning in different educational settings, from pre-five to post-sixteen. It also implies comparative studies of learning in different contexts beyond the boundary of the institutionalised settings: what kinds of learning take place in the home, the community and the workplace as well as in school or college? What effects do the interconnections between these settings have on learning?

Such a new impetus to comparative studies would, many acknowledge, require 'some rejuvenation in a crusty old domain of educational studies'. Some new tools will be needed to study the nature and quality of learning which are sensitive to the context in which learning is taking place.

Inter-disciplinary

Adequate exploration and analysis of the purposes, tasks and conditions of learning in its different settings will require colleagues from different disciplines to work together. Inter-disciplinary study would counter the tradition of not working together in education: 'we are fragmented, working in our separate tracks'. The intellectual demand to explore the interdependence of analytical frames would have the effect of strengthening the intellectual discourse and professional coherence of the field.

There will also be a need for evaluation of multi-disciplinary work. Does it deliver its promise? What are impediments to it and how can they be overcome?

Collaborative

The need for comparative and multi-disciplinary research suggests the value of study teams comprising different kinds of disciplinary knowledge and experience. This mode of collaborative research can be achieved in a number of ways: within the same department, across departments in the same institution, and between universities. There can be value in each of these forms of study: learning is exemplified in the mode as well as the purpose of the research.

Research sponsorship can play a role in breaking down the (sectoral and disciplinary) boundaries within education, encouraging cross-field and collaborative study.

Focus

Educational research, it is argued, needs to focus on developing a practical theory of the values, purposes, conditions and practice of active learning which can be brought to bear upon, and refined as a result of analysing, the issues of learning embedded in the layers of historical change affecting individuals, institutions and communities. One approach to such a practical theorising of active learning seeks to develop analysis of three interdependent processes which include:

Practice

Learning is the process of discovering our distinctive agency as persons and how this grows out of and leads into the capacity to learn with others to create the contexts in which we live and work. There is no solitary learning. We develop as persons with and through others. The unfolding agency of the self, learning 'to make our worlds', can thus only grow out of cooperative action, the conditions for which are inescapably social and public.

Institutional capacity

The motivation and capabilities of citizens to learn will depend much upon the capacity of the multi-institutional systems. Within post-16 systems, institutional arrangements which enable active learning may be characterised by: curricula which connect learning to creative innovation in employment and the community; pedagogies that reinforce responsibility and initiative through independent as well as cooperative learning; participative decision-making and partnerships which support collaboration between institutions and across sectors.

Cultural formation

While the nature of learning as progression towards agency and the development of capacity is always subject to institutional structuration, this process, in turn, is deeply shaped and inscribed by the cultural and national formations of any society. To understand learning we must grasp the 'habitus' which defines the very notions of ability and capacity, as well as who should have access to learning opportunities that will develop their agency. The cultural traditions of the public domain are also a significant influence upon agency.

Themes

It was said by participants at the Birmingham seminars that the 1993 Report to the ESRC, presented by the Working Party which John Gray chaired, was still regarded as significant and relevant in many respects although there were some gaps which needed to be clarified and explored. Thus, in this final section, ideas for future research in the field are described in terms of a number of broad headings: stages of learning; learning in different contexts; policy issues; learning in a post-modern world; and learning at the centre.

1 Stages of learning (to be explored comparatively)

Early Learning. There is increasing recognition amongst policy makers as well as education researchers of the significance of early learning for educational achievement within primary and secondary school. A recent OECD report reveals the weakness of provision in the UK and the scale of the problem. If, as seems likely, 'pre-five education' is likely to become one of the most important areas of growth, then development needs to be based upon major programmes of research which include studies of the nature of early learning, the relationship of nursery provision and the family, and patterns of effective professional collaboration.

Learning in School. A number of contributions suggested there was a need for further research to develop understanding of the interaction of the several reforms which have been implemented within schools as a result of the Government's legislative agenda. John Fitz made this case well: 'While we have a foot inside the school gate, we haven't ventured in strength and depth into the classroom to explore how and whether the macro-system has impacted on classroom discourses, interacting practices and on the processes of how learners learn to learn.' Halpin and Troyna reinforce this analysis:

> Instead of being defensive about educational studies and educational research we should engage our energies in consolidating existing strengths and developing new ones. These include taking further forward and possibly into the classroom itself the relationship between systemic and institutional reform and children's learning; and engaging in forms of theoretically informed cross-national policy analysis that give priority to the investigation of particular universalising tendencies, most notably moves towards site-based management and the commodification of education.

This kind of research would require, Fitz believes, 'a new or different rapprochement between various educational disciplines'. Other significant issues for research could include:

- boundary crossing studies: break down the focus just upon school; focus on the key issue of the intersection between school and the family, between the school and the workplace;
- action research in relation to school-based teacher training and teachers' role in developing that area;
- issues of gender and learning remain amongst the most significant and urgent in the field (including equality of opportunity for women and the underachievement or disenchantment of boys);
- school organisation and its relationship to increased performance;
- the relationship between a 'competency' and a 'knowledge' curriculum: the impact of NVQs;
- teaching and learning and its relationship to economic competitiveness.

Higher Education. Research into higher education, and into education and training beyond sixteen, has been neglected. Within higher education research has in the past focused upon issues of funding and structure. Now studies are needed of new styles of student-centred, active learning as against the entrenched subject-centred pedagogies. Another important proposal for development included:

- using the teaching skills of lecturers in HE Departments of Education to train other professionals and lecturers across the higher education sphere.

Adult and Continuing Education. Within continuing education (lifelong learning) there are new trends and directions which need study, especially in relation to health and the environment (green issues).

2 Learning in different settings

Education research, many are increasingly willing to argue, has been too pre-occupied with learning within the statutory sector, and within institution-alised settings within that sector. There is a need for research into how people learn in the different contexts of the home, community and work as well as within the formal boundaries of school, college and university. Kathy Sylva emphasised the need for research on tools for studying the quality of learn-ing in a variety of settings inside and outside the school. The theories of learning we require are likely to be both topic and context specific:

> We need to develop new tools for studying the quality of learning. The old tools have assumed a monolithic theory of learning, that there is one theory of learn-ing. The new tools for a theory of learning need to be much more domain spe-cific: they will be sensitive to the topic being learned, and they will be much more sensitive to the setting or the context in which the learning is taking place.

This analytical perspective could lead to valuable comparative educational studies. For example, a study could concentrate on the individual as a reflec-tive learner throughout all phases of education, exploring what was common and what different between the phases/contexts of learning. This approach would be highly relevant to adult learning and learning in higher education. Related studies could include:

* the relationship between assessment procedures, associated pedagogies and context;
* the theory of pedagogy and learning in different contexts;
* understanding educational relationships and educational conversations in different contexts.

3 Policy issues

The education policy process itself was identified as in need of research. New ways of intervening in policy contexts were required while the actual processes of policy implementation needed to be understood more precisely than at present.

In terms of substantive issues there is growing understanding that future research in the field of education should be much more broadly based than it is at present. Anne West argued:

> Even using a narrow definition of what constitutes education, there is a paucity of research about macro-policy issues – resourcing of education, post-16 edu-cation and training, higher education and other forms of education and train-ing for adults, both in work and out of work. There is also a need for more

education research that has a European focus; whilst there is some at present, there is much that can be learned from the systematic examination and analysis of the systems in operation in other European countries. Using a broader conception of education, there is no doubt that education should be more at the centre of key issues facing our time – social, economic, cultural and environmental.

Discussion emphasised a number of key areas for policy development and research:

Information technology. The implications of the new 'information highway' and all the networking it implies need to be the focus of a major research programme. The possibility of schoolchildren in the UK 'Internetting' with schoolchildren elsewhere in the world offers extraordinary educational possibilities. The questions are endless. What is the impact of IT on learning? Who will be empowered by the new technologies? Will students be more in control of what and how they learn? Or will the programmers gain in control? Will teachers lose their capacity to shape the curriculum and the sequencing of teaching and learning? How is IT integrated into the wider curriculum? Does the new technology imply a greater individualising of the learning process or conversely an increase in the possibility of collaborative learning? Do the new technologies imply a passive role for the learner or explicitly encourage the agency of the learner? Will IT accelerate innovation in education? What are the implications of the information availability for school library resources?

Socio-cultural change and cities. Cities present a key predicament for modern nations. Many cities appear to contain enclaves of deprivation, pollution and crime and yet there is an emerging understanding, as expressed in the 1994 Reith Lectures, that the cultural vitality of cities is becoming the key to national economic and cultural regeneration. Research is needed to understand what it is to live and learn in these crucibles of change.

Some of the deepest structural changes in our society are located at the heart of cities: the collapse of employment, the restructuring and feminisation of work, the redefinition of the family, increasing poverty. The Borrie and Rowntree reports serve to indicate that multiple inequalities in disadvantaged communities are on a sharply increasing gradient. Research is needed to develop understanding of the impact of these changes on education in the city: for example, what it is to learn in contexts of structural change and disadvantage. There is need for imaginative strategies to kindle the motivation of young people to learn in such contexts of change. It requires rethinking of provision and pedagogies. Tim Brighouse's 'university of the first age' illustrates the kind of creativity required.

Yet some cities have become the centres of a new global network. Their success grows out of a vision to develop and sustain their attractive local cultures, recognising that enterprise and innovation grow out of forms of living which encourage creativity. Research is needed into the conditions of creative learning in the global city.

Learning and wealth creation. There has been too limited a grasp of the paradigm shift in skills and learning required for social and economic regeneration. A much more enriched conception of work and wealth creation is needed. Not only does 'social wealth' (e.g., preventative community health care, or environmental repair) add to the quality of life, it clearly adds economic value as well as saving public expenditure. Furthermore, rethinking the nature of work cannot be separated from the social and cultural relations (between the sexes, races, and generations) which define who works and thus the social conditions of economic growth. In this analysis, public policy has had too impoverished a conception not only of work but also of the personal capabilities and powers needed; the institutional capacity required to support the learning of new capacities; and the participation needed to discuss and legitimate the cultural reconstruction of wealth and work. Research is needed to develop understanding of these issues.

Health. Health issues of smoking, drinking, drugs, solvents, nutrition, exercise, Aids have become major issues for education and social policy. Research is needed into the prevalence of these and other behaviours and the risk to personal development. Study is needed about why young people do and do not adopt healthy life styles as well as what kinds of health intervention programmes are successful in influencing the attitudes and behaviour of young people. A theory is needed of the principles and practice of health education. Such a theory would be able to connect health issues to conceptions of learning and teaching within school and within the wider community.

4 Learning in a post-modern world

The transformations of our time are altering fundamentally the structure of experience and the powers and capacities needed to live in a post-modern world. The changes raise deep questions for the government of education and for the polity in general about:

- *what it is to be a person.* Is a person a passive being or possessed of powers that define his or her essential agency?
- *whether there is any such thing as a society and what it is.* Is it an aggregation of individuals or some form of social and linguistic community?
- *what should be the nature of the polity.* What is it to be a member and with what rights and duties? What distribution of power and wealth is consistent with justice and freedom? Who should take decisions and how? What forms of accountability and representation define our democracy?

Any effective response to these questions will require a capacity for renewal and for learning, from the institutions of our society as much as from each individual confronting the changed circumstances in private life. Issues for research include:

- learning, self-identity and subjectivity;
- learning, civility and civil society;
- learning and the politics of difference;
- how education can promote active citizenship and enhance social solidarity in societies which are increasingly plural and individualistic;
- whether the nation-state will have a role in education and what forms of democratic control are possible;
- what models of knowledge and culture might underpin the curriculum in so called post-modern societies.

Research is needed into the nature and conditions of agency in the post-modern world. How do institutions work within their multiple publics to generate agreements about identity and purpose in learning? How do a civil society, citizenship and the politics of difference underpin learning to become a person and a community in a post-modern world?

5 Learning at the centre

Some voices argue the need for researchers to be sponsored into the learning/educational issues which lie at the centre of many of the critical issues facing the modern world. Michael Bassey has been prominent in this respect arguing that while issues of learning within school will properly be a continuing concern for researchers, nevertheless beyond these there are matters which lie outside the classroom, affect people of every age, and are central to the future of humankind:

> There are perhaps five billion people on the planet Earth. How can they learn to avoid potential disasters that are associated with famine, environmental pollution, over-population, resource exhaustion, extinction of wild-life species, and ecological disruption? How can they learn to contain aggression, avoid adult bullying, prevent vandalism, stop wars? How can they learn to stop racial hatred, ethnic cleansing, genocide? How can they learn to use medical knowledge to reduce the incidence of disease? How can they turn growth economics into steady-state economics? How can they learn to organise their political affairs so that the democratic ideal of the open society can prosper?

For Bassey and others, these are educational problems.

> They are about learning. They require sociological research and psychological research which will inform our understanding of these phenomena as educational problems and they require educational research which will inform the judgements and decisions of people learning how to handle these problems. They require the focused intelligence of multi-disciplinary teams of researchers with as much attention being paid to effective dissemination of results as to the cre-

ative development of new insights. They should be on the agenda of university departments of education throughout the world for they are the significant issues of today and tomorrow.

IV CONCLUSION

Educational studies, like many other fields of study, is experiencing the pressures of change facing higher education, and controversies surrounding the need to clarify the purpose and foundations of its work. The willingness to engage in such a debate reveals strength within the field, and the seminars, while illustrating differences of perspective, nevertheless indicated the potential to create a meta-frame of shared assumptions about educational research. Strategies for the future include developments at the level of the Department, the field of study and the sponsor.

At the level of Departments of Education

The new paradigm sets the agenda for the Departments of Education of the future – an institution which is the centre for action research on learning throughout society. It will require a significant shift of culture for some DEs – both to broaden their conception of education and to generate a flourishing ethos of independent, theoretically based research. Others, however, are already there. The approach of many institutions for organising and managing the development of such a research culture includes:

- strategic planning: identifying and prioritising institutional strengths, and planning to ensure a coherent and balanced profile of research;
- resource programming to establish the infrastructure for research continuity;
- team-working to encourage cohesion and shared responsibilities for research;
- networking within the university and between institutions to enable flexibility and interdependence;
- staff development and appraisal to consolidate research skills.

Underlying all these developments in the excellent DE is the preoccupation with producing a culture of research; one which generates a shared commitment to analysis, to open discussion, and to learning. In the new paradigm the good institution becomes an inquiring organisation whose culture and practice are oriented to action research on the nature of learning throughout society.

At the level of the field

A number of strategic developments were proposed to support the education research community. These involved questions of identity, organisation, communication and assertion.

(i) Identity

The sense of an emerging disciplinary identity was encouraged by the broad agreement for the 'need to strengthen the sense of the education research community and of an education community'. Both of these communities need support through networks and other means.

(ii) Organisational development

Many are clear that educational studies needs to forge clearer organisational relationships with other departments in their institutions. The variety of existing relationships is recognised. Sometimes DEs are located in social science faculties, sometimes they are quite separate. DEs themselves have a great variety of practices in establishing formal links with other disciplines which might include the arts and sciences as well as the social sciences. There is every reason, many argue, for educational studies to maintain linkages with related social sciences and other applied fields such as social studies. The arguments for organisational interdependence were pressed particularly strongly by Deem, Ball, Halpin and Troyna:

> We need to break out more from our own departments and forge academic relationships with cognate disciplines, particularly sociology, political science, psychology and economics.
>
> (Halpin and Troyna)

> Mergers or alliances will not offer magical solutions to the ills of educational studies, but more relationships with social policy would not go amiss. And some colleagues in some sites have been developing these.
>
> (Ball)

Beyond the institution, the education research community also needs to develop multi-disciplinary networks through 'special interest groups' across the country.

(iii) Communication

Researchers need to learn to be more sensitive when communicating their findings so as to reflect the needs of different audiences: 'If you are speaking to ESRC you might want to emphasise the relevance of your findings to certain social science disciplines; when you're talking to a policy group or a teacher group you might want to emphasise another orientation' (Helen Simons). It was also generally acknowledged that the community of education researchers needed to be much more active in communicating and promoting their work:

> We need to consider ways of taking greater control over how our research is reported in media other than academic journals and books. Despite the fact that all of us have considerable experience of handling newspaper, radio and TV journalists our work is often misrepresented and insufficiently reported by them. Unlike politicians who seem able successfully to package what they want to say, the products of our research are mostly reported in ways that do not do justice to its significance.

> (Halpin and Troyna)

> If education has theoretical contributions to make to the social sciences in general it may need to become more ambitious and make its influence felt in cognate disciplines via publications which are not education-focused. The corollary of that, however, is that educationists may need to make a considerable effort to map what is going on in other disciplines.

> (Fitz)

'The community of researchers needs', Tricia Broadfoot concluded, 'to be more assertive, to take a more pro-active stance with politicians and funding bodies so that the "public domain" can develop an enhanced understanding of the purposes and strength of educational research.'

At the level of the sponsor

Finally, sponsors have a key role to play. As Rosalind Driver pointed out: 'There are undoubtedly educational dimensions to most domains of human activity. From a pragmatic point of view, the research that tends to get support, however, relates to education in formal settings where there are institutional interests at stake.' An appropriate lead from sponsors is thus essential to steering the strategic developments encouraged in this report: principally a much broader conception of educational issues to be researched and more imaginative collaborative studies within and between institutions.

NOTES

1. See Ranson (1993).
2. See Skidelsky (1993) – *Hansard*, 7 December, col. 882–3.
3. See Harvey (1993), Mouffe (1993), Altieri (1994).
4. See McCabe, *The Times Higher Educational Supplement*, 1995, 10, 3.
5. See MacIntyre (1990; 1995).
6. See Nixon *et al.*, (1995).

REFERENCES

Altieri, C. (1994) *Subjective Agency*, Oxford, Blackwell.

Bassey, M. (1994) Why Lord Skidelsky is so wrong, *The Times Higher Educational Supplement* 1, 21, January.

Gellner, E. (1988) *Plough, Sword and Book*, London, Collins.

Gray, J. (1993) *Education Research Working Group Report* (ESRC), January.

Halpin, D. (1995) Editorial, *British Journal of Educational Studies*, 43, 1.

Halpin, D. and Troyna, B. (1994) *Researching Education Policy: Ethical and Methodological Issues*, London, Falmer.

Harvey, D. (1993) Class relations, social justice and the politics of difference, in J. Squires (ed.) *Principled Positions*, London, Lawrence & Wishart.

Hobsbawm, E. (1994) *Age of Extremes*, London, Michael Joseph.

MacIntyre, A. (1990) *Three Rival Versions of Moral Enquiry*, London, Duckworth.

MacIntyre, A. (1995) A partial response to my critics, in J. Horton and S. Mendus (eds.) *After MacIntyre*, Oxford, Polity Press.

Mouffe, C. (1993) *The Return of the Political*, London, Verso.

Nixon, J. Martin. J., McKeown, P. and Ranson, S. (1995) *Encouraging Learning: Towards a Theory of the Learning School*, Milton Keynes, Open University.

Pimenoff, S. (1995) Seeking for the truth, *Guardian Education*, 11 April, p. 6.

Ranson, S. (1993) The management and organisation of education research, *Research Papers in Education*, 8, 2.

Ranson, S. (1995) *The Future of Education Research: Learning at the Centre* (a report to the ESRC).

Ranson, S. (1996) Towards a theory of learning, *British Journal of Educational Studies*, Vol. 44, no. 1, pp. 6–26.

Responses to Section One

4

SOME SIGNIFICANT DEVELOPMENTS?

Caroline Gipps

In this chapter I will respond in the main to the (1992) report of the ESRC's working party chaired by John Gray. The report very usefully, in my view, sets out at the beginning both a definition of the field and some areas of strength. It is important that any review which attempts to look forward to developments in the future is based upon a realistic and fair critique of the current state of play; I believe that Gray's report does this commendably, and thereby betrays its intellectual/academic origins. The key requirements he outlines for the future (to develop strategies for promoting theoretical advancement; to initiate ways of further improving the methodological contribution; and to demonstrate practical significance to the wider world) are clearly crucial to maintaining a profile (or even an existence) for educational research on any scale. I will return to the vexed issue of demonstrating practical significance later.

RECENT CHANGES

First I wish to point out that since 1992 some changes have taken place within the wider context of research funded by three major agencies: the DfEE, SCAA (the School Curriculum and Assessment Authority – now the Qualifications and Curriculum Authority – QCA) and the ESRC itself. Gray makes two points: 'For the foreseeable future the greater preponderance of non-ESRC funding for research on education is likely to be for studies of an essentially applied and short-term nature'; 'Contractual restrictions on publication are also likely to inhibit the development of rigorous research.' Gray (1992) pp. 4 and 9.

The DfEE has undergone quite a significant change in approach to research, no doubt following on from the merger of the Departments of

Education with Employment. It is well known that amongst government departments education has had a low priority for research while employment has always seen research as an important element of its strategy. During the summer of 1996 the DfEE ran a series of four research liaison seminars in the areas of pre-16 education, 16–19s, adults in the labour market and developments in the labour market. The DfEE aimed to draw on these contributions to help formulate its research plans; and, after the 1997 General Election, it built on them in undertaking a more fundamental review of educational research. The fact that the DfEE is conducting such a review after discussing the potential direction and content of educational research with members of the research community and others is very much to be welcomed.

Furthermore, the DfEE has recently funded a five-year longitudinal study of the effectiveness of preschool education of various forms at a cost of around £1.48 million: this has, by any light, to be seen as a real commitment to high-quality, policy-related educational research. It is designed in a rigorous way, involving longitudinal studies, and therefore is expensive in terms of DfEE funds and university staff time. This again is a welcome development.

QCA, whilst not funding theoretical research as such, has shown a shift in its attitude to research, researchers and a research agenda, with regular meetings of researchers involved in assessment. Whilst the timescales are still short, there is a commitment to open evaluation and to some research on underlying issues; for example, SCAA funded a study to evaluate consistency in teacher assessment which was carried out in liaison with the NUT. The report of the evaluation of national assessment in 1995 at Key Stage 3 carried out by Exeter University was a considerably more open document than many of those produced in the early stages of the national assessment programme. Similarly both the science and the maths test development teams have been analysing performance on the national tests at Key Stage 2 in depth in order to identify issues of performance which can be used at a diagnostic level. All these are positive moves away from a preoccupation with applied, short-term research.

By contrast, the ESRC now has more of an instrumental approach with an important focus on users and impact, together with a theme-driven research programme which is heavily applied. We thus have a system of funding in which three major players are drawing closer together: there is less polarisation amongst major funders and the two extremes are softening.

Another important change is the contractual position on publication and copyright. The first major funding body that, to our knowledge, has changed their contracts on these points is the Department of Health (DoH). University ownership of copyright, and the right to publish a certain length of time after the submission of a final report to the sponsors, are now a part of DoH research centre contracts. We believe that this change has been influenced by pressure from the universities in order to claim from HEFCE (the Higher

Education Funding Council for England) that element of their funding which is based on GR (generic research). For research to count as GR in HEFCE terms, and therefore to bring block grant funding to the university concerned, it must be in the public domain. HEFCE will not shift on this point and therefore it appears as though government departments/funding bodies are being urged to move on this themselves (one imagines that it is probably the weight of science and medical departments in major universities which has pushed this forward). Following this, the Institute of Education in London was able to negotiate similar publication and copyright clauses in a recent DfEE contract. It also appears that at least one university who had a large contract with SCAA was able to publish virtually what they wished at the end of the research, suggesting that SCAA too was softening on this issue where appropriate. The exchange of letters which Professor Helen Simons and I had with Sir Ron Dearing and which were reprinted in *Research Intelligence* (autumn 1995, issue no. 54, p. 21) indicated SCAA's position at the time:

> the principle on which SCAA has operated since its creation last year is that research and evaluation work conducted for the Authority will be published. This is a principle to which we want to adhere; it is also consistent with the government's Code of Practice on Access to Government Information.

Sir Ron did however list a number of situations in which full publication would not be appropriate. This is a helpful principle and we welcome a climate of research co-operation where publication is discussed openly and is presumed to take place rather than not.

STATUS AND TRAINING OF RESEARCHERS

Another important issue which is addressed in Gray's working party report is the training and status of career researchers. There have been developments here too, for instance, in the CVCP (Committee of Vice Chancellors and Principals) concordat with the research councils on 'Contract Research Staff Career Management'. This concordat involves not only the ESRC (and other research councils) but also CVCP, SCOP (Standing Conference of Principals), COSHEP (Committee of Scottish Higher Education Principals), the Royal Society and the British Academy. This concordat is to be welcomed for its agreement that conditions of employment for research staff should match those for other staff employed by universities, and for its focus on review and mentoring of contract researchers, including in-service training and supervision. The concordat is an important step forward for contract research staff, but will do nothing to address the real problem for contract researchers which is that of the short-term nature of their contracts (although of course many lecturing staff now operate on short-term contracts as well).

Clearly large research institutions, such as the Institute of Education, will need to consider further ways of using their HEFCE core grant to provide some security for career researchers, with more part-time research lectureships and more underwriting of rolling contracts. In this way we can give our talented researchers the chance to stay in the system if they choose. A traditional route for educational researchers has been to move sideways into lecturing posts, since the posts tended to have, if not longer contracts, certainly more security attached to them. That situation has also changed, and in two ways: fewer university lecturers are being appointed, and those who are, are not often on long-term contracts. Many researchers do not in any case wish to move into lecturing jobs since they prefer to focus their time and energies where their main skills are – that is, in doing, and writing up, research. It is possible that we will see in five years' time a smaller number of high-status research institutes/departments of education with HEFCE-funded staff carrying out research as our major research cadre; this is the way in which many academics outside education wish to see future developments going and was a recommendation of the Dearing Report. HEFCE research money would be concentrated in a smaller number of universities with those universities doing the bulk of the research in the field. Whether that is likely to happen in education is not at all clear, and if it did, what would be the impact on our ability to continue involving many teachers in practitioner or action research?

THE RESEARCH ASSESSMENT EXERCISE (RAE)

The major force which is driving research activity for most members of staff in education departments in this country is not ESRC funding, or even external research funding in general, but the RAE. I was recently a member of the RAE Panel for Education and read through every submission from every university department for education in the country. Now, looking again in detail at the Gray and Ranson ESRC reports, it is quite clear that there is a gulf between those of us who are fortunate enough to get ESRC funding (we are indeed a very fortunate few) and others: most of our colleagues are doing research without funding, developing their scholarship and working with teachers, or working with funding from a very different range of sources, usually on much shorter timescales. The timing of the ESRC application and award procedure is also now out of sync with modern academic life: the take-up time between applying for a grant and being able to use the money is too long, and yet still academics apply for them. This is of course because they provide two absolutely key components in which researchers are interested: freedom to carry out the research unencumbered once the proposal has been accepted, and prestige.

IMPACT ISSUES

I now return to the issue of impact. This has always caused anxiety amongst educational researchers. Over fifteen years ago I was involved in an evaluation of the Assessment of Performance Unit (APU). The APU was the first national assessment programme which this country had; modelled on the American NAEP (National Assessment of Educational Progress) system it designed high-quality assessments across English, maths, science and modern languages. The research programme was expensive, but the assessments were of high quality. The quality of the data produced was high and many reports were written about children's performance at different ages which were designed to be of use to teachers. Teachers never read the reports and one of the key anxieties for the APU was the limited extent to which their results and findings were taken up and used. However, we can now see, fifteen years on, that the APU has had a tremendous impact on assessment worldwide. The APU was the first to design true performance-based assessments with rigorous administration and marking schemes. Teachers were trained as markers by the research team and these skills have fed into the training and development of teachers for practical assessment and marking both at GCSE and national assessment level. Current developments in the USA to produce usable performance assessments are building on this APU work. The early SAT tasks for the National Curriculum assessment programme which were, in diagnostic and formative assessment terms, probably some of the best instruments designed for teachers, came out of the experience of the APU development. Furthermore we know that the SAT tasks 'trained' Key Stage 1 teachers to become extremely competent assessors in terms of close observation, assessing against criteria (more or less closely) and moderating the results. The APU is a good example of how money spent on research *does* impact on teachers' practice, although in a far from simplistic route. Weiss (1980) uses the phrase 'knowledge creep and decision accretion' to convey how research knowledge gets only slowly into policy deliberation and may begin to affect policy not by a single clear decision but through a more diffuse process of influence (or, as the ancients phrased it: *scienta dependit in mores* – knowledge works its way into habits).

Boyd and Plank (1994) argue that the role of research and policy studies in problem formulation cannot be overstressed for this is how ideas get on to the agenda for discussion and policy-making, whether by accretion or more explicit access. They point out that as long ago as 1978 Getzels demonstrated the generally underestimated impact of basic research on pedagogy on thinking and problem formulation in education. Boyd and Plank argue that the generally slow diffusion of research findings and ideas through knowledge creep and decision accretion may actually be beneficial in that in this way ideas and implications from research have to work their way through people's acceptance and capture their imagination.

In reviewing the perennial question of why research and policy studies in education are so often undervalued ('Why is it that the support for educational research is declining while questions about education and the political attention directed toward education [are] increasing?' – Heyneman, 1992, p. 7), Boyd and Plank come up with four possibilities. *First*, many people believe that educational research and development efforts have little pay-off: the slow effects often obscure the pay-offs of research; moreover education has a specific problem in that everyone is familiar with the process of schooling and therefore has a view about the appropriateness of ways of, for example, maintaining discipline and order in schools, or the teaching of reading. *Secondly*, impact is not so much a dissemination problem as an incentive problem: teachers have, in the past, had few incentives to do a better job. Combine this with the fact that teachers have little free time to engage in reading and development, then the lack of interest in research results is hardly surprising. (However, schools which are involved in whole-school improvement efforts with joint professional development schemes clearly buck this trend.) *Thirdly*, is a lack of consensus within the educational research community. This seems to be an issue for education within the ESRC panels: whilst the psychologists and economists and lawyers have close agreement about what is 'good' research, and what is the right way to go about it, educational researchers are not generally so encumbered by clear certainties. This in itself some see as a hindrance to the profession whilst others feel it is a source of its vitality and excitement. *Fourthly*, the field is heavily politicised: groups differ on many fundamental questions in the domain of education thereby disagreeing even on what sort of research should be done (the vexed issue of researching class size is a good example).

These last two points, in particular, indicate that current moves towards coherent thematic planning for research as argued in the Gray report and by David Hargreaves would help to raise the profile and value of educational research. Whilst accepting that there are different, and legitimate, research approaches (rather than arguing about whether one approach is better than another) we should develop our skills across a range of research methodologies and use those which are most appropriate to the topic. In a recent paper (1996) Andy Hargreaves explores issues to do with university-based research and research knowledge and how it can be made more useful to teachers. Amongst the principles that he sets out in his agenda for postmodern professional knowledge generation and utilisation are these: to diversify what are to count as legitimate forms of knowledge about teaching and education; to broaden the forms of discourse through which research knowledge is presented; to widen what it means to be a teacher to include skill and practice in systematic inquiry; to redesign educational policy processes so that teachers can become agents of policy realisation rather than conduits of policy implementation; and to widen what it means to be a university professor or researcher in education to include practical and policy work with other educational audiences and constituencies.

FUTURE PRIORITIES

We need as researchers to read more and write less. This is not a flippant observation; it is a serious comment on how little time we as academic researchers have to address properly other people's writing. Not just in our own research areas, where of course we do keep up, but in reading more broadly across the field in other social science areas and in research methods in general. A wider reading across these areas would allow us all to be more reflective, to build on what others write, and would break down barriers across the cognate disciplines. We need regular reviews of research findings, along the line of those being commissioned by OFSTED at the moment, and also more academic reviews of recent research such as those produced by the American Educational Research Association. I understand that BERA is planning to set up a system for this in the near future. All of this, I am convinced, would lead to a much higher-quality product.

We must continue to involve teachers in research activity: as partners in research projects, as action researchers in their own right and as researchers doing higher degrees. We clearly also need to think much more creatively about how to involve teachers in disseminating and using results of research. (As an example, one idea that we are trying to put forward is that when teachers mark tests, alongside the marking key should be an analysis of the most common errors and what these are likely to mean in diagnostic terms and for appropriate teaching follow-up. In other words, the aim is to build the diagnostic information into the marking process so that teachers look at this information at the same time as they are doing the marking rather than as a separate step.)

It is important to try to develop co-ordination across the DfEE, QCA, ESRC and other funding agencies/bodies in addressing thematic priorities for educational research. David Hargreaves' suggestion of a national forum which would play a role in determining and co-ordinating such an agenda of thematic priorities is, I think, a useful one.

Given the politicisation of education as a field, multiple sources of funding for research must remain. Given the tremendous importance of education to our society and the small sums which, as Gray's report shows, are spent on educational research in this country, it is surprising that there is no education subcommittee within ESRC with earmarked funds for education. The recent suggestion that HEFCE funds for educational research be transferred in large measure to the Teacher Training Agency (TTA), is not, in my view, appropriate since the TTA does not have the same independence of government as does ESRC or the universities. The traditional freedom of universities to engage in research which may be politically unacceptable, or of a basic theoretical nature, is a very important one and that route to educational research must not be lost.

REFERENCES

Boyd, W. and Plank, D. (1994) Educational policy studies: overview, *International Encyclopaedia of Education*, Vol. 4, pp. 1835–41.

Getzels, J. W. (1978), Paradigm and Practice: on the impact of basic research in education, in P. Suppes (ed.) *The Impact of Research on Education: Some Case Studies*, National Academy of Education: Washington.

Gray, J. *et al.*(1992) *Frameworks and Priorities for Research in Education: Towards a Strategy for the ESRC*, Swindon: ESRC..

Hargreaves, A. (1996) Transforming knowledge: blurring the boundaries between research, policy, and practice, *Educational Evaluation and Policy Analysis*, Vol. 18, no. 2, pp. 105–22.

Heyneman, S. (1992) Educational quality and the crisis of educational research, *CIES Newsletter*, Vol. 101, no. 2, p. 7.

Weiss, C. (1980) Knowledge creep and decision accretion, *Knowledge: Creation, Diffusion*, Vol. 1, no. 3, pp. 381–404.

5

THE SILENCE OF THE SHADOWS: EDUCATIONAL RESEARCH AND THE ESRC

David Hamilton

This is my third comment on the ESRC report on *Frameworks and Priorities for Research in Education: Towards a Strategy for the ESRC*. I welcome the opportunity, and the open remit offered by the editors of this volume.

I first submitted a few hurried comments when the report was circulated early in 1993. Dissatisfied with those efforts, yet feeling that the report was important, I prepared more extended comments for the BERA conference held in Oxford (September, 1994). My comment had the title 'Clockwork universes or clockwork oranges?', and the version I subsequently prepared for the *British Educational Research Journal* (*BERJ*) included the subtitle, 'on the reform of educational research and the refinement of educational practice'.

The editors of *BERJ* returned the paper to me for revision. One of the reviewers felt that I should have included a more extensive summary of the ESRC report; and even suggested that one element of my argument might be libellous. I was insufficiently moved by these suggestions and, crowded by other tasks, I turned to other things.

Nevertheless, interest in my conference comments was aroused elsewhere. Having been quoted by John Elliot in a recent issue of the *Cambridge Journal of Education* I began to receive requests for copies. To meet this unexpected demand (two copies to date) I posted my *BERJ* submission on the Internet site of Liverpool University Department of Education (http:\www.liv.ac.uk\education), where it can be consulted and/or retrieved as a hard copy.

On this, my third opportunity to comment, I will not repeat the arguments of 'Clockwork universes or clockwork oranges?' Instead, I will offer a complementary set of comments. I restrict myself to the abridged text and, in particular, to the section on 'the need for review'. Further, I have chosen to

focus on one long-term issue – the shadowy yet persistent empiricist and positivist inheritance of British educational research. Finally, I have written these
notes such that, with the remainder of this volume, they could be explored
during an ESRC-recognised course of research training. On such occasions,
however, I might also start with another question for the ESRC: is the notion
of 'research training' as oxymoronic as 'military intelligence'?

POSTPOSITIVISM

The ESRC report appears to make no mention of the fundamental changes
that have entered Anglo-American educational research since the 1960s. The
only allusions that I can find are oblique references to 'increasing levels of
conceptual and methodological sophistication' and to the 'substantial' United
Kingdom contribution made in the 'methodological' area of 'qualitative
approaches to data-gathering'.

I would put a different spin on these allusions. The rise of so-called qualitative research has been an epistemological rather than a methodological
breakthrough. It arises from Kant's re-evaluation of empiricism in the eigh-
teenth century, and comparable twentieth-century re-evaluations of positivism
associated with, among others, Wittgenstein, Vygotsky, Kuhn and Habermas.
Anglo-French positivism was launched in August Comte's *Cours de
Philosophie Positive* (6 vols, 1832–42) and John Stuart Mill's *A System of
Logic* (1843). Post-Kantian tensions occupied much of mainland European
thought during the nineteenth century and the first half of the twentieth century, but these debates spilled over into the Anglo-American arena with the
appearance of Thomas Kuhn's *The Structure of Scientific Revolutions* (2nd
edn, 1962).

Since that time, Anglo-American educational research has had to come to
terms with the Kantian premise that all knowing is presumptive and that,
therefore, all observations and facts are theory laden. Indeed, both
Wittgenstein and Kuhn had used the same optical illusion (Jastrow's
duck/rabbit) to illustrate this feature of modern thought: *viz.*, that there is
more to seeing than meets the eye (see Campbell, 1988, p. 64).

I came to these ideas through the *The Structure of Scientific Revolutions*
and also through a comparable interruption made within the mainstream of
educational research. In the same seminal paper in which Michael Scriven
(1967, p. 40) advanced the distinction between formative and summative
evaluation, he also argued that curriculum evaluation should include not only
the 'gathering' of information but also the 'justification' of the curriculum
goals previously adopted. 'Why?' questions, he proposed, were no less important to the scrutiny of curricula than 'what?' or 'how?' questions.

Thus, whenever I am asked to teach 'evaluation', I build the course around the distinction between 'weak' and 'strong' evaluation (my labels). Weak evaluations raise questions of the form 'Does the programme meet its goals?', whereas strong evaluations also include evaluation of the goals themselves.

I have tried to remain faithful to Kant's caution and Scriven's injunction. Like many others, I have generalised them to my research practice. Postpositivist research becomes a 'critical' or 'hermeneutic' activity. It attracts these descriptors because it incorporates the scrutiny as well as the advancement of theory and method.

Postpositivism, therefore, is an inclusive label. It relates not to a field of research nor to prescribed procedures. Rather, it is a perspective on research – which I can illustrate with reference to 'qualitative' research – one of the approaches identified in the ESRC report.

As noted, I regard the spread of qualitative research as directly attributable to the impact of postpositivism. Any quantitative proposition (e.g. 'here are two cups') necessarily entails a prior qualitative question ('Are these entities both cups?'). Mindful of the fact that the Latin word *qualis* means 'what kind of?', qualitative research has come to prominence because it prioritises qualitative questions over their quantitative counterparts. Qualitative research, therefore, does not preclude quantitative analysis, it merely engages more strongly with the justification of category systems, typologies and taxonomies (different names for the same thing). Thus, self-confessed qualitative researchers are likely to give more time and space to problems associated with the justification of the theories and methods of the status quo. In turn, of course their empiricist and positivist colleagues find them unreasonably argumentative, disruptive, pedantic, unhelpful. Compare, for instance, my essay on the OFSTED review of school effectiveness research (Hamilton, 1996) with the authors' rejoinder (Sammons *et al.*, 1996).

Qualitative research is a diverse practice, not a neat label. Without attention to justification, it can be just as empiricist as its positivist counterparts. The substitution of endless interview transcripts for equally voluminous summaries of test data is merely the substitution of one form of empiricism for another.

But why is discussion of postpositivism missing from the ESRC report? Here is a suggestion. Postpositivism eschews linear technocratic models of causality. Accordingly, it cannot be reduced to a social engineering model. It regards education as a complex social practice. It is not a network of levers that operates with 100% efficiency. Nor does it operate through the distribution of packets of digitalised information. Education, teaching and, above all, school teaching are mediation not transmission processes. The difference between postpositivist research and its forerunners is not between good and bad research, nor between easy and difficult research. Rather, it is about different ways of representing the world and interfering in its workings.

TEACHING AS A RESEARCH-BASED PROFESSION

This brings me to my second comment on the ESRC report. Earlier critics noted that it says very little about the relationship between teachers and research except, perhaps, in its reference to action research as an influential methodology. Indeed, I affronted one of *BERJ*'s reviewers with my conjecture that the report had been written using a template supplied by the natural science tendency of the ESRC. Yet I am not arguing, in response, that education is a human science. I go further – to propose that education is an occupational science. Here I find common cause with the Teacher Training Agency's claim that teaching should be reconfigured as a research-based profession.

I recognise that the discipline of educational studies entered British universities in response to local efforts to upgrade the status and practice of schoolteachers. If universities are to retain such a mission, their departments of education need to take a principled position on the relationship between research and (school)teaching. In the process, they must distinguish themselves from university departments (e.g. philosophy, sociology) which have a different connection to the occupational structure of the labour market.

In other words, departments of education must take up a position on the refinement of 'practice' rather than the extension of knowledge. For example, when I read masters degree dissertations, I always seek an answer to the question: how does this work relate to the candidate's professional practice? (Rather than: how does this work contribute to the advancement of knowledge?)

I feel that the ESRC should develop a more elaborate position on the relationship between knowledge and practice. I recognise that this is not a trivial question. It cannot be collapsed into the theory–practice dualism. It must come to terms, for instance, with the fact that the seventeenth-century scientific revolution rendered practitioners the object of science; whereas the eighteenth-century Enlightenment repositioned them as the subjects of science. Is it an accident, for instance, that Manchester Grammar School chose Kant's slogan *sapere aude* as its motto; and that a one-time pupil of that establishment, Lawrence Stenhouse, made much of the same idea – 'have courage to use your own understanding' (see Stenhouse, 1983, p. x)?

WHAT IS RESEARCH

By the same token, the ESRC report might have given a little more space to the question: what is research? I tend to think along the following lines. Human beings have always tried to ease, assure or extend their futures. They have sought to enhance their collective chances of survival by reducing the possibility that they will be overtaken by extinction. To do so, they have domesticated the natural world – turned it into a homeland.

Over the same period, humans have extended their powers of observation and record-keeping. They have accumulated their experience and they have used it to prefigure the future. Concurrently, these practices have also become partitioned, institutionalised, professionalised and bureaucratised. The ESRC, like its report, is a consummate expression of these annexation processes.

Yet all humans still retain their investigative powers. They – or we – try to think ahead and, in all kinds of ways, probe the future. The pursuit of such domestication may seem remote from the mysteries of modern science (yet see Latour, 1987). It still, however, can be validly designated as practitioner research. But where do such inquiries fit into the future plans of the ESRC? And what version of research – the domesticated or the annexed version – is to feature in the future plans of the Teacher Training Agency?

REFERENCES

Campbell, D.T. (1988) Qualitative knowing in action research (1978). Reprinted in *Methodology and Epistemology for Social Science* (selected papers edited by E. S. Overman), Chicago, IL, University of Chicago Press.

Hamilton, D. (1996) Peddling feel-good fictions, *Forum*, Vol. 38, no. 2, pp. 54–6.

Kuhn, T. S. (1962) *The Structure of Scientific Revolutions* (2nd edn), Chicago, IL, Chicago University Press.

Latour, B. (1987) *Science in Action: How to Follow Scientists and Engineers through Society*, Cambridge, MA, Harvard University Press.

Sammons, P., Mortimore, P. and Hillman, J. (1996) Key characteristics of effective schools: a response to peddling feel-good fictions, *Forum*, Vol. 38, no. 2, pp. 88–9.

Scriven, M. (1967) The methodology of evaluation, in R. Tyler, R. Gagne and M. Scriven (eds.) *Perspectives on Curriculum Evaluation. AERA Monograph Series on Curriculum Evaluation*, Chicago, IL, Rand McNally.

Stenhouse, L. (1983) *Authority, Education and Emancipation*, London, Heinemann.

6

RESEARCH, DISSENT AND THE REINSTATEMENT OF THEORY[1]

David Bridges

There is much that I agree with in the chapters of both Gray and Ranson – some good sense in the first and perhaps rather more educational vision in the second. They leave me, however, with two particular concerns arising out of both what has been said and what is missing, and it is on these that I shall focus.

RESEARCH AS DISSENT

I start off from the assumption that a democracy requires institutionalised systems of dissent which serve a democratic citizenry by offering informed critical commentary on the activity of those in power and offering plausible alternatives to the policies which those in power are proposing or pursuing. This principle is no doubt contestable, but it is where I start from and it informs my concern. A formal parliamentary opposition and a free press are among the institutions which have traditionally been expected to play this role, though in the UK today it is difficult to see that either seriously live up to this expectation.

If we turn to the educational scene more specifically, the picture gets worse. The removal from office of senior civil servants who fail to support government policies with sufficient enthusiasm and the erosion of their independence by their being obliged to support the party political activity of ministers undermine the opportunity for even the private voice of dissent in the ministerial office. What used to be firmly *Her Majesty's* inspectors, but are now directed by a political placeman, have lost all credibility as a voice independent of the political will of the Secretary of State. The Secretary of State was

[1] This contribution was submitted in November 1996

endowed by the Education Reform Act 1988 with so much power to act by regulation that the control of educational change was effectively taken out of the forum of Parliament. The powers of the local education authorities were much reduced and their inspectors and advisers, to whom parents, teachers and local councillors could once have looked for an independent opinion, have been decimated in numbers and distracted by their need to make a living in a competitive market. Lecturers in colleges and departments of education were, under the last government, systematically disparaged and criticisms were eagerly taken up by a compliant press. Where, then, today and in the future can a citizenry turn for an independent critical voice on educational matters and how can we protect any such voice or voices from the forces still at large that seek not merely to control the practice of education but also to control the terms in which this practice is debated?

Predictably, no doubt, I want to reaffirm the crucial role of the education research community in sustaining an informed, independent voice (or, more accurately, a variety of voices), and I would like to see this principle reflected more strongly in any policy recommendations which come from this community. I have no doubt that Gray and Ranson would all share this commitment in principle, but there are a number of points where the chapter by Gray steers dangerously close to its erosion. While they acknowledge that 'Research has an important contribution to make in the change process', that role seems to be largely conceived in terms of supporting or informing the agenda for change which others have dictated rather than in challenging the direction or nature of that agenda (something which Ranson both urges and illustrates rather more effectively). Their reference to a national research effort guided on the Australian model by a set of national priorities, and their desire for 'a measure of coherence' is also worrying. Why not a national Educational Research Board with a national education research agenda? – and then Secretaries of State can put their own appointee as chair and fill the board with their own sympathisers . . . and down goes another of those irksome institutions of dissent. (Compare, if you like, precisely what is happening in the Teacher Training Agency's approach to research.)

Happily Gray concludes that responsibility for ensuring the continuing development of research does not currently rest with any one organisation – nor could it, but one would like to see a more positive commitment to the *functional desirability* of the principle of decentralised, multisite, unco-ordinated research – to the principle of anarchy in the research community and to a structure for research which, like the Internet, inherently eludes attempts at its control.

To say all this is not to ignore the other imperatives which bear upon the research community (and which are well represented in the chapter by Gray) to address through our research the practical problems thrown up by government policy. Nor is it to suggest that researchers should never undertake work for government departments. What it does suggest is that in a review of research such as this we should give careful attention to ways in which a research community which is doing both of these things can simultaneously honour its duty of dissent to a wider democratic community. This seems to me to indicate the following:

- Maintaining a strong position in relation to the conditions which govern contracted research for government and in particular the independent publication of research findings; ensuring that there remain plentiful sources outside and independent of government which are prepared to support an independent research agenda and one which can generate critical dialogue around government and alternative policies - a principle which makes me nervous of the suggestion in Gray's chapter that ESRC should establish better channels of liaison with, for example, the Department for Education and Employment.
- Ensuring that research is published in a form which does actually reach this wider audience.
- Ensuring that the universities, which provide the institutional setting for this activity, support researchers who run into the political flak which can accompany effective critical questioning of the activity of government or other powerful bodies.

I have written so far about the duty of dissent *vis-à-vis* government, because this is the institution which perhaps most vividly threatens this dissent. But there is a different form of stifling in which the research community can be readily tempted to collude. In some political climates it is easy to understand how researchers feel themselves allied with teachers against government policies many of which both groups view as damaging to the education of children. When both are under fire it is natural enough that they find some mutual comfort in mutual support. The role of teachers' friend, even qualified as 'critical friend', is a seductive one to the researcher. But in so far as the duty of dissent is rooted in a view of the necessary conditions for the maintenance of a democratic community, it is a duty which is entirely catholic in its application, and it extends to the teaching profession and indeed to the education research community itself. As Ranson points out, 'That educational studies has engaged in a public debate must be considered a considerable virtue'. Beleaguered as we are under external criticism, we retain nevertheless a duty to ourselves and to a wider community to maintain a critical dialogue which is accessible to a wider public – a duty which I hope this publication will show us to be honouring.

RESEARCH, THEORY AND THE REINSTATEMENT OF PHILOSOPHY

Gray addresses relatively briefly but straightforwardly the issue of theory in relation to educational research. It is noted that in recent years . . . the development of theory has either been seen as unfashionable or been pushed off many researchers' agendas by the pressures of short-term, narrowly focused studies; that for an area of research in the social sciences to sustain its vigour . . . it needs to develop strategies for promoting theoretical advancement; that researchers in education need to keep abreast of developments elsewhere if they are to sustain the theoretical vigour of their enquiries

and that 'ways must . . . be found for ensuring that as much theoretical benefit as possible can be gained' from the essentially applied and short-term work which is likely to receive funding. There is however little in the chapter to indicate how these principles might be honoured in practice or to develop a more sophisticated perspective on the variety of relations between 'theory' and the research enterprise. Revealingly too, though the group acknowledge the place in educational research of psychology, sociology, linguistics, economics and anthropology, there is not a single reference to what philosophy or history might contribute to the development of either theory or methodology – but more of this shortly.

Ranson's chapter is more overtly critical of the failure of educational research to live up to the expectations which Gray sets out. It is increasingly acknowledged that educational studies has become too isolated from key theoretical debates of the period. This neglect of theory has impoverished its research. But in response he offers a fruitful picture of the sources of educational theory and its location in the space between 'subjects' and between subjects and practice – a field that is not only a space for the disciplines separately to explore their ideas in, but will offer forms of knowing that can contribute significantly to the traditional academic disciplines of social science.

I am less concerned that educational research will contribute to social science (though this is a perfectly honourable aspiration) than that the thinking (the theory, if you like) which informs educational research is drawn from the richest and most radical seams of current and historical intellectual life. In my observation the theory that comes out of empirical research in education rarely represents much of an advance on the theory that went into it – or, to personalise the point, it is the intellectually most richly endowed researchers who seem to be able to provide the most stimulating and provocative analyses however modest the empirical research they engage in. All this suggests to me that engagement with big ideas of the past and the present (from sources worldwide and not just a parochial Anglo-American community), debate about theory, a culture of intellectual inquiry and a readiness to ask questions about the fundamental features of human understanding and experience are necessary conditions for fruitful research in general and will indeed provide a sufficient arena for some research enterprises. In other words a particular piece of educational research may simply be occupied with some of these theoretical questions and will not necessarily have to involve empirical inquiry at all – though this distinction is, as I have argued elsewhere (Bridges, 1996) itself a problematic one (see Quine, passim and Kuhn, 1970).

Ranson clearly recognises most of this, but, strangely, attributes the necessity of it to living in a *postmodern* world whose 'transformations' raise 'deep questions for education and for the polity in general'. The questions he identifies are: *What is it to be a person? Is there such a thing as a society? And what is it?* and *What should be the nature of the polity?* These may indeed be among the central questions facing people in the postmodern world – but so also have they been the central questions facing people in the Enlightenment, in the Renaissance and indeed in classical Greece and Rome. And Ranson, who quotes Alasdair MacIntyre with approval, must surely recognise that attempts to answer these and kindred questions have constituted the core of philosophical writing for over 2,000 years. Yet philosophy (no more than history) gets a single acknowledgement here as not just a contributory discipline to educational studies but as a foundational source of thinking both about the nature of educational research and the status of the claims to knowledge and understanding which it makes, and about the ontological, existential and ultimately moral substance of educational inquiry. Its invisibility or unacknowledged presence in these documents, as well as in a dozen similar commentaries on contemporary educational research, is a sad reflection on the ahistorical nature of much of this contemporary educational commentary and inquiry and the intellectual disconnectedness of many of those who pursue it.

REFERENCES

Bridges, D. (1996) Philosophy and educational research: a reconsideration of epistemological boundaries. Paper presented to BERA annual conference, Lancaster, September, and to be published in a special issue of the *Cambridge Journal of Education on Philosophy and Educational Research*, 1997, Vol. 27, no. 2.

Kuhn, T. (1970) *The Structure of Scientific Revolutions*, Chicago, IL, University of Chicago Press.

Quine, W. (1953) *From a Logical Point of View*, Cambridge, MA, Harvard University Press.

Quine, W. (1960) *Word and Object*, Cambridge, MA, MIT Press.

7

SUBVERTING THE DOMINANT PARADIGM

Michael Bassey

Visiting San Francisco recently I was bemused by a car bumper sticker which said 'Subvert the dominant paradigm'. Reflecting on it, I have realised that it is what Stewart Ranson seeks to do in arguing for 'a new paradigm that moves the field [of Education] from its perceived position at the periphery to the centre of analysis and purpose within the social sciences and in relation to the key issues facing society'. He identifies five dimensions in his new paradigm: 1) broadening educational research to embrace all learning in society; 2) developing a theory of learning which is motivational and responds to complexity of contexts; 3) moving from training models based on transmission to learning models based on action research; 4) creating a distinctive discipline of educational research which forms a central focus for the social sciences; and 5) locating education at the centre of public policy.

Ranson's ideas are exciting, constructive and challenging – even if occasionally his meaning is difficult to follow. But what is missing is an analysis of the different ideologies that currently fire different political leaders and future-minded thinkers. Ranson's analysis doesn't face up to either the question 'what is education for?' or the question 'what direction should educational improvement take?'

I have identified at least six different ideological stances of self-professed educationists and I suggest that critical discussion of these is an important contribution to the future of educational research. In part my recognition of these has come from the writings of Stephen Ball and I described some of them in an article in the *Guardian* (16 April 1996). Here they are:

The *cultural-restoration educationists* define education in terms of the transmission of traditional culture by authoritative teachers. For them teaching needs to focus on subjects which are traditionally valued and defined in a national curriculum. The acquisition of worthwhile knowledge is more important than engaging in creative or critical processes: whole-class teaching methods are valued. There should be formal relationships between teachers and learners. Assessment should be by examination, not coursework. Selection by academic ability will enable new grammar schools to develop which teach in traditional ways. Parents are significant in terms of choosing schools for their children.

The *industrial-training educationists* define education in terms of future adult work in a society where economic growth must be the major concern. For them teaching needs to promote habits of punctuality, self-discipline, obedience and trained effort, and needs to provide appropriate skills and knowledge which will contribute to the creation of industrial wealth. League tables help parents choose schools for their children. Technical innovation is valued – for example computer learning. Industrial management styles should be developed in schools and colleges with performance-based salary increments for effective teachers.

The *equal-opportunities educationists* see education as a means of redressing inequalities in our society. They want all children to have equal chances of succeeding through their own endeavours and irrespective of parental wealth, social class, race or gender. They are totally opposed to private education. They are against selection of children into different schools, or streams within schools. They are in favour of democratic processes within schools and of mixed-ability teaching. Formal examinations disadvantage anxious children and so should be replaced by coursework assessment. Collaborative learning, self-assessment by pupils, education of the emotions and an emphasis on respect for others are important. There is ambivalence about the role of parents in education.

The *élite-and-underclass educationists* see education as a means of restructuring society into a small élite and a large underclass. The élite can be selected by the education system and then must be given an education suitable for their future role as managers, scientists and technologists. The underclass need an education which will: 1) train those who get jobs with the skills needed for the job; 2) inculcate a moral code which protects the interests of the élite; and 3) develop a compliant and unquestioning attitude which accepts their place in society. Competition is not only the way of developing the élite; it is the way of enabling the underclass to accept their inferior status. It follows that assessment by formal examinations is important as is the formal inspection of schools. Reflection and research are potentially dangerous activities because they may challenge the fundamental premise of this stance.

The *learner-centred educationists* define education in terms of social nurture of the individual and full development of personal potential. To this end they look for innovation in curriculum, pedagogy and assessment which is justified by professional experience, research evidence and logical argument. The emphasis is learner centred, constructivist, democratic, and collaborative. Motivation is very important and there is a strong orientation towards individual performance and graded assessments. Formative assessment by teachers and self-assessment by learners are important. There is a strong interest in educational processes which focus on cognitive skills, problem-solving, creativity and critical thinking. They hold to the concepts of the reflective practitioner, of action research, and of challenge-and-support inspection, as means of improving practice. Parents play a key part in the education of their children and school should recognise this.

The *environmental educationists* share many of the values of the learner-centred educationists, but put a green perspective to education, which for them should prepare pupils for a postindustrial future which is economically sustainable, ecologically stable and humanly convivial.

Personally I reject the cultural-restorationist stance because it ignores the future and the permanence of cultural regeneration, and I reject the industrial-training stance because it perceives the future in terms of economic growth and fails to recognise that that is pushing the planet to ecocatastrophe. I utterly reject the élite-and-underclass position as morally unacceptable. I accept the equal-opportunities and learner-centred stances as moral and appropriate, but insufficient because they do not respond to the ecological predicaments that face humankind. Of the six ideological positions described it is the environmental stance that I embrace – on moral and intellectual grounds: but I do so with the guilty awareness that I do very little to advance its case.

The contemporary writer Andrew Dobson's book *Green Political Thought* is helpful. He develops ideas suggested earlier by writers like E. F. Schumacher (1973) and Ivan Illich (1973). Dobson (1995, p. 1) vigorously distinguishes between the technological-fix view of the future, which represents 'a managerial approach to environmental problems, secure in the belief that they can be solved without fundamental changes in present values or patterns of production and consumption' and what he calls 'ecologism' which holds (*ibid.*) that 'a sustainable and fulfilling existence presupposes radical changes in our relationship with the non-human natural world, and in our mode of social and political life'.

The technological-fix view is clearly linked to the educational ideas of the industrial trainers (who seem at present to be dominant in Parliament on both sides of the House) while ecologism provides a philosophical basis for the environmental educationists. Dobson (*ibid.*, p. 112) shows the relationship between green philosophy and education when he says: 'we must get to know the land around us, learn its lore and its potential, and live with it and not against it', and again when he writes (*ibid.*, p. 198):

> Ecologism envisages a post-industrial future that is quite distinct from that with which we are generally acquainted. While most post-industrial futures revolve around high-growth, high technology, expanding services, greater leisure, and satisfaction conceived in material terms, ecologism's post-industrial society questions growth and technology, and suggests that the Good Life will involve more work and fewer material objects. Fundamentally, ecologism takes seriously the universal condition of the finitude of the planet and asks what kind of political, economic and social practices are (a) possible and (b) desirable within that framework.

I suggest that it is with such a mind-set, or ideological stance, that Ranson's concept of creating a distinctive discipline of educational research, which forms a central focus for the social sciences and of locating education at the centre of public policy, makes sense.

REFERENCES

Ball, S. (1990) *Politics and Policy Making in Education*, London, Routledge.
Dobson, A. (1995) *Green Political Thought*, London, Routledge.
Illich, J. (1973) *Tools for Conviviality*, London, Calder & Boyars.
Schumacher, E. F. (1973) *Small is Beautiful: A Study of Economics as if People Mattered*, London, Blond & Briggs.

Section Two

8

IMPROVING THE QUALITY OF EDUCATIONAL RESEARCH

Michael Beveridge

INTRODUCTION

In October 1995 David Hargreaves and I each produced a report on the current state of educational research for the Leverhulme Trust. These reports had the same terms of reference and both combined elements of research foresight with an analysis of the strengths and weaknesses of current research. David and I consulted extensively with each other and with research and user communities but the views in each report were those of its author. My contribution to this present volume contains a synthesis and extension of some of the issues raised in my report, some of which were raised at the one-day BERA conference in May 1996 from which this volume emanates.

It hardly needs saying that education is morally, politically and economically crucial to the shape of modern society. But we do sometimes need reminding that talking and thinking openly and constructively about educational research issues are also important. It is in this spirit that the views in this chapter are offered. It is accepted from the outset that I can only offer one picture, my own. It may not be a view that many of my colleagues will entirely share or perhaps even recognise. It is however offered in sincerity and, it is hoped, will not be seen either morally or intellectually judgemental. I value the opportunity presented by this volume to engage in this dialogue in the knowledge that I will be saying nothing new to many readers; and in the hope that there is never a definitive last word on educational research.

This chapter looks beyond the short-term needs of education. It identifies some problems between users and researchers in education, and suggests ways of bringing these groups together to examine future research questions. The intention is to help the process of establishing an educational culture which is more able and prepared to use research to influence education policy. This kind of dialogue is difficult, leads to disagreements and reveals the weaknesses of research; but these should not be reasons for not engaging in it. There is of course a danger that excessive examination of the research process will lead to moribund meetings and repetitive reports. In the present chapter I will try to avoid both by not repeating the work of recent similar exercises. Nor will I try to lend weight to my views by abundant referencing. This chapter is part of a dialogue: a genre requiring a certain lightness of style and personal subjectivity.

The Leverhulme review set some difficult questions which touch on some deep divisions in both education and social science. Some researchers accept that research could establish 'non-trivial' educational truths which persist across space and time, while others do not. Also we know that doing educational research which impresses practitioners and policy-makers is difficult. Short-term educational effects tend to be easy to demonstrate, but also tend to be obvious to practitioners. Long-term effects are extremely difficult to demonstrate conclusively; and these are of most interest to policy-makers and parents.

Other difficulties abound. Educational research tends to find problems rather than solutions. Research about solutions is often seen as merely evaluation which is not judged by many in the research community as being intellectually significant. It could even be argued that researchers are more interested in studying and explaining education's failures rather than its successes. If so, then it is no wonder that those politicians who are looking for examples of good practice find the research community problematic.

These dialogues take place against the background of the relatively insecure status of educational research. And it is important that educational research continues to gain confidence. Hence debate must be constructive and open. This will assist communication between researchers as well as between themselves and user communities.

However, communication should not be enhanced at the expense of flexibility. It would, in my view, be a mistake to argue a priori for single common aims and methods which must be agreed by all educational researchers. Some of the respondents in the Leverhulme review made comments, particularly about action research, which seem to suggest this way forward. I believe that educational research needs the methodological pluralism of other social sciences. Arguments about methods are important, but the way in which this debate is conducted reveals the level of maturity of the discipline.

The discussions and deliberations of the review have led me to two general conclusions. The first is that there is little chance of relevant and important knowledge finding its way into education unless the outcomes of research are actively sought out by practitioners. Users of research need to be able to understand it, evaluate it, reject it when it is contextually inappropriate and think out its implications for their own practice. Some individual teachers, schools, teacher educators and policy-makers can and do 'use' research. However, how, when and why this occurs is not well understood, apart from the obvious fact that some people choose to cite evidence in support of their own prior beliefs and to confirm their current practices. A great deal more needs to be known about the process of research utilisation.

My second general conclusion concerns the several recent reviews on aspects of educational research in the UK sponsored by what is now the ESRC. These are discussed more fully later in this chapter. Authors of these are among the contributors to this volume and they will be making their own cases. My conclusion is that I remain less convinced than these earlier reviews (Nisbet and Broadfoot, 1980; Gray, 1992; 1995; Ranson, 1995) as to either the overall quality of educational research or its value for money. I say this in the constructive spirit mentioned earlier because I believe there are ways forward. And I fully acknowledge the high quality of the best work.

The 1980 review by Nisbet and Broadfoot examined the educational research scene in North America and Europe and also considered the views of leading UK researchers. They provide a list of reasons why research fails to make an impact in these countries and they also describe some important features of the policy implementation process. Their report is an interesting piece of social science which characterises the 1980 situation. They identify educational research as an important part of a 'reflective culture' of education, which in their view is a symptom of a healthy and democratic system. While I would not take issue with the politics behind this view, it is no longer an adequate justification for substantial research expenditure. Specific examples of positive outcomes of research must nowadays be identified to justify future investment.

The Ranson and Gray reports, together with Light's (1995) review of research on human development, seem to me to have been largely preoccupied in identifying categories of research or themes which give the overall research effort some ideational coherence. This they have done reasonably successfully but I remain unconvinced that the resulting 'inclusive' programmes will, without substantial change in the educational research culture and reorganisation of the research infrastructure, rectify the 'unplanned' and 'incoherent' way in which research is produced, and which these reports identify. It is tentative suggestions as to these cultural and organisational changes which are the main focus of this chapter.

THE FUTURE CONTEXT

The Leverhulme review sought comments on the following questions about the future:

What major problems are likely to be met in education over the next ten to twenty years? What research is being done in relation to these problems? What is its quality? What research might be needed to throw light on, help to influence about, or contribute to solving, the problems identified?

Interestingly the academic respondents were remarkably diffident about giving specific suggestions for future research. In general they preferred to focus on problems facing education in relation to its changing future context. The topics they raised most frequently concerned 'learning to learn' and its relation to flexibility:

> The most promising line of work for facilitating responsiveness to change is on 'metacognition' i.e., the development of awareness of one's own learning processes. Such 'reflective practices' appear to be the main way of overcoming resistance to change, since some of the main consequences are an increase in the flexibility of learning and the ability to see problems from different perspectives. Metacognition is concerned with learning to learn and therefore enables students to take responsibility for their own learning and not remain dependent on explicit tuition. The net result is a decrease in the tendency to stick rigidly to well entrenched skills and ideas.
>
> We need to rethink and redesign what school is about, especially how we assess performance. We must move away from credentialism, performance indicators and towards ideas that promote rich learning, i.e., facilitating generalisation and knowledge transfer, ensuring that students are capable of communicating ideas and concepts, developing learning to learn and other meta skills.
>
> The challenge for the next few decades seems to be how to reconcile the conflicting needs of individuals and control, the problem of how to maximise flexibility and freedom while maintaining integrity and quality.

The importance of research into information technology in education was emphasised by numerous respondents. This was usually linked into the points illustrated above:

> What differentiates the rapid, effective learner of new knowledge/concepts from the slow and pedestrian? This work could take account of new sources of information (IT).
>
> The UK is at a choice point between a high value, high wage economy and a stratified elite plus low wage economy. The choice will be determined by our ability to maintain and improve educational standards and to have the high standards at the top end operate further down the heap. The Japanese dominance of quality manufacturing has been enabled by changes in management/training techniques which drop the training of even quite abstract subjects down the production hierarchy. New information technology is rapidly shortening our training cycles and requires a more generalised and effective literacy, with yet to be created communication skills.

It can be argued that while we have a mass of evidence on pupil attitude to learning with new technologies which gives a very positive picture of its potential we have limited research on the actual learning gains made with different types of multimedia applications as measured against learner characteristics and their prior achievement levels. What we do have suggests a much more complex picture of how learning would need to be individualised and supported if we are to avoid suboptimal and disappointing results from incorporating the new media into the learning environment. I note with some dismay, for example, that not a single article in the *British Journal of Educational Technology* presented 'hard' data of this kind from 1991–1994 inclusive.

Respondents were well aware that research needs to focus on learning outside formal education, and again links to information technology were reinforced:

Relatively new and under-explored issues related to post-compulsory education, learning in the workplace, informal learning, technology-mediated learning, learning in the community, etc. will achieve greater societal importance and visibility. So it would be a strategic error to reinforce a definition of 'education' and 'educational research' which located them exclusively or even primarily in the context of formal schooling. Instead, we should seek to strengthen our national capacity to undertake work on learning, the support of learning, and learning contexts throughout the lifetime of the learner.

There is inadequate work in significant 'learning' outside of formal education. Examples of topics are the impact of parental involvement in extending reading and writing in the 8–16 year range, the role of fathers in parental education and the sensitivity of parental education programmes to the needs of different cultural groups.

The work context for educational research was also emphasised by many respondents:

Recent evidence suggests that the amount of training in companies is not related to their success at innovation, but the amount of training needs analysis is so related. This appears to indicate exactly that we do not know what training should be done.

Work on expertise seeks to identify what is unique to a domain of learning and so needs to be learnt by someone from another discipline. Secondly, it seeks to establish what prior learning can already be deemed to be shared by people from different disciplines. These questions also relate to the issue of learning to learn and metacognition.

There was also some support for the view that there is a lack of good research on teaching:

There is amazingly little research on what exactly characterises good tutoring or teaching. What work there is reveals surprising results. For example skilled teachers do not seem to overtly provide corrective feedback of the kind that behavioural models might predict. The work at Carnegie Mellon on the ACT theory of cognition is an example of educationally applied high quality cognitive science research.

Overall these responses were interesting and represented a genuine attempt to give objective replies to our questions. Respondents did not engage in self-serving exercises which merely emphasised their own interest, but they clearly did not feel that it was appropriate to produce lists of specific research projects, although we have no doubt that they would have done so if encouraged by suggestions of funding.

In my view respondents are correct to suggest that education will become more flexible and life long. There will also be changes in the relationship between learners and teachers, especially in the way learners will become customers in a diverse market of educational provision. There will be an increase in the need for information about the type and quality of learning facilities that are available nationally, regionally and locally. This information must be accurate, current and intelligible to users.

It is not my brief in this chapter to argue for a specific agenda for educational research but the changing scenario does, I think, indicate some research priorities which will tax our methodological and organisational ingenuity. The development of appropriate information systems requires that some important issues are addressed immediately. Some of these relate to current areas of research; others require new programmes of work.

My own view is that two main inter-related issues arise for educational research in relation to the new developments in education. These are:

1) How to take best advantage of developments in communication technology.
2) How to produce high-quality, useful, policy research in this changing educational context.

Fortunately the UK is in the vanguard of research on the ways learners interact with computers and on why they learn successfully. For example the Centre for Research on Development, Instruction and Training (Nottingham) and the Human Communication Research Centre (Edinburgh) are studying detailed aspects of the learning process. Other important work in this area includes that of Light (Southampton), Hoyles and Sutherland (London and Bristol) on LOGO, Goodyear (Lancaster) on Tutoring Systems, and at the Open University. The catalyst for this work was the availability of desktop computers but the result has been to refocus the attention of cognitive scientists and psychologists, as well as some educational researchers, on learning processes. This is an important shift of emphasis which is to be encouraged.

However, I suggest that while this research has been timely and appropriate, it will require much development if it is to provide an adequate research background to enable IT to be used to best advantage in the new educational context. Currently educational software is designed with little reference to research into learning. The 'Superhighway' will soon make a vast range of information available and this will be used in ways that may not be optimal for learning.

The new problem is how to guide learners along appropriate information pathways. The research questions are, in their most general form: can learners use the new systems which present information? How do they do this? How do they learn it and how can they be taught to do it better? Furthermore, as suggested above, learning is now a life-long experience and 'learning to learn' new information presented in novel ways will be the most useful outcome of education in the future. There are encouraging signs that the research community is aware of the issues. In addition to those already mentioned I would note the work of Heppel (Anglia) which studies children using networked home computers. Recent ESRC themes and programmes certainly include this area. However, much new thinking needs to be done. Work of both a theoretical and methodological nature is required if research is to make progress. It is going to require an interdisciplinary approach in which few educational researchers are experienced. We need to combine sociological accounts of changes in educational provision with the work of cognitive science on learning processes. Only if this occurs will we be able to study 'learning to learn' in practice.

An additional and important question for research in education in the emerging information age concerns the nature of educational organisations themselves. The new ESRC themes and its initiative on the 'Learning Society' both emphasise that organisations need to be able to learn. Educational organisations in particular need continually to adapt and relearn how to deliver learning in changing contexts. How, when and why organisations learn is a crucial research area.

There has in recent years been a growth in research into school management and effectiveness. This work is going to need refocusing to accommodate to the information age. Despite the enormous expansion in training and research in educational management, very little has been associated with the relationship between management and teaching and still less between management and learning. We need to bring together research teams to tackle this problem. These groups must combine research skills in organisation theory and decision-making, the study of learning environments and the cognitive and social processes of teaching and learning. We will need new and better theories to address these questions in an interdisciplinary way. Unless such developments occur attempts to study organisational effectiveness in education will founder as the context changes.

The second of the inter-related issues stemming from the changing educational context referred to earlier concerns the nature of useful policy research. The changing nature of educational provision and usage cannot be assumed to be either value free in its impact, or to be consistent with the aims of either society or government. Issues of inequality across ethnic groups, gender and socioeconomic groups will require continuous investigation. Nor can it be assumed that the increased flexibility in provision will serve the needs of industry and commerce any better than at the present time. This question will also need more systematic study.

Furthermore these policy issues should be connected to economic analysis. At present many people in education believe economics to be essentially about accountancy procedures. They fail to understand the wider sense of economics and its relation to value. However, despite the ESRC study group and the quasi-markets seminars, there is a scarcity of good economic work on education. Economists are clearly in need of encouragement to engage in this area of study. For example, a survey of the papers published by UK economists in the five leading economics journals between 1991 and 1994 revealed no work on education. An interdisciplinary centre for policy studies in education would be an important development. It would aim to improve on the currently unhappy relationship between the research community and education policy-makers which was apparent from our Leverhulme review.

A few of our respondents in this review saw something of a politically motivated conspiracy in the poor link between policy and research in the UK. For example

> The political commitment to social and economic equality is lacking. As a result there is little research on the consequences for schools of social dislocation and unemployment. As things stand at the moment inequalities in schooling will continue to contribute to the construction and reproduction of social hierarchies.
>
> The politics of education on a macro level are such as to render a neutral mechanism for linking theory and practice an impossibility.

Clearly these views have, in themselves, a political perspective. Hargreaves, in his report, comments that some critiques of government policy which have emanated from the academic world have spuriously claimed the objectivity of social science when in fact they are ideologically driven. The obvious cases are less worrying than the general suspicion that government and policy-makers believe that all educational research is inherently politically biased, unless it is controlled by strict commissioning and monitoring procedures. Unless a relationship of trust can be developed then the chances of research assisting education in taking advantage of the potential of technological change will remain remote. Trust of course will need to be mutual and might involve some academics in acknowledging that not all government policies and statements on education are inherently flawed. Merely disagreeing with a government does not make for a sound principle of quality control.

THE SOCIAL SCIENCES AND EDUCATIONAL RESEARCH

During the last four years I have been a member of the ESRC Research Grants Board and have also been Dean of the Faculty of Social Sciences at Bristol University. These experiences, together with the responses to the Leverhulme report's terms of reference, indicate to me that educational research could usefully look at answers to the following questions:

> Which research, especially basic research, is being conducted in the social sciences which has important implications for education and educational research? How might transfer across and interaction between interdisciplinary fields be made more effective?

As I hope is apparent throughout this chapter I am arguing for an interdisciplinary and collaborative approach to educational research. Not surprisingly therefore I believe the questions posed above to be very important; but first a word of caution.

Education as an area of study has in the past suffered from inappropriate attempts to apply theories from the social and behavioural sciences. Sweeping generalisations were made, for example, using Piaget as a theoretical justification for discovery learning and Bernstein as an explanation for differences between social classes in educational attainment. This situation must be avoided but given the tendency of educators to want simple, easily applied, solutions it can easily occur. This is especially likely if social scientists adopt weak techniques of dissemination just to satisfy funding conditions. They need to have a real interest in communicating their work. Most teachers remain ignorant and deeply sceptical about social science. This is unfortunate because, in the move away from grand theory, social science has been making progress in the study of specific problems with practical applications. My recent ESRC and university roles, referred to earlier, have instilled in me the strong view that we have much to gain from the work of the social and behavioural sciences; and furthermore that they also benefit from addressing educational questions. As an example let me take cognitive science:

> Cognitive science is producing a shift towards process modelling. It is studying the roles of analogy, external representations, the 'self explanation effect'. Deductive, inductive, abductive reasoning, implicit versus explicit knowledge acquisition, social factors and the role of language in collaborative learning, the value of mixed modes of teaching, and cognitive apprenticeship.
>
> (A Leverhulme respondent)

As this comment shows, cognitive science is now addressing issues which are important to education. These developments have the potential to lead to a better understanding of the processes of teaching and learning, especially if we can encourage the involvement of educational practitioners. Developments in the study of expertise indicate that the intuitive knowledge of gifted teachers gained through experience will begin to be characterised in ways which can be communicated to new recruits to the teaching profession. The idea that only teachers understand teaching will be less easy to sustain in future. But practitioners will only become interested if out of the complexities of research come some useful ideas.

Cognitive science is also developing models of how learning develops over time and which take account of the structure of the tasks and the way they are taught. Work on small-group teaching and peer tutoring shows that there may be many pathways to learning. Cognitive science is also showing how information technology can be used creatively to expand rather than narrow down children's learning environments. There is an urgent need for this research because designers of educational software are currently no better informed by research than textbook authors were fifty years ago.

However, closing the gap between cognitive science and education will also require that some cognitive scientists change their approach to investigating learning and teaching. Teachers are concerned with learning by individuals over an extended period of time and in different contexts, and cognitive scientists need to take account of this in their research. For example, recent work in cognitive science on 'situated cognition' needs to be related to educational researchers' studies of classrooms which have attempted to describe the 'meaning making' activities which lead children to learn. This latter work is highly interpretative and relies heavily on the subjectivity of the observer. It also typically fails to test these interpretations in any systematic way. This research into the scenes and situations of classroom life lacks good theory as to which scenes and situations are important. Nevertheless this work is attractive to practitioners because it presents data in narrative form from which they can recognise events similar to their own experiences. This narrative work on 'meaning making' must begin to come together with cognitive science to study the long-term retention and use of both knowledge and skills. Studies of the individual learning histories of children would seem to be a possible way forward. These must take account of the scenes and situations they encounter in home and school. Such studies would need to be carefully framed in terms of their aims and objectives, and linked to ongoing developments in cognitive science.

While commenting on the basic research in the social sciences in relation to education it should be noted that work in a number of areas of social policy and welfare has little current connection to educational research. The academic structures of university departments of education separate them from other policy units. Hence the study of the ageing society, changing family structures, labour mobility, changing employment structures, poverty, homelessness, health, crime and racism takes place with little contact with education. Many of the methods used in these studies are not in common use in educational research. For example, increased work using new techniques for analysing large data sets would be particularly appropriate in education, which has broadly kept abreast of developments in qualitative methods.

As indicated earlier, one of the most promising areas of work in which further collaboration between education and other social sciences would be sensible concerns the topic of 'learning in organisations'. Management science is very actively exploring this area using a variety of methods and theoretical approaches. Currently, our understanding of educational organisations is influenced by, and is contributing to, this area of work and it is to be hoped that this dialogue continues. Schools, colleges and universities need to become able to learn more readily, especially if the changes in education indicated earlier become reality.

BEYOND SOCIAL SCIENCE

Although rarely made in the UK, there are also important connections to be established between education and neuroscience. Unfortunately there is a serious mistrust of biological explanations of human behaviour amongst education professionals, as exemplified by the response in the media to Professor Plomin's new MRC unit on behavioural genetics.

This attitude is preventing many UK educationalists from engaging in some potentially important developments. For example in cognitive neuroscience there is much debate about the 'modularity' problem, which concerns the separateness of intellectual faculties. Research into both normal and special populations has provided some intriguing examples of children with exceptional abilities, e.g. graphic reproduction, memorisation and numerical ability. The neurological processes which produce these abilities may underpin talents children show in normal education, e.g. chess playing, foreign languages and mathematical skills. A number of general theories have been developed which require refinement. For example, in the area of language, grammatical modules may be separate from the more socially and culturally influenced areas of semantics and pragmatics. The work in this area, technical though it is, suggests many interesting possibilities for assessment, learning and teaching. It would be, in my view, a serious mistake if the enormous advances in knowledge of human neurobiology were to be rejected as unimportant for education. I am not advocating a crude sociobiology. And it is not possible in the context of this chapter to spell out the many possible ways in which neuroscience can work with education. But recent neurolinguistic research into both Down's syndrome and dyslexia provides examples.

The application of the methods of cognitive psychology and, to some extent neuroscience, to education has been recognised in the USA in the discipline of instructional science. It is time for this development to occur in the UK, but this must be carefully and systematically monitored. As one respondent said: 'Educational theory needs to be grounded in basic theory and developed from it, but it is necessarily distinct from it. It is dangerous to apply basic theories to education. We are after all experimenting with other people.' Linking educational research more closely to other disciplines raises problems of transfer of information between disciplinary fields. It presents a staff training and development problem which most universities and colleges would find difficult to solve given current structures and resources. One possible solution is establishing a few interdisciplinary research centres. Such centres would require strong and talented leadership from the outset if they are to avoid fragmentation into disciplinary groupings. Centres of this type have existed for some time, and can be successful. The danger can be that the conceptual clarity and methodological rigour of the individual disciplines are lost. Even high-quality staff must be led in ways that ensure this does not happen.

Most of our respondents to the Leverhulme review were in favour of a pluralism in research methods and models, but whether this view merely represents a liberal attitude, rather than a genuine taste for pluralism, is unclear. Acting as a member of a research grants board has shown that there are, in fact, considerable differences between educational researchers as to what they believe represents quality work. In general, however, these differences are no greater in education than in the other social sciences. But it does still present a problem for the reviewing process. Some of the differences about research stem from different disciplinary approaches, some have political undertones and others come from the acceptability of research to users. There is no immediate prospect of a solution to these difficulties, but it is hoped a more mature culture of research will emerge in due time. This will require a more widespread, and deeper, understanding of the technicalities of research methods. My experience is that many research grants are reviewed either positively or negatively without high-quality objective technical evaluation. The role of recognised centres of methodological excellence is important in solving this problem.

AN EPISTEMOLOGICAL HEALTH WARNING

Any move beyond established disciplines requires that clarity of thought is not abandoned. Interdisciplinary work often lacks rigour especially in applied social science. Knowledge and understanding of different areas of work will not in themselves avoid the need for careful thought. There is much confusion, in my view, in social science generally and education in particular between disciplines, methods and philosophical views. Arguments about methods can obscure, and even replace, epistemological analysis. Of course there is much that can and has been said about the comparison between the physical and social sciences. Issues such as replicability, truth, the discovery of laws, falsifiability and objectivity have received much consideration in comparisons between the two domains. Furthermore, philosophical traditions from Descartes to Husserl and Heidegger have revealed, at the very least, that the view that natural science can explain all aspects of the human condition is questionable. It is not appropriate to summarise or continue these debates in this chapter, but it is important to realise that some of the tensions within the educational research community are connected to serious intellectual issues.

An example based around the important practical problem of student motivation will serve to illustrate the situation. Motivation, as reflected in the time and effort given to study by learners of all abilities, is a concern of all teachers. And despite the general connection between educational success and economic prosperity for both individuals and nations, many students do not, at least in the UK, just recognise this and work hard to succeed in their learning. It is an important research question as to why this is the case. And policy-makers and practitioners are very interested in the answers.

The key question concerns whether motivation can be studied independently of the cultural meanings and values of the students. Is motivation, as many psychologists have assumed, a characteristic of individuals who can be said to belong to measurable motivational categories, e.g. having high achievement motivation? And is there an association between motivation and biological factors? Or, on the other hand, is motivation connected to Heidegger's 'basic modalities of the world', such as our separation from others, our anxieties about the future and our fear of death? None of which seem, at least at first sight, to be easily amenable to measurement using either questionnaires or biochemical techniques.

Many disagreements about educational research, its value and its usefulness have elements of this type of intellectual difficulty. Obvious examples include disputes about intelligence, ability, assessment and even teaching. And despite my avowed enthusiasm for cross-disciplinary knowledge and understanding I am aware that more 'information' will not on its own resolve epistemological problems.

My real concern is not that these epistemological issues arise, but whether they are being thought about and considered carefully enough. The drive to empirical social science, which, despite the short-termism associated with research assessment, is a welcome move away from 'armchair' deliberation, has left educational research short of thorough intellectual analysts. There are a growing number of technicians but very few thinkers and scholars. There is even in some academic institutions a prevailing anti-intellectualism which runs alongside views that all understanding and clarity of thought come from the 'reality' of the classroom. This 'natural attitude', to use Husserl's term, is in itself an intellectual position but it is doubtful whether many of its protagonists understand its nature.

UNITS, CENTRES OR DEPARTMENTS

Whatever the results of the Research Assessment Exercise (RAE) it is not clear that educational research is currently served best by the existing organisational structures and cultures. I have suggested that we need to foster 1) a higher standard of technical understanding which would raise the quality of the research review process; 2) better support for the interdisciplinary work which is needed in some areas; and 3) increasing the chances of long-term programmes on a sufficient scale to give useful answers. Establishing strong research groups would contrast with the current situation, as perceived by several of the Leverhulme respondents. For example:

> I have a strong impression of individualism, of researchers working in isolation from each other, dabbling in a rather amateurish way at issues which are too big to be tackled by lone researchers.
>
> Much educational research in the UK is too small and narrowly structured to make a significant impact on educational policy.

As always if informed decisions are to be taken by funding bodies the research community needs to have clear specifications of research programmes and clear examples of relevant quality work. And equally important, as another respondent indicated: 'It would be useful to identify examples where university or institute based researchers have created successful partnerships with field based practitioners leading to the direct open continuous testing and application of findings.' The creation of strong research groups, if it is to occur, must not be allowed to exacerbate problems of dissemination. They must work with users and be encouraged to seek funding from them, as engineers and medical researchers do on a large scale.

Do we need to change the research culture as exemplified by a typical university department of education? The answer to this question is, in my view, inevitably 'yes'. In his Leverhulme report, Hargreaves has described the way differences between subject areas and disciplines makes it difficult for staff in typical university education departments to work together and reach agreement. This is particularly important because as one respondent put it: 'There is no sense in trying to apply research unless consensus has been reached. It is unethical to seek to apply ideas that have not met with general acceptance unless people volunteer for experimental education.' On a more positive note, by examining the practices within these institutions, we can investigate whether the social processes, which might lead to consensus, do exist. Do people see themselves as part of a corporate organisation, as research centres often do? Is information shared? Do people attend talks and seminars beyond their own immediate interests? Do they talk to practitioners and discuss these conversations with their colleagues? And, does the career structure in higher education value the results of these activities? The answer to all these questions could, in principle, be 'yes', but history and current circumstances, including the workload of staff, make it difficult to be confident that this is in fact the case today.

I suggested at the BERA seminar in May 1996 that a typical university department of education has a culture of mutual tolerance between staff, but no shared desire to engage with difficult issues on which they might differ. This benign culture lacks the social will and the necessary processes which lead to the synthesis of ideas which the user communities are looking for. I deliberately overstated my case at the May meeting and do so again in the dialogic spirit of this volume. I therefore await the arguments and evidence that my own perceptions are not shared. If, however, I am at least partly correct then some changes are overdue.

If my remarks so far appear somewhat critical, let me set them in the context of the current record by asking the following question: how good is the record of education in promoting the application of ideas, concepts and findings to educational practice? This question raises important but complex issues. Hargreaves in his report quotes a number of respondents who believe the general record of research application to be poor. Some, however, were less critical:

> Some of the research on school effectiveness, on science education, on pupil assessment, on accelerated learning and on equal opportunities, for example, has been very successful. In general, classroom action research has contributed much to improvement in practice in localities, but is largely unrecorded. However major issues like the teaching and learning consequences of different class sizes, relative effectiveness of different forms of nursery provision, the creation of academic cultures in schools and university entrance procedures, for example, have been almost untouched.

This is a reasonable statement of the relative levels of research impact in these areas; however, whether any work has been 'very successful' in a direct way is perhaps doubtful. It is possible to provide a positive rationalisation of the impact of research. As already noted, influential members of the educational research community have explained the importance of research to practice through a diffuse impact model. Research is said to filter into the educational culture, to heighten its powers of self-criticism and to influence practice in indirect ways. This is the conclusion of the Nisbet and Broadfoot (1980) review and was echoed in the 1995 BERA presidential address. There is undoubtedly some truth in this position. But it must be regarded as a weak defence when set in the context of the research expenditure patterns described by Hargreaves in his Leverhulme report.

The solution to the problem of research impact requires two main courses of action. The first is raising the quality of research and researchers. The important factors are research time, training, better reviewing procedures, centres of excellence and better links with other disciplines. These developments should focus on doing research which helps the teaching of individuals.

Much research effort is wasted producing global averages of infrequent observations of children. These data are of little use to teachers, partly because they mask the effect of different forms of instruction.

The second course of action on research impact starts with recognition of the difficulties the education system has in assimilating new information and acting on it. Even if research-driven policies can be agreed, which means dealing with the political issues, the implementation process is complex and typically very slow. Recent OECD reports on the integration of children with learning difficulties suggest that implementing significant policy changes can take up to ten years. They must be planned and agreed by all parts of the system that might be affected, including parents and employers. They require additional resource, especially staff time; and finally they require highly motivated initiators. The idea that research can be implemented merely by explaining it to a few teachers or lecturers is naive in the extreme.

The evidence from medicine and engineering, which are more systems orientated, shows how a cultural shift to a systems approach and away from the primacy of the individual teacher or lecturer is required. There are signs in, for example, new whole and interschool policies which involve parents that this change may be occurring slowly. However, certain parts of the education system, for example the primary, secondary and university sectors, still implement significant changes without consideration of the consequences for each other. Changes in the secondary curriculum are often discovered by universities when students arrive there. However, all change needs monitoring and evaluating. New education policies can be wrong, and should not be allowed to persist if this is the case.

RESEARCH AND THE USER

But how do government, business, heads, teachers and teacher educators relate to, influence and in turn become influenced by educational research? Can more effective models of interaction between 'producers' and users be created in order to improve the focus of research, its quality and character, and its dissemination?

One Leverhulme respondent gave a clear answer to the first part of this question by identifying the associated behaviours: '. . . going to conferences, meetings and reading. If people do not engage in these behaviours then they won't be influenced by research.' This must be correct. Another respondent, who argued strongly that there is good research with educational implications that fails to make an impact at the chalk face, suggested a biannual newsletter which summarises findings from all the major agencies, gives a quick critique of the research methodology and an evaluation of the sense of the findings. This is an interesting and sensible proposal which may well find commercial support.

Perhaps telematics can now make a major difference in creating new communities of researchers, researched and users of research. This is possible but, as several large EU-funded projects have shown, there are ways not to do this. It needs careful planning and there is a research base from which to learn.

As noted earlier, the relationship between government and researchers is particularly problematic. No one in England or Wales fulfils the function of the Scottish HMI as mediator between government and research. As one respondent said:

> It seems clear that government and the research community have different expectations of educational research. The experience of APU is a case in point. Expensively funded, it could not answer the political question of whether standards were falling or rising. There needs to be a much more sophisticated understanding of the relationships between policy and practice in education amongst all those likely to engage in the relevant debates.

By no means all educational issues require research for their solution. We must not get into the situation characterised by Christopher Ball where the 'management of data becomes an impediment to thought'. Comments on the ESRC priority issues, made by potential users, suggest that this may be happening. They were worried that the research agenda is steered by topicality with educational institutions. For example ESRC was investing in some areas where the policy debate was already advanced, e.g. inner cities, apparently ignoring others where strategic and basic research investment was much needed, e.g. assessment and learning.

There have been a number of recent attempts to categorise types of research in terms of the social relationship between researcher and researched. For example Kemmis (1991) produced a crude, but useful, typology of the social relationships implicit in educational research on the basis of distinctions between 'third person', 'second person' and 'first person' research. 'Third person' researchers take the view that reliably predicting people's actions is the same as having explained them. The people being researched are researched in the third person (he, she or them). Second person research, or interpretative research, aims to understand people's actions through a researcher, who is a knowledgeable observer, has an interest in educating those researched about meaning, significance, nature and consequences of their actions in the context of the human, social and historical circumstances under which they act.

First person or 'action' research is both subjective and objective in the sense that the researcher treats him or herself and his or her colleagues as both subjects and objects in a process of critical reflection and self-reflection. There is a growing tradition in education that this is the most effective research method when attempting to improve education.

As I have already said there is good reason to support each of these approaches where appropriate. But making this judgement is not a straightforward task. The different methods present different problems of quality evaluation and dissemination. No method should have priority but must be suited to the aims of the research and the constraints of the potential audience.

My general conclusion on the current scenario concerning users is that the education research community does need to ask itself some searching questions. Why, for example, are Coopers & Lybrand, the management consultants, major players in the world of educational consultancy? Why have university departments not attracted this money?

Would it be possible to develop research impact indices? Consideration of this problem might be a useful way of starting to consider improvements in funding policy.

CONSIDERATION OF THE LEVERHULME REVIEW AS COMPARED TO THE RELEVANT (1992 AND 1995) REPORTS ABOUT EDUCATIONAL RESEARCH TO ESRC

The terms of reference of the ESRC reports have to be inferred from their discussions and recommendations. Perhaps due to differences in these terms, the recommendations of the present chapter are different in some important respects, especially in relation to the organisation and structure of the research enterprise. However, the major points of agreement are as follows:

1) Attempts to define educational research as independent from the general field of social science are unhelpful and likely to lead to methodological weaknesses.

2) In some key areas the development of theory is the most crucial issue. This, together with the refining and development of research methods and training of a larger cadre of research workers, is most important. The present chapter supports the conclusion that the most interesting phenomena of education are best studied in real time and require longitudinal research designs. The ESRC report suggests that methods of compressing the period of data captured to fit the constraints of short-term funding should be developed. This requires methods which combine qualitative and quantitative measures. This approach is important, but funding some longitudinal work is going to be necessary to answer some of the most pressing research questions.

Research infrastructure is also identified as requiring considerable strengthening. The ESRC report recommends a network of centres of excellence with satellite groups focusing on specific research agenda. This is similar to the ideas put forward here. However, funding the network through a National Educational Training Board is, as they indicate, likely to require a very significant increase in expenditure on educational research. One of the weaknesses of the ESRC report is that it lacks the sustained arguments which might justify its increased expenditure to any policy-makers with enough money to support this type of network.

The ESRC report argues that the quality of education proposals for research grants compares favourably with those from other disciplines. This conclusion is largely based on funding rates and, of course, takes no account of the possibility that educational referees are using different standards. There is no hard evidence to suggest that this is the case, but I have already suggested that there may be some problems with the review process for educational research proposals. The two most obvious are that some referees favour either qualitative or quantitative research irrespective of the problems being studied. And, secondly, that some referees are rejecting proposals on the grounds that the results would not immediately be in a form that could be communicated to the practitioners. This latter factor is we think one reason why the ESRC report concludes that basic research is currently underfunded in education.

As has been said earlier, there are conditions under which peer review is not to be trusted. For example, when mutually self-supporting groups dominate a research area they lead to unreliable judgements of both the positive and negative type. And when professional rivalry and insecurity are at a high level, research methods become the focus of disagreement.

In the ESRC report, the main areas being funded by ESRC were classified into eleven categories. These were preschool and primary education, learning processes and methods, teaching methods, curriculum, exams and assessment, humanities, science education, further and higher education, organisation and resources, and education and training for the disabled. At that time two-thirds of total funding was going to just two of these areas, exams and assessment and further and higher education. The report concludes that in a number of research areas funding has been extremely modest, for example, £250,000 in one year on primary education.

In recent years, ESRC has been identifying themes for research and as part of this process has commissioned a number of brief reviews of its research support. One of these concerned human development and learning. The list of projects it identified suggests that the conclusion of the ESRC's 1992 report that the national research effort is incoherent and unplanned is still true. This report notes the importance of archiving good data studies for subsequent investigation through secondary analysis. Connected to this is the problem of analysing qualitative data. Since the ESRC report there have been significant advances in the UK in this respect. However the extent to which these new methods are widely used is currently unclear; but new Internet facilities are being actively used to exchange ideas in this area.

The recommendations of the ESRC report concerning the four focus areas of learning in education settings, management and organisation in educational institutions, enhancing professional training and development and informing policy development, do seem to be somewhat unadventurous. There is no particular reason to quarrel with the list nor with the subsections within it. However, it does seem to reflect an attempt to include virtually all work in which researchers were engaged at the time. Although each area is carefully discussed and evaluated and contains many interesting suggestions we feel that the categories are to some degree arbitrary and their justifications somewhat pragmatic. Unfortunately the recommendations are not connected clearly to the issues of methodology and research structure which are highlighted in the earlier parts of the report. This is a difficulty which some of the organisational suggestions in this chapter might overcome.

The 1992 report's general comments on the way the research community is struggling to develop its skills in a situation of uncertain employment and underfunding still pertain. In the subsequent three years since the report there has been a substantial push for research in many university departments of education, especially those in the new universities. Many of the respondents in the Leverhulme investigation expressed concern that the RAE, which is driving these developments, is leading to quantity rather than quality in research. It mitigates against long-term programmes of work and methodological care, both of which cannot be easily achieved in the short term. The ESRC report notes that a relatively small number of groups have achieved international status. This is still true, although the volume of research will have increased.

The ESRC report emphasises the success of research networks and suggests that two or three of these should be initiated each year. This support could be supplemented by a programme funded by other bodies. The report's recommendation to establish policy forums is in line with the analysis of the present chapter.

The 1995 update of the ESRC report notes that, of the original 1992 proposals, the 'Learning Society' initiative emerged for funding, but it is unclear why, although it is consistent with the analysis presented earlier. The suggestions for further initiatives which emerge are

1) learning and literacy in preschool family settings;
2) the potential of new technologies especially in science and mathematics;
3) learning to learn, with particular reference to the context specificity of different teaching approaches; and
4) cost effectiveness, finance and productivity in educational institutions.

The last three of these initiatives are consistent with the areas of research highlighted in this chapter.

CONCLUSION

I have suggested that we need closer ties with social science and other disciplines. And that multidisciplinary centres of excellence can, and should, be established with the appropriate resource and leadership. Such centres could, for example, study children and classrooms in relation to their social, economic and cultural context. I agree that some good work of this kind does get carried out – I am arguing for ways of doing more and better research.

On a final note I must again stress that I am concerned to bring practice and research closer together. Many people in the educational community are sceptical about this being possible, while others seem to me to have abandoned the idea of carefully accumulating evidence across situations to produce general principles. My case is that, unless some of the issues I have raised can be addressed, then the future of research as a contributing force to educational change and improvement is at best uncertain.

REFERENCES

Gray, J. *et al.* (1992). *Frameworks and Priorities of Research in Education: Towards a Strategy for the ESRC,* Swindon, ERSC.

Gray, J. (1995) *Education: A Review of ESRC Supported Work,* Swindon, ESRC.

Kemmis, S. (1991) Improving education through action research, in O. Zuber-Skerrit (ed.) *Action Research For Change and Development,* Aldershot, Gower.

Light, P. (1995) *Human Development and Learning: A Review Of ESRC Supported Work,* Swindon, ESRC.

Nisbet, J. and Broadfoot, P. (1980) *The Impact Of Research on Policy and Practice in Education,* Aberdeen, Aberdeen University Press.

Ranson, S. (1995) *The Future of Educational Research. A Report on ESRC Supported Work.*

9

A NEW PARTNERSHIP OF STAKEHOLDERS AND A NATIONAL STRATEGY FOR RESEARCH IN EDUCATION

David H. Hargreaves

The structure of government and the modes of organisation of social science have large effects on the fate of social science research.

(Weiss, 1995, p. 138)

Each stakeholder group is entitled to state its wants and to assert them as the needs to which society should pay attention ... tensions and conflicts are inevitable and even necessary ingredients of development ... We can look forward ... to strengthening through negotiation the shared interests of the many groups in the improvement of education.

(CERI, 1995, Chap. 6)

A QUESTION OF QUALITY

The idea of a forum, which would bring into dialogue the various stakeholders in education to help shape a national strategy for educational research, is not a new one. The form of such a forum and its functions should, however, be determined not on the principle that, in an age when better liaison between research and user communities is generally held to be desirable, a forum is a convenient way of meeting this vague objective. Rather, its form and functions should relate to the weaknesses in the research enterprise that might thereby be cured and the aims and objectives that might thereby be more fully realised. Improving the quality of educational research should be the principal motive for establishing a forum and a national research strategy.

What are the weaknesses of educational research in the UK? There is no straightforward answer to this question. A major difficulty is that educational research is not easily defined. In a round-table discussion of quality in educational research at the conference of BERA in September 1994, the following statements were made by the four main speakers:

> I suggest that quality in educational research requires the outcome of research to have a significant and worthwhile effect on the judgements and decisions of practitioners or policy-makers towards improving educational action.
>
> (Michael Bassey)

> High quality research should ... help the understandings of those involved in any way in education, providing them with information and relevant viewpoints.
>
> (Wynne Harlen)

> What distinguishes educational research is its relationship to practice ... For many educational researchers it is the practical outcomes, the effective procedures and 'what works' that signify research progress and research quality.
>
> (Gwen Wallace)

> The highest quality educational research is that concerned with the creation and testing of education theory. Its quality may be judged by the extent to which it reconstitutes educational theory in the sense of developing more appropriate forms of explanation than those which exist at present for the educational development of individuals and communities.
>
> (Jack Whitehead)

The sentiments here do not diverge in any significant way from Sir William Taylor's (1973, p. 3) succinct definition of twenty years earlier that educational research is concerned with 'advancing our knowledge and understanding of the educational process, and helping policy makers, administrators, teachers and pupils to achieve their objectives'. Other definitions recognise that because education is a field, not a discipline, educational research is heterogeneous in its aims, character and style. Yet this pluralism is not by any means seen by all researchers as a benefit: there are serious disputes about what constitutes sound and acceptable research. This may explain why in their response to our strategic review of educational research,[1] the Executive Council of BERA seemed to find it difficult to comment on the terms of reference in any clear or detailed way, not least on matters of quality. The council was only too aware that their members have strongly held but highly divergent views on most of the questions: how could the council then represent the association as a whole and not the many sectional interests? The resulting submission shows that the council, in attempting to avoid offending some members, side-steps all the difficult or interesting questions and is driven to state what is dangerously close to the platitudinous:

(i) We welcome the chance to contribute to this [review], and hope that there will be opportunities for all of the 2000+ educational researchers in the UK to contribute as the review proceeds.

(ii) Educational Research currently faces many challenges and BERA as an association is doing all it can to help it to thrive, be well resourced, and achieve an effective impact on policy and practice.

(iii) There is a place for policy-driven research, but there is also an important place for educational research that is not driven by political expediencies. It is extremely important that a reasonable balance is maintained between [*sic*].

(iv) The priorities developed by the ESRC working group on 'The Future of Educational Research' in 1993 are still highly relevant.

(v) Dissemination of educational research findings is of course vital, as well. The responsibility for this needs to rest with policy makers as well as researchers. Some government departments and organisations are much better at making use of research in their decision-making than others.

(vi) Many funding agencies are now tending to put research out to tender. The approaches used vary quite a bit, and organisations that do not employ an open tendering procedure (such as the DfE) can create suspicion about how they allocate their funds for research.

(vii) There is a real need to ensure a better career structure within educational research. Good researchers develop as a result of training and experience of working on educational research problems in a well resourced team. Current trends have tended to make the careers of young researchers very uncertain, and as a result the number of good researchers coming through the system may be diminished. Funding policy does therefore need to be improved to address this issue as well as the others listed above.

Recent reviewers evidently struggle to give some semblance of coherence to the diversity of educational research. Take, for example, this definition in the recent review of educational research in Australia (McGaw *et al.*, 1992, p. 7):

Educational research is a very diverse enterprise that coheres around a broad set of common concerns. Since these concerns are *ultimately* about aspects of educational practice, educational research is essentially an area of applied research ... concerned with teaching and learning, with curriculum, with educational contexts, with knowledge of the social characteristics of students and teachers and with the management, organisation and funding of education.

A British example is provided by the ESRC's working party (Gray *et al.*, 1992, p. 5):

The scope of research on education is immense. It takes its agenda from several sources. The policies of government continue to be prominent. Given the multi-disciplinary nature of research in education, educational activities and institutions provide important test-beds for the theories and hypotheses deriving from other areas of social science. Psychology and sociology have been particularly influential... This group draws its priorities primarily from the realities of school and classroom life. The circumstances and conditions under which teachers and pupils interact and learn are at the heart of the research questions.

The multidisciplinary character of educational research is a problem as well as a strength. To a greater or lesser degree, much research is linked, in both theory and methods, with the broader social sciences, especially psychology and sociology. Attempts to draw distinctions and demarcate boundaries, as has recently and persuasively been attempted by Bassey (1995), are fraught with difficulties.

Finally, many educational researchers tend to be defensive about the quality and value of their work. They know that they are regarded as having relatively low standing in the status hierarchies of higher education and they know that at least some practitioners in schools and colleges are scornful of the value and usefulness of research. These concerns destroy the security and openness in which constructive self-criticism flourishes. Yet it is undeniable that the users of educational research are more critical of quality than researchers themselves: 'Educational researchers tend to take a positive view of the development of their field and of their own accomplishments. But policy-makers and practitioners often take a different and more critical view' (CERI, 1995, p. 15). Determining weaknesses in educational research is, then, a matter of judgement, not evidence. Each critic of educational research tends to adduce a different set of weaknesses, depending on his or her stance on a number of issues. My conviction that 'the improvement of educational practice' (to use the term that was once at the heart of BERA's mission statement) is central to the purpose and character of educational research greatly influences my selection of the main weaknesses of educational research, which I take to be six:

1) The low level of involvement of stakeholders in educational research.
2) The low level of application of educational research.
3) Excessive reliance on peer review in the funding of research.
4) Weak co-ordination among researchers and funders.
5) The non-cumulative character of much educational research.
6) The lack of large centres for educational research.

Let us consider each of these.

THE LOW LEVEL OF INVOLVEMENT OF STAKEHOLDERS

In comparison with other fields of professional research – say, medicine and engineering – the extent of user involvement in educational research is very low. In medicine there are some full-time researchers, but most, including those who hold university teaching posts, are also medical practitioners in the way that very few academics in the field of education are involved in teaching in schools.

Since I have discussed the similarities and differences with medical research elsewhere,[2] let us consider the case of engineering.[3] Here much of the funding comes from business and industry, there are strong links with firms and research is continuously subject to judgement as to the commercial value of its application. The timescale for this return is variable but the general view is that it has in recent times dropped from around fifteen years to three. There is consequently a strong industrial 'pull' which influences research policy and practice. The engineering community is research led, with companies drawing upon universities to update themselves on new developments. The university-based engineers usually have substantial industrial experience and are convinced that it is essential to maintain their connections with the industrial base. Some successful universities have established centres in which industrialists and academic engineers work together.

Many research ideas originate in the industrial context. University research is funded, the research councils apart, substantially by industry.[4] Engineers take a positive attitude towards putting research into practice and industrial enthusiasm is a major force in their research culture. Conscious of users' tendency to short-termist views of research, engineers in universities and research institutes are adept at cross-subsidising their 'blue skies' research with money from shorter-term commercial R & D. It is recognised that some blue-skies research will lead nowhere, but some will become the foundation for major developments, including applied work, at a later stage.

Engineers expect the solutions to practical industrial problems to generate high-quality theory. An example is Hooke's law which sprang from meeting demands for a navigation clock. University-based engineers are, like all academics, subject to peer review on judgement of quality and applaud the usual criteria such as citation indices and other measures of influence. But they also stress client satisfaction and agree that a key criterion of their success is the extent to which their ideas are applied in industry.

It is evident that the engineering user communities are more involved with research and exercise greater influence over the research agenda than is the case in education. Happily, and very much under the influence of the ESRC, educational researchers are increasing the involvement of practitioners in projects. Moreover, at local levels many of the teacher training institutions are, as they move to more school-based teacher training and continuing professional development, establishing closer ties with users. At the national level, however, relations between researchers and users remain tenuous.

THE LOW LEVEL OF APPLICATION

Relatively little educational research leads to applied outcomes in either the policy or practice in education and this was acknowledged by researchers in our survey:[5]

> In my view educational research has rather a poor record in 'promoting the application of ideas, concepts and findings to educational practice' . . . It must be admitted that some research has been of poor quality (in relation to educational need and to general standards in the social sciences) and it has rightly been ignored.

> At the moment there seems to be a huge gap between research and practice.

> UK record in this area is dreadful. Central problem is that education researchers typically have little concern for (or interest in) their professional audience – teachers and parents – and write mostly for each other.

> It is not so much the epistemology of the social sciences that is important but the failure to address questions to which policy makers need an answer.

> Much 'basic' research in social science is not seen as relevant to education because it addresses theoretical issues of significance to academic disciplines rather than the concerns of the practitioner.

> There are no clear mechanisms by which research can be discussed with policy makers and politicians and the implications considered for practice. . . There seem to be a number of missing links - between practitioners and researchers and between researchers and policy makers.

> One [of my concerns], to put it quite bluntly, is that the standard of much research writing in education is poor. . . Too often the audience of the paper is forgotten in the rush to write it.

There are understandable reasons why direct influence on policy-making is unusual: politicians decide policy on the basis of values alone rather than in association with relevant evidence, unless the evidence is consonant with their values; they usually work to very short timescales and will not risk putting their policies to trial; and in recent years much educational work on policy has been highly critical of right-wing governments. It is, however, much less easy to defend the low levels of application by practitioners, especially schoolteachers.

The most common response is to explain the record of the application of educational research as a consequence of poor dissemination. Some blame researchers, some blame funders, some even blame the teachers:

I guess that the record [of educational research] is poor. . . I do not think the problem is so much a matter of methodology but that researchers have not proved competent at disseminating their findings in such a way as to make them accessible.

I think the biggest problem is that many researchers have not had the ability, the readiness or the time for effective dissemination.

The usual method of dissemination is in-service education and failure to ensure the wider assimilation of the recommended processes and techniques is routinely attributed to the failure of the in-service training and staff development. Research activity examining the factors influencing the methods of translating research findings into common practice should be increased.

The difficulty has been going beyond a relatively small percentage of practitioners who see the importance of educational research . . . for their own work.

In the UK there is a problem with credibility of educational research and a lack of willingness on the part of practitioners in the school context to act on research findings: a structure for dissemination of findings must be articulated.

I guess the record is poor. In fact we seem to have bred a generation of teachers who denigrate research as being something 'out there somewhere' and of no use or relevance to them.

Though educational researchers see dissemination as a problem, little is done about it. At the 'macro' level, Postlethwaite's (1984, p. 197) sensible suggestions that

it is very important that researchers forge or strengthen links with policy-makers from the inception of a major national research project. . . [T]here are different levels of policy-makers from the Minister . . . the various divisions in the ministry, the curriculum developers, the teacher unions, and the school principals and teachers. It is important to have links with them all

have largely been ignored. In consequence, at the 'micro' level most requests for research grants continue to offer a conventional dissemination strategy of publications in journals and books and perhaps a conference for interested practitioners and policy-makers. But since, in education, publication in journals and books rarely contributes to its application to professional practice, such dissemination strategies are hopelessly thin. At the same time funding agencies do not always respond favourably to including in research grants a substantial budget for dissemination.

Some researchers defend themselves on the grounds that educational research has in the past rarely been shown to have any direct impact on policy and practice and so (by a *non sequitur*) can never be expected to have any direct effect. Some have even adopted the view that empirical educational research designed for application is largely pointless and that research is best seen as critiques of policy and practice. Indirect influence has been more readily documented and so, the argument runs, can be accepted as the normal character and legitimate goal of research. 'The relationship [between educational research and policy],' reports Kogan (in Husen and Kogan, 1984, p. 48), 'is held by most observers to be insidious, subtle and non-linear rather than direct and decisive' which helpfully lets researchers off the hook of application as well as active co-operation with users. In much the same way, the mixture of optimism and defensiveness is evident when Taylor (1973, p. 200) writes that educational research

> exerts its influence by helping to determine the agenda of problems and difficulties, and in providing some of the elements that shape individual and group orientations towards particular issues... Although the influence of research in education on staffroom conversation and school committee decision is more tenuous and indirect ... it is none the less real and is growing. All this points to the need to be aware of simplistic assumptions regarding the actual and likely pay-offs from research. Some of these are readily traceable, but most make their way into thinking and practice less directly – through the literature on education ... [and] through courses, conferences and lectures... The fact that ... most discussions about education, except among researchers themselves and some of the professionals in universities and colleges, contain few explicit references to research, is no real guide to its influence and certainly no basis on which to calculate its usefulness in cost/benefit terms.

The same line is readily adopted when research shows impact to be negligible. Witness Nisbet's (1995, p. 78) comments on

> a small-scale study, funded by S[cottish] E[ducation] D[epartment], on the effectiveness of dissemination of two projects, *Problem solving in the primary school* with a sample of 32 teachers and *The marketing of further education* with 10 FE staff. Almost all said they had neither seen nor heard of the reports, a result of serious concern. However, this is an over-simple (and possibly invalid) measure of the effectiveness of dissemination, unless the samples were the sole target audiences of the two project reports. Research sometimes may have a direct effect, but often its impact is in the form of a 'trickle-down effect', questioning practices, procedures and assumptions which have been adopted unquestioningly in the past.

A leading American authority (Weiss, 1995, p. 141), noting the very few examples of direct or immediate impact, speaks of research as 'a form of continuing education for busy officials. It gave them insight into the nature of social problems and the institutional structures that sustained them. Once in a while it changed their priorities'. Some of the influence of research in any professional field will properly be indirect, adding to the general enlightenment. It is the severe lack of evidence of direct influence, and the unwillingness of researchers to regard this as a problem, which seems to mark out educational researchers from researchers in other professional domains. The comments cited thus far, especially those from our survey, seem to confirm that there is a *prima facie* case to answer over the quality and impact of educational research. They may not be typical: our sample was small and biased, and those who responded may have been more critical than those who did not. On the other hand our method of culling opinions offered a degree of anonymity that encouraged candour. Take the academic respondent who said

> I don't think the rest of the world shares the priority given to educational research by university academics ... it was seen as 'ivory tower' and of little direct relevance to practitioners. One headteacher of my acquaintance summed up the prevailing attitude in schools by saying: 'If research is any good it confirms what I already know and therefore don't need to be told again. If it doesn't confirm what I already know it is probably no good'. I deplore this attitude but we are fooling ourselves if we don't think it is widely held in schools. .. In my view, therefore, it is only a small minority in the world of education outside universities who genuinely believe in research as a means of improving education.

Does he seriously misrepresent a typical headteacher's attitude to educational research? There is one recent small-scale study by Saha *et al.* (1995, p. 115) of a hundred American and Australian headteachers' attitudes to educational research which concludes that 'the typical school principal judges research knowledge to be very valuable, describes him or herself as a regular, thoughtful user of that knowledge, states that he or she learns from that knowledge and that research knowledge may be flawed but nevertheless relevant'. The figures given in this study stretch credibility to the limit. Only 7% of school principals think research is of little or no value and 71% think it is usually valuable or invaluable. Fewer than 2% say they are hostile to research and two-thirds claim they are regular or enthusiastic users of research. But Carol Weiss (1995, p. 146), a leading international figure on issues of policy application, had already warned against taking such findings at face value:

> Are there some kinds of research that are more likely to be used than others? ... We know from earlier research that it was fruitless to ask decision makers to tell us. They themselves did not know. They knew what the socially acceptable answer was, but they did not know what they really did.

Saha *et al.* (1995) interviewed headteachers face to face; and the heads knew the authors were eminent educational researchers. Is it really likely that they would find it easy to admit if they did not value or use much research? Headteachers are not in principle against educational research: the point is rather that they, like their representatives with whom I talked,[6] think it could be better and more useful.

A telling anecdote was told by a colleague at the BERA conference in May 1996. She reported how a school of which she was a governor was writing policies in relation to an impending OFSTED inspection. To be helpful, she supplied the working parties writing the policies with some user-friendly summaries of relevant research. Though these were politely received, little use was in the event made of them. The teachers were more interested in what fellow practitioners in other schools were doing. Colleague practitioners, not researchers, were the reference group that mattered.

EXCESSIVE RELIANCE ON PEER REVIEW IN THE FUNDING OF RESEARCH

Educational researchers also take their colleagues as their major reference group. Users are peripheral to most educational researchers most of the time: it is colleagues who matter more, because of the overwhelming power of peer review. Peer review has legitimacy for them; its exercise is inescapable and has substantial effects. In a conflict between peers and users, peers will, other things being equal, win decisively.

The most important and prestigious research projects are those funded by the ESRC or the major charitable foundations. There are several reasons for this: these bodies fund other kinds of research apart from educational research; they support research which is explicitly social scientific and is not necessarily of immediate relevance to policy or application; they do not seek to control the direction of the research through their own steering groups; they do not reserve the right to control the publication of research results; and for their refereeing system they adopt a form of peer review to guide funding decisions and the evaluation of outcomes.

By contrast, many government agencies now commission educational research with a very close prespecification of research objectives and methods, leaving relatively little scope to the researchers; adopt very tight timescales, often expecting results within a year or less; demand a high degree of control over the publication of any research findings, provoking among researchers the understandable fear that if the findings do not support or are inconsistent with (political) policy directions, conclusions will in effect be suppressed; and make relatively little use of peer review.

Peer review is valued by educational researchers, as by other kinds of researcher, for the good reason that it avoids reliance on political or user whim or bias: the research deemed most worthy of support is that judged to be of high quality by those with demonstrable expertise in the field. Peer review is seen as a linchpin of both research quality and academic freedom.

There are, however, some known weaknesses in peer review.[7] For instance, if members of a discipline or subsection of a discipline referee one another in highly favourable terms using less stringent criteria or apply agreed criteria less stringently than another discipline or subsection, then they may gain a disproportionate number of research grants. This is a very real hazard when research funds are in short supply relative to demand and it becomes known to reviewers that unless they award exceptionally high grades to their disciplinary peers the research will go unfunded. Funding bodies tend to trust the reports of the best-known people in the field, and studies have shown that reviewers tend to review more favourably people they know personally. Reviewers are favourably influenced by track record – even though in practice the best-known researchers, holding many research grants, do less of the actual research themselves than the less well known directing a single project. On the other hand, reviewers may judge unduly harshly those with whom they see themselves in competition for research awards and prestige. Reviewers may sometimes be biased against research proposals that are high in novelty or risk. Interdisciplinary research (commended by many of those submitting evidence) may be treated by reviewers with greater caution than research which falls within the mainstream of a single discipline, and may fall foul of a negative judgement from just one of the disciplines involved.

All these possibilities of distortion in peer review might apply to education as to any other field: there is too little British research on the topic. My concern is, however, not so much with the mechanics of peer review. It is with the deeper problem, in professional fields of research, of determining the proper and most beneficial role of users in generating and maintaining research of the highest quality and how the role of users is to be balanced against that of peers. If research is judged by all with an interest or stake in that field as being in good shape, then peer review will be effective in promoting quality, within a desirable climate of academic freedom over the selection, execution and publication of research. If, however, a field is not regarded by all with an interest or stake in it as being in good shape, then peer review maintains financial support to research, preserves the status quo and inhibits the emergence of corrective reform. Peer review systems which are seriously adrift from the relevant user communities are in danger of being self-nurturing, self-communicating, self-validating and self-perpetuating.

This, I believe, is the position with educational research in this country. In engineering research there is a tension between peers and users, but the tension can be creative rather than damaging, in part because sound and regular relations with users have become routinised within the culture and in part because the importance of user pressures and the legitimacy of meeting user demands are shared by the academic community and thus become a natural component of peer review. None of this obtains in education, where in my judgement:

- the criticisms that many educational researchers have of the overall quality of educational research are justified;
- users are justified in believing that too little educational research is relevant and useful to practice and policy-making;
- researchers have become estranged from user communities and protect their position by laying the blame elsewhere – the problems of dissemi-

nation, the indirect nature of the impact of educational research, the deficiencies of commissioned research, the failure of teachers to attend to research findings, policy-makers' suspicion of research, etc.; and

- the peer review system plays a key role in maintaining the status quo and inhibiting reform that would

  - create a richer partnership between researchers and users;
  - produce a more healthy balance between user and peer influence on the funding of research and the evaluation of its outcomes; and
  - generate research of higher quality, relevance, usefulness and cost-effectiveness than now obtains.

A proper partnership between researchers and users means the involvement of users at all stages of the research process – formulating a research strategy; selecting the topic for research; formulating the research design; carrying out the research; applying and disseminating the outcomes; and evaluating the outcomes.

THE WEAK CO-ORDINATION AMONG RESEARCHERS AND FUNDERS

There is weak co-ordination among funders and among researchers, and between funders and researchers. That funders are, at least officially, rather weakly co-ordinated is understandable, because there are so many of them. The advantage is that educational researchers may take an application sequentially to several funders and eventually get it accepted by one after initial rejection. The disadvantage is that nobody knows until a very late stage whether an area is being heavily funded or relatively neglected. The agenda for educational research is not planned; it is something discovered in retrospect.

Researchers working in the same area, especially if it is relatively new, may take some time to learn that a team in a different institution is working on the same or a related set of problems. The National Foundation for Educational Research (NFER) does its best to create a useful register, but because this takes time to compile and depends on returns from researchers, the register's value is limited in the co-ordination of researchers during the active phase of their projects.

THE NON-CUMULATIVE CHARACTER OF EDUCATIONAL RESEARCH

Much educational research is non-cumulative[8] in part because few researchers seek to create a body of knowledge which is then tested, extended or replaced in some systematic way. A few small-scale investigations of an issue which are never followed up inevitably produce inconclusive and contestable findings of little practical value to anybody. Replications, which are more necessary in the social than the natural sciences because of the importance of contextual and cultural variations, are astonishingly rare.

Reports of educational research are, of course, replete with cross-references, but these are often merely decorative, attesting to the author's familiarity with relevant material. Given the huge amounts of educational research conducted over the last fifty years or more, there are relatively few areas which have yielded a corpus of research evidence regarded as scientifically sound and as a worthwhile resource to guide professional action. In many educational areas a line of research ends because it goes out of fashion, rather than because the problems in it have been solved or the dominant theory is now well established.

Part of the problem is the lack of long-term funding of particular areas of work. Few funders will support a single project for more than four years, which is too short a time in most fields of educational research in which to build a sound body of knowledge. It may be significant that neither of the two ESRC educational research centres, which usually get guaranteed funding for ten years, is in a university department of education. Sustained research on a topic would be more likely if there were more research centres.

THE LACK OF LARGE CENTRES FOR EDUCATIONAL RESEARCH

At present, there is only one very large institution which can mount educational research of high quality across a wide range of specialisms and themes – the London Institute of Education. Much of the rest of the educational research enterprise is dispersed across a range of relatively small teacher training institutions. To achieve more high-quality research of national and international significance, and to achieve the degree of excellence that can reasonably be expected for the amount of public and charitable money invested, there needs in my view to be more centres of excellence with larger groups of researchers working in closer association with mainstream social scientists. This the education research community has hitherto firmly resisted: when there are so many small units, it appears to be in each unit's interest to preserve the status quo.[9]

It is accepted that not every university should support, say, a department of biochemistry, let alone one of eminence for its research. Most universities are involved in teacher education, especially initial training; but it does not follow that all their teaching staff should be engaged in research. Although the top-rated institutions for educational research tend to be the larger ones, it is not possible to demonstrate that larger centres would produce better research. I suspect, however, a greater concentration of research resources and personnel would, combined with a stronger relationship between researchers and users, lead to better educational research.

TOWARDS SOLUTIONS

Solutions, like problems, are a matter of personal judgement and preference; the ones I favour naturally reflect in part my nominated weaknesses. While the research community will inevitably be divided on the nature and extent of weaknesses in the record of educational research, there may well be greater agreement on measures that might contribute to improvement. The urgency is that research budgets in all fields are under scrutiny as researchers become more accountable to funding agencies, user communities and the general public. Some recent developments[10] suggest that faculties of education may soon have to defend their research budgets.

Any discussion of the future of educational research should, I suggest, include the need for the community to

- take as a primary purpose *the involvement of user communities*, especially policy-makers and practitioners, in all aspects of the research process, from the creation of strategic research plans through to the dissemination and implementation of policies and practices arising from or influenced by research activities and findings; and thereby achieve a more even balance between users and peers in the influence they exercise;
- establish the machinery for creating *a national strategy for educational research*, including the formulation of short and long-term priorities, with some mechanism for co-ordinating the work of the various funding agencies to increase knowledge of all parties about what topics are being funded for what reasons and what relevance the outcomes of research have for policy and practice; and
- create more *centres of excellence* which can take forward not merely research projects but research programmes and which have the infrastructure to support research of the highest quality on a particular theme on a sustained basis, and thereby achieve an international reputation.

GREATER INVOLVEMENT OF USER COMMUNITIES

Creating a new partnership between researchers and user communities should be at the heart of any reform, in part because success here will help to solve so many other problems. Partnerships must (and of course do) exist at the level of the individual research institution and individual research project. All that encourages this is to be applauded, as I applaud the pressure the ESRC is putting on researchers to demonstrate consultation with and involvement of users. Such action is, however, insufficient in itself, for it does too little to change the culture and the routine practices of users or researchers; indeed, there is a danger of researchers playing at user involvement in a superficial and rhetorical way because the rules of the 'game' of obtaining funding and doing research have not really changed. Users must play a real role in shaping the direction of educational research as a whole, not just in influencing a local project in which they happen to be involved; and researchers need to know that users are powerful partners with whom many aspects of research need to be negotiated and to whom in a real sense the research community is in part accountable.

A NATIONAL STRATEGY FOR EDUCATIONAL RESEARCH

This means, in my view, that it would be desirable to establish a National Educational Research Forum. It would not itself fund any research: its function would be to establish a continuing dialogue between all the stakeholders and to help to shape the agenda for educational research and its policy implications and applications.

The idea has been aired before. In their report to the ESRC, Gray *et al.* (1992, p. 25) suggest:

> the development of policy forums. Policy-makers and practitioners often complain that research in education is irrelevant to their concerns. Some of it may be but more could be done to bring the various partners together. If the energies of these groups could be enlisted in establishing research priorities then they would be less likely to dismiss the outcomes.

On this view users are mainly involved in determining (general) priorities and then in learning about outcomes rather than playing an active role in each stage of the whole process and thus shaping it in what are potentially new ways. Moreover, the forums – note the plurality of them – are suggested in vague terms, without specified functions, core funding or leadership. Nothing has been done to create these forums. The report by the CERI (1995) is more specific, but since the audience is international there is inevitably much generality in the recommendations. It is very easy for the stakeholders in any country to affirm their commitment to partnership whilst being indifferent to setting up the machinery to make it a working reality.

To make progress with a National Forum we must move from pious hope to a clear definition of what such a body might do and how the necessary groundwork might be undertaken. There is perhaps a useful parallel to be made with the idea of a General Teaching Council (GTC). Many have argued for a GTC, but it has taken John Tomlinson and a group of enthusiasts to create a GTC in waiting. If one is eventually created, it will have been helped by this preliminary work.

The forum's members would be formed from a mixture of researchers, policy-makers (especially national and local government), practitioners (principals, heads, teachers), representatives from funding bodies (research councils, major charities, smaller trusts) and relevant lay persons (governors of educational institutions, parents). The mechanism for selecting the members would need to be devised with some ingenuity. The organisation, with a small permanent staff, would need to be led by a person of eminence who could be trusted by all parties and who could take the initiative in shaping the agenda for the discussion of all matters relevant to educational research and educational policy-making and practice. It would provide the arena in which all kinds of stakeholder could talk to one another in that necessarily broad and open conversation about matters of educational interest in which research 'is just one element in the complex mix of experience, conventional wisdom and political accommodation that enters into decision making' (Husen, in Husen and Kogan, 1984, p. 31).

Building on these interchanges, the forum would, on a regular basis (say every four to five years), conduct or commission a review of current achievements, omissions and problems in educational research, leading to a research foresight[11] exercise, involving researcher, user and lay communities, and the establishment thereafter of a *national research strategy*. Such a strategy would inevitably be in broad outline, based on the forum's conclusions concerning the most desirable research (the priorities especially of users) and the most practicable research (based especially on researchers' knowledge, skills and experience).

The outline strategic plan would then be shared with all the community involved in educational research, the individual bodies of which, whether a major funder like a research council or charitable trust or a minor player like an individual researcher, would make their own decisions in the light of, but without being bound by, the national strategy. The staff of the forum would play a major role in keeping major players informed of what other players were doing, and would in due course publish the emergent match between research activity and the guiding national strategy. Such feedback loops between a national strategy and the constant decision-making by funders and researchers are essential to better communication, co-ordination and coherence in educational research. In this way the forum staff would have a duty to keep the research and user communities informed as to progress within the national strategy; to keep a register of current and recent research; and to encourage and support the various forms of networking that are essential to good-quality and sustained communication, co-ordination and collaboration among researchers and stakeholders. Improved co-ordination should enhance the cumulative development of research on which successful application rests.

Experience with foresight exercises and machinery to co-ordinate disparate bodies suggests that the processes involved in a National Educational Research Forum would be just as important as the outcomes; indeed, the outcomes would not be achieved without the successful management of the key processes – gaining the commitment and confidence of the parties concerned; ensuring clear and open communication between them; achieving consensus on ways of working and the determination of priorities and so on. I suspect the research community would be less enthusiastic than the users, since they would fear loss of autonomy in the choice of research topic, methods of investigation and ownership of findings. There would indeed be some loss of autonomy, but it would be offset, particularly in the medium to long term, by far more research which is closely related to policy and practice, which is carried out in partnership with users, and which leads to outcomes which are far more likely to be disseminated and implemented. Researchers may claim that users have short-termist views about research, which means users want quick answers to today's most salient problems rather than complicated longer-term solutions to problems which are emergent. In this the academics are right: users are indeed preoccupied by short-term issues, and for perfectly understandable reasons. Users accuse the academics of neglect of the short term, and in this they too are right. This tension between short and long term, between user and researcher perspectives, can be resolved only through more discussion and hard negotiation.

It is through the sustained interaction between researchers and users that many of the persistent weaknesses in educational research can be tackled. There is a need for commissioned research and there is a place for unconstrained inquiry or 'pure' research: there should be 'decision-orientated' research where the question posed is that of the policy-maker or practitioner as well as 'conclusion-orientated' research where the question arises from a researcher's hunch or hypothesis (Cronbach and Suppes, 1969). It is not a case of advancing the claims of one against the other, or even of striking a balance between the two. It is more a question of establishing a continuing dialogue between the stakeholders out of which will come the learning and accommodation on all sides. Policy-makers will find that there are good reasons why they cannot get direct or simple answers from researchers over a short period and that educational research nevertheless has indirect benefits by clarifying and reconceptualising the nature of educational questions and answers. In their turn, educational researchers cannot expect to be funded unless they are prepared to devote far more energy and ingenuity to addressing policy-related and practitioner-led questions that require investigation and solution. There is no reason to believe that the funding of good 'blue skies' research, or of basic, long-term research without immediate application should be under threat – provided that the funding bodies (who should retain their existing powers) continue to believe in its importance and users are persuaded through the forum to value it more highly than they do at present.

Researchers should accept as legitimate the increased pressure to pay more attention than hitherto to users' immediate and pressing problems.

The forum would need to have secure funding for its small permanent staff, for the activities involved in the research foresight exercise and for the construction of the national research agenda. It would almost certainly need to come, at least in the longer term, from the Department of Education and Employment.[12] The forum would need to be led by an energetic champion of educational research who had high credibility with all the relevant communities.

The functions of the National Educational Research Forum, then, would be to

- support continuing dialogue about the directions for and quality of educational research among the stakeholders;
- promote and support sustained networking among stakeholders;
- review educational research on a regular basis;
- hold a research foresight exercise every four or five years;
- devise with the stakeholders a national strategy for educational research;
- support educational researchers and the funding agencies in their implementation of the national strategy;
- monitor and co-ordinate research activity in the light of the national strategy; and
- provide information about research activity to all the stakeholders.

In the UK the concept of national is always ambiguous. It could be a forum to cover the whole UK; there could be separate national forums in each of the four countries; there could be a joint one in England and Wales. I incline at this stage to the last of these three possibilities, not least because the Scots have in any event already created their own version of a forum,[13] as they have of a GTC, and those south of the border should learn from the Scottish experience.

The establishment of the forum along these lines would not solve all the problems and weaknesses in educational research, nor would it suddenly make research influence direct rather than indirect. It would, however, slowly change the culture of educational research to good effect and bring education into line with comparable professional fields, such as medicine and engineering. In the absence of a forum or some equivalent, there is no reason to believe that over the next decade educational research will contribute more effectively than it has done in the past to improving the quality of the education system.

CENTRES OF RESEARCH EXCELLENCE

Creating centres of research excellence is a difficult task.[14] A university department of education (UDE) should be identified as a centre of research excellence only when it is of an appropriate size, the research record is of high quality and there is a demonstrable collaboration with one or more social science departments in the same university. Ideally such centres should be reasonably well distributed around the country, because they need to take a regional lead in forging the partnerships between researchers and user communities at the local level and in representing the region's interests at national level. In this way the centres of excellence should forge stronger partnerships than has hitherto been usual among social scientists and users. In addition, research centres should play a significant role in advanced teacher education and training within each region.

One option would be for the Higher Education Funding Council (HEFC) to change the formula for allocating 'R' money in the field of education so that institutions with 5 ratings are given a significant increase at the expense of those with a 3 or below who might be given nothing at all. Leaving those with a 4 rating with their present level of funding ensures a degree of regional competition with the 5s – and a potential regional alternative should an existing 5 go into decline. To prevent the isolation of the lone scholar or research group in the low-rated institutions, the regional centres of excellence should involve scholars in local institutions in relevant scholarly activities and offer local fellowships and secondments.

It has to be accepted that many of those who play a vital role in teacher education, namely those who come to teacher training after a distinguished career in schools, need not themselves become researchers. This is a perfectly respectable position and it is absurd to pretend that all teacher training institutions of good quality need to have a major research function. Teacher training institutions might then fall into one of two categories suggested some years ago:

• Teaching-only institutions (with no HEFC research funding, no research students, few if any research staff, most academics having teaching functions only) – the majority of faculties of education.
• Teaching and research institutions (with HEFC research funding, research students and most academic staff having both teaching and research duties), with one or two of the best in each region becoming centres of excellence;

In addition, a small number of research centres, focusing on a single major theme, normally attached to a UDE or to a social science department, should be established.

There are, in the UDEs, a huge number of so-called research centres, which are one-man-and-a-dog affairs. There are ESRC-funded educational research centres, such as the Centre for Research in Development, Instruction and Training (Nottingham University). There are several other important centres, such as CEDAR (Warwick University). But the UK lacks research centres on the scale of those in the USA – such as the Centre for Research in Assessment, Evaluation and Testing at UCLA (funded to around $5 million per annum) and the other seventeen R & D centres (mostly funded at around $1million per annum) on topics such as education in the inner cities, mathematics teaching and learning, educational finance and productivity, adult literacy.

'Educational R & D personnel are more heavily concentrated in higher education than are R & D personnel as a whole' (CERI, 1995, p. 48). There is room, especially in the area of policy analysis and policy evaluation, for independent research centres and 'think-tanks' which enter into some kind of association with a university. In the USA bodies such as the Brookings Institution, the Rand Corporation and the Johnson Foundation, as well as graduate schools of public policy which thrive much more readily than in Britain, have played a very significant role in education policy analysis and development. The emergence in Britain of similar institutions with a research arm would be beneficial. Part of the reason for suggesting that independent research centres, think-tanks and bodies concerned with public policy analysis be funded to undertake educational policy analysis and related research is the failure of teacher training institutions to develop policy analysis in appropriate ways. Martin Trow (1984, p. 265) has proposed a stringent criterion for the policy analyst:

> Perhaps the most important distinguishing characteristic of the policy analyst as contrasted with the academic research social scientist in the university is that he or she is trained, indeed required, to see and formulate problems from the perspectives not of the academic disciplines but of the decision-maker. In his work he accepts the constraints and values of the decision-maker – the political pressures on him, the political feasibility of a proposal, its financial costs, the legal context in which it will operate, the difficulties of implementing it, of shaping organisation, of recruiting, training and motivating people to work in the service of its purposes. He is, if effectively trained, sensitive to the benefits and costs of programmes, to the trade-offs in any decision, and to the alternative advantages of government and the market in achieving social purposes. In a word, he tries to see problems from the perspective of the decision-maker, but with a set of intellectual, analytical and research tools that the politician or senior civil servant may not possess. He is, and is trained to be, the researcher in government at the elbow of the decision maker, or if not in government, then serving the 'government in opposition' or some think-tank or interest group which hopes to staff the next administration or agency on the next swing of the political pendulum.

Many sociologists of education now see themselves as engaging in policy analysis, but they do not meet the above criterion nor are they training their students to do so. Funding independent research centres, think-tanks and public policy units, which tend to find it difficult to get core funding as well as research grants, could and should further develop policy analysis and the training of the next generation of policy analysts. Such a challenge to university-based educational research and analysis from bodies outside the UDEs, or even outside higher education, would exert some healthy pressure towards development and change in the UDEs' domination of educational research. Indeed, such an independent centre might take responsibility for the National Forum.

A flourishing set of organisations or units concerned with educational policy analysis would enjoy a complementary and symbiotic relationship with the UDEs. As Trow has pointed out, policy analysts are under little pressure to publish, are not subject to peer review, and manage their careers in a relatively closed and private world rather than the international openness of the scholarly community. But they have less access to research evidence and some research methods; they sometimes – by the pressure of working within tight time-frames, sharply defined problems and what are regarded by politicians as feasible solutions – have to work within narrower perspectives than academics free from such constraints; and they enjoy less independence in forming opinions and making judgements and standing by them. But they do have the enormous advantage of constant access to policy-makers. Necessarily they have had to acquire a full understanding of policy-makers' ways of thinking, working and decision-making, and thereby develop insights into the art of speaking and writing about policy in clear and persuasive ways – a feature notable for its absence in most writing by educational researchers. Policy analysts, then, are potentially a powerful bridge between the academic educational research community and policy-makers – a bridge that is sorely needed if educational research is to emulate the relatively greater success evident in other professional fields.

NOTES

1. This was conducted by Michael Beveridge and myself in the academic year 1994–95 and funded by the Leverhulme Trust.
2. See my lecture 'Teaching as a research-based profession', Teacher Training Agency, April 1996.
3. In a study funded by the Leverhulme Trust, Michael Beveridge and I conducted interviews with a number of professors of engineering. These remarks are based on the evidence of the interviews.
4. With the exception of construction engineering, which in this country (unlike Japan) funds little research.
5. According to the responses to the question *How good is the record of educational research in promoting the application of ideas, concepts and findings to educational practice?* made in the survey conducted by

Michael Beveridge and myself from which the quotations are taken.

6. I interviewed the President and General Secretary of the Secondary Heads Association, who responded immediately to my invitation and talked with me for about two hours.

7. See, for instance, United States General Accounting Office (1994).

8. Some writers seem unduly dogmatic and pessimistic in denying any cumulative character to social science, rather than acknowledging it as a greater problem in the social sciences than in the natural sciences. Take for instance the following: 'Knowledge about policy questions is 'not cumulative in a scientific sense, partly because the problems are intractable and also because the environment changes so that old solutions do not fit the new circumstances' (Rein, 1976, p. 23).

9. This probably explains the ESRC working party (Gray *et al.*, 1992) recommendation that the council could help educational research by changing its policy on research centres, scaling down the size and duration of the grant to fit the large number of small research bases in the UDEs. This self-serving recommendation proved to be popular with the ever-hopeful educational research community – but not with the ESRC.

10. Including the report *Research Capability of the University System*, produced by a group appointed by the National Academies Policy Advisory Group – which consists of the British Academy, the Conference of the Medical Royal Colleges, The Royal Academy of Engineering and the Royal Society – and chaired by the Master of Selwyn College, Cambridge, Sir David Harrison.

11. In developing my view on the role of research foresight in educational research I have been strongly influenced by the report *Technology Foresight: A Review of Recent International Experiences*, written by Ben R. Martin (of the ESRC Centre for Science, Technology, Energy and Environment Policy in the Science Policy Research Unit, University of Sussex) for the Office of Science and Technology, Cabinet Office. I am grateful to him for letting me see his report.

12. In Australia, the McGaw review (1992) proposed the establishment of an Education and Training Research Board to bring together stakeholders and proposed a small levy on education expenditure to fund it. This was strongly opposed by those on whom the levy would fall, including university vice-chancellors and tertiary education authorities. The recommendation has not been implemented to date.

13. See the contribution in this volume by Sally Brown and Wynne Harlen.

14. See CERI (1995) for a summary of the conditions for the creation of healthy centres of excellence.

REFERENCES

Bassey, M. (1995) *Creating Education Through Research*. Newark, England, Kirklington Press.

Centre for Educational Research and Innovation (1995) *Educational Research and Development: Trends, Issues and Challenges*, Paris, OECD.

Cronbach, L. J. and Suppes, P. (1969) *Research for Tomorrow's Schools*, London and New York, Macmillan.

Gray, J. *et al.* (1992) *Frameworks and Priorities for Research in Education: Towards a Strategy for the ESRC*, Swindon, ESRC.

Husen, T. and Kogan, M. (eds.) (1984) *Educational Research and Policy*, Oxford, Pergamon.

McGaw, B., Boud, D., Poole, M., Warry, R. and McKenzie, P. (1992) *Educational Research in Australia: Report of the Review Panel, Strategic Review of Research in Education*, Canberra, Australian Government Publishing Service.

Nisbet, J. D. (1995) *Pipers and Tunes: A Decade of Educational Research in Scotland*, Edinburgh, Scottish Council for Research in Education.

Postlethwaite, T. N. (1984) Research and policy-making in education, in T. Husen and M. Kogan (eds.) *Educational Research and Policy*, Oxford, Pergamon.

Rein, M. (1976) *Social Science and Public Policy*, Harmondsworth, Penguin Books.

Saha, L. J., Biddle, B. J. and Anderson, D. S. (1995) Attitudes towards educational research knowledge and policy making among American and Australian school principals, *International Journal of Educational Research*, Vol. 23, no. 2, pp. 113–26.

Taylor, W. (ed.) (1973) *Research Perspectives in Education*, London, Routledge & Kegan Paul.

Trow, M. (1984) Researchers, policy analysts, and policy intellectuals, in T. Husen and M. Kogan (eds.) *Educational Research and Policy*, Oxford, Pergamon.

United States General Accounting Office (1994) *Peer Review: Reforms Needed to Ensure Fairness in Federal Agency Grant Selection*. Washington D.C., USGA.

Weiss, C. H. (1995) The haphazard connection: social science and public policy, *International Journal of Educational Research*, Vol. 23, no. 2, pp. 137–50.

Responses to
Section Two

10

A RESPONSE FROM OUTSIDE THE UNIVERSITY SYSTEM

Seamus Hegarty

These two chapters throw down the gauntlet to educational researchers. They paint an unflattering picture of educational research, discerning major short-comings in terms of quality, relevance and value for money. The recommendations for action are no less challenging than the analyses, calling as they do for radical changes in the organisation and conduct of research.

It is worth remarking that robust critiques from informed colleagues are to be welcomed. Whether or not one agrees with them, it is a mark of some maturity – and essential to progress – that divergent views can be discussed in a rational way. And what a relief it is to be critiqued by people who know what they are talking about and are not driven by dogma or prejudice.

Both chapters draw on analyses of educational research, analyses that focus on current weaknesses, to make a case for various reforms. Hargreaves advocates a national forum which would establish a continuing dialogue between all the stakeholders in educational research and, by articulating a national research strategy, help to shape the agenda for action. Beveridge focuses more on changes within the working structures of educational research – better links with other disciplines, changes within university departments of education, more long-term research programmes and closer attention to the user–researcher interface.

Hargreaves poses a particular difficulty for the respondent: how to comment on a chapter where one agrees with the conclusions but questions the route to them. Actually, it is a bit more complicated. The general thrust of the recommendations – better links between researchers and 'users', greater coherence in the national research effort and more centres of excellence in research – is entirely right but some of the detail is, to say the least, debatable. Likewise, the underpinning analysis does, for all its sweeping assertions, make some telling points.

Let me start with the analysis. After an initial foray into matters of definition, Hargreaves details the six main weaknesses of (British?) educational research as he sees it: low level of involvement of stakeholders; low level of application; excessive reliance on peer review in funding allocation; weak co-ordination between researchers and funders; non-cumulative character of educational research; and the absence of large centres of research.

As one reels punch-drunk from this barrage, it is tempting to confess to the error of one's ways and promise to go look for a proper job. But still, even as oblivion sets in, one cannot help but notice that some of the targets are still standing. The punches have certainly been forceful but not particularly discriminating. Thus, while it is true that stakeholders are – inexcusably – ignored in some studies, in others they are closely and appropriately involved. Indeed, the very point of many studies is precisely to articulate the perspectives of stakeholders other than policy-makers and ensure that they contribute to policy formulation.

Even if this onslaught is a valid critique of some educational research, it suffers from being too sweeping. There are numerous counterexamples which suggest at the very least the need for a more refined critique. And of course it perpetuates the familiar neglect of research conducted outside the university sector. Aside from large bodies such as the National Foundation for Educational Research (NFER) and the Scottish Council for Research in Education (SCRE), a great deal of research is conducted in local education authorities and elsewhere to which much of the analysis simply does not apply.

It may well be that university research is as dire as Hargreaves says – a truly uncomfortable situation if true, given the importance that academe attaches to research relative to teaching – but there is undoubtedly much excellence as well. One can readily cite work in assessment, primary teaching, special educational needs and other areas where research findings are cumulative, there is considerable impact on practice, stakeholders are involved and so on.

The more important point, however, is that educational research is not all of a piece. So far as this debate is concerned, there are significant differences linked to funding source: the Higher Education Funding Council (HEFC), research council, government or charity. Thus, peer review is dominant in ESRC funding but less so elsewhere, co-ordination between researchers and funders is far higher with government than with HEFC, level of application varies across sectors and so on.

The more interesting – and fruitful – questions have to do with why some research is relevant and some is not. Could some answers be found in the funding arrangements (part of the context missing from the critique)? The biggest single source of funding for educational research in this country is the £27 million given to the universities by the HEFC. So far as the outsider can tell, the degree of either strategic planning or accountability in respect of this research expenditure is modest, not least in comparison with the tight parameters within which research outside the university sector is conducted. It is at least plausible to suppose that a more strategic disposition of some or all of this £27 million would address the weaknesses identified by Hargreaves and would give better value for research money into the bargain.

What of Hargreaves' recommendations for action? Here he is on surer ground, at least as far as his guiding principles are concerned. Who could disagree with the involvement of user communities, a national strategy for educational research and centres of research excellence to take it forward?

Some of the detail is troubling, however. Take user communities. Given the compass of educational research, the users are a large and heterogeneous group, from teachers to employers, from parents to psychologists, from journalists to policy-makers. If we seek users' involvement 'in all aspects of the research process, from the creation of strategic research plans through to the dissemination and implementation of policies and practices arising from or influenced by research activities and findings', the logistical and resourcing implications are immense. The aspiration is worthy but is it sensible? Research time and budgets are not elastic, and user involvement on the scale advocated could only be achieved through a considerable diversion of both.

Creating centres of excellence in research is vital to achieving progress, and Hargreaves is right to insist on this. Where they should be located is another matter. Certainly, many of them will be in universities, but every single one? The case might be tenable if university research was uniformly good. By Hargreaves' own account, it is mediocre to bad – hardly an enticement to put all one's research eggs in the university basket.

Some of the most outstanding centres of excellence in social science research are in fact independent bodies with no university affiliation. This should not surprise anybody. While the university environment offers certain advantages for the conduct of research, there are drawbacks as well, particularly when one is seeking to maintain a sizeable research programme over a period of time. Centres of research excellence need staff who are full-time research professionals, capable of working within a business ethos, and supported by a dedicated infrastructure and professional development. Doubtless, universities can and do establish such centres but, to date, the track record of the independent centres is rather more impressive. It is likely, therefore, that the most productive way forward is a systematic mix of independent and university-based centres; that, I believe, would maximise the chances of capitalising on the strengths of the two sectors and minimising their weaknesses.

Beveridge draws on his Leverhulme study on the state of educational research, conducted in parallel with a similar study by Hargreaves, to raise key issues for the future. Specifically, he identifies central research themes, considers what education and educational research can learn from social sciences research, and makes proposals for the organisation of educational research and the promotion of research impact.

The two big issues posed for future research are capitalising on developments in information technology and ensuring that research is conducted which serves policy needs. What is suggestive about the latter is the proposal that such research should be set within a resources context. He notes the paucity of good economic analysis of educational issues and is surely right to highlight this as a significant deficit.

The broader social sciences context is discussed but briefly. The particular example chosen for detailed attention, however, is highly pertinent and intersects with many current concerns. Beveridge sees cognitive science – and indeed neuroscience, which takes us outside the social sciences – as capable of contributing much to education. It could stimulate highly focused investigations into instructional variables and bring a new dynamic into our understanding of the core processes of learning and teaching. By implication this would necessitate a fresh approach to assessment and the development of new assessment devices.

The vista set out here is an attractive one and it would be folly on the part of educational researchers to ignore it. As Beveridge points out, however, genuinely interdisciplinary work is not easy. If it was, presumably there would be much more of it! The account given here is tantalisingly brief: the epistemological difficulties are outlined and some of the practical problems hinted at, but it falls some way short of a comprehensive statement about interdisciplinary research.

Beveridge shares Hargreaves' conviction that research has a limited impact, and they are at one in being unimpressed by the 'Enlightenment' notion of impact proposed by Nisbet and others. Beveridge does go a little further with his acknowledgement of 'the difficulties the education system has in assimilating new information and acting on it'. This is a step in the right direction but, I would argue, does not go far enough. Practical people draw on a variety of knowledge sources in order to act intelligently. This is as true of teachers and other educational actors as it is of doctors and engineers. Research findings are – rightly – one strand among many in the web of knowledge that influences action. Moreover, their input is frequently indirect and mediated through assessment instruments, curriculum materials, pedagogical practices and even the very language that educators use. As an example of language embodying research findings, reflect on the use of 'pupils with special educational needs' as opposed to 'handicapped pupils'. This shift derives in part from research evidence that the traditional categories of handicap have limited educational relevance and that many pupils' difficulties in learning stem from an interaction between innate and environmental, including school-based, factors. The fact that the underlying research is not to the fore in special educational needs discourse, and indeed may be entirely tacit for much of the time, does not in any way vitiate it or nullify its impact.

Beveridge and Hargreaves challenge the educational research community to address its weaknesses and they make concrete proposals to assist in doing so. While one can take issue with some of the detail, this broad thrust must not be ignored. If educational research is to fulfil its function of building up our understanding of educational processes and improving educational provision, ways must be found of tackling present limitations in its organisation, conduct and dissemination. Robust criticism can help in this task by sharpening our understanding of the true state of educational research and clarifying the options for action. In this context the two chapters serve us well and should be welcomed accordingly.

11

MISLEADING PROGNOSES?
EDUCATIONAL RESEARCH IN ACTION

Roger Murphy

I am delighted to have this opportunity to respond to the chapters of Professors Michael Beveridge and David Hargreaves, who are of course themselves highly respected researchers, whose own work has over the years had a great influence upon social scientists, educational researchers and indeed educational practitioners. Paul Atkinson (1986, p. 48) in a review of the growth of ethnographic research, comments on the enriching effect that it had on research in education in the 1960s, and picks out the work of the 'Manchester school' (where David Hargreaves did his early work), which allowed educational research to start to get beyond the input/output level of analysis of schooling represented for example by the Plowden research:

> Until the 1960s sociological research in the area of education all too often treated the school as a 'black box': researchers were generally content to measure the 'input' (e.g., social class, family background and individual ability) and the 'output' (e.g., attainment and occupation) whilst the process of schooling remained largely unexplored . . . In Britain this [research into school processes] received its initial impetus from researchers working in the anthropological tradition (Hargreaves, 1967; Lacey, 1970).

The work of David Hargreaves (1967), Colin Lacey (1970) and Stephen Ball (1981) and others undoubtedly represents one of many strong cumulative traditions in educational research – exploiting methodological advances in other social science areas to advance research, theory and practice in education. Such work has broken new ground, developed new theories and been used extensively by practitioners, teacher educators, decision-makers and large numbers of other stakeholders to inform their decisions, practices and general level of insight into the complexities of educational processes and institutions. I doubt whether such work would have been commissioned by a 'National Educational Research Forum', and it is my view that we should take careful note that this work emerged from the intellectual exploration of university researchers working in prestigious university departments committed to scholarship and the development of knowledge. I know that Hargreaves and Beveridge value this aspect of research as well, but in my view their general line of argument could easily damage its survival in the years to come.

In the early 1970s I was given the opportunity as a recent social science graduate to take up an SSRC (later to be renamed the ESRC) studentship. No topic was prescribed and I was left to establish one with the help and support of my university supervisor. I was at the time sharing a flat with two people (stakeholders I suppose), who were following a course to prepare them to teach religious education in schools. The course was heavily influenced by the research of Ronald Goldman (1964; 1965). Goldman (1969) later referred to himself as the 'Dr Beeching of Religious Education', because his research had been seen as causing many branches of RE teaching to be abandoned (Dr Beeching had a few years earlier closed down much of the railway network in the UK). To cut a long story short I decided to conduct research following up the work of Goldman, which seemed to me to be highly suspect and driven more by ideology than anything else. Thus my first experience of sustained research in education was gained in a university department, of psychology as it happens, in the mid-1970s. This was both profoundly rewarding and at the same time highly disappointing. The excitement of engaging in original research, of immediate relevance to a major area of teaching in schools, which quickly yielded findings that challenged the new teaching orthodoxies in RE, was tempered by what seemed like the impossible challenge of making any kind of impact upon the world of RE teaching. RE teachers it seemed had bought Goldman's books or heard about them through LEA advisers or the media and their minds appeared to be made up. Research in education was all very well but how did one manage to make an impact on practice?

This experience was followed by a move to a research unit of a GCE examination board. Here I was to gain my first real experience of 'policy and practice-related research in education'. Within a few weeks of being asked to conduct a piece of research I was being chased by professional officers of the board and others anxious to get the results so that they could consider their implications for the revision of syllabuses and examination practices in the coming year. Twenty years later I still get enormous satisfaction from working on educational research which relates obviously and immediately to concerns about policy and practice. I am currently working on projects commissioned by the DfEE, the Qualifications and Curriculum Authority (QCA), the School Curriculum and Assessment Authority (SCAA), the NHS, the English National Board for Nursing Midwifery and Health Visiting, the Southwell Diocese and a charitable trust fund. All these projects relate in different ways to questions, issues and concerns of people working in educational settings (including but in no way exclusively school settings). The stakeholders in such projects are very real and are very involved both at the commissioning stage and during the research and when it comes to discussing and implementing the results. At the same time these projects involve multi-disciplinary teams involving quite a range of discipline areas. The project for the NHS which relates to an evaluation of an initiative to promote new approaches to in-service training for GPs in London, involves a health economist, sociologists, GPs, experts in public health and community medicine, as well as educational researchers. A very large majority of educational researchers in the UK work in this way. Their involvement with practitioners and policy-makers is very close, and their research already benefits a great deal from a level of stakeholder involvement which Beveridge and Hargreaves appear to think is so rare.

It is clear that research in education is conducted by all sorts of people in all sorts of situations and the extent of direct impact on policy and practice varies somewhat between cases. Educational research is itself a very complex phenomenon – not easily typified and analysed, and anyone who imagines that there are simple solutions 'to improving its effectiveness' needs to look a little harder and study a little more of the evidence. Perhaps what would be beneficial would be some 'Manchester school-type anthropological work' into the complex worlds occupied by those engaged in research into education. There are, as many will know from their own experiences, many unusual customs and phenomena to be experienced, and an anthropologist alien to such a world would have a difficult job trying to shape an account of what characterises it.

My own major point of conflict with Michael Beveridge's and David Hargreaves' chapters is their dismissive attitude to most of what goes on in the field of educational research at present. Of course UK educational research is not perfect and in my recent BERA presidential address (Murphy, 1996), like many other BERA presidents, I explored a range of different ways in which educational researchers could make an even more effective contribution to educational policy and practice. Also as a member of the Education Panel for the recent Research Assessment Exercise (RAE) I spent several months wading through returns to our panel from 104 universities and over 2,800 academics working in the UK. This research, as the resulting profile of grades indicated, varied from outstanding to poor. Nevertheless the results of the 1996 RAE show that 30 departments, containing 1,236 researchers, gained the highest grades of 4, 5 or 5*, indicating returns judged to contain a majority of research of high national standing along with a good level of internationally recognised work.

I believe that educational research in the UK has a good track record. Its impact can be seen to have quite an influence on policy-makers, practitioners and researchers around the world. The stereotype of educational researchers inhabiting narrowly defined worlds in university departments, isolated from the cut and thrust of educational practice is not one that I think stands up very well to rigorous scrutiny. I would be more than happy for anyone to draw a random sample of researchers from the thirty grade 4/5/5* university departments and investigate whether their research involved close contact with practitioners and other stakeholders such as parents and policy-makers. I would be equally happy to see such an investigation conducted into the many educational researchers who do not work in university departments. A great deal of excellent research has been done by educational researchers working in LEAs (for example the ILEA Research and Statistics Division's work was held in high international regard), the National Foundation for Educational Research (NFER) and other educational bodies such as the GCE examination boards.

In 1995 Patricia Broadfoot and myself compiled an edited volume, as a tribute to the work of Desmond Nuttall, one of the very many excellent educational researchers working in the UK during the last thirty years (Murphy and Broadfoot, 1995). Anyone reading that volume could not help but be struck by the cutting-edge nature of Desmond's work. He always worked at the interface between research, policy and practice. His interactions with educational stakeholders were central to his work as a researcher whether at the NFER, Schools Council, Middlesex Regional Examinations Board, ILEA or the three universities where he held chairs. He is just one more example of what I regard as a good educational researcher, and there are many more – a perspective which seems to me to be barely stressed in the overview provided by Beveridge and Hargreaves. Furthermore one of his key areas of research, education assessment, illustrates I believe another very strong tradition of cumulative research, which has greatly influenced policy and practice over the last fifteen years (Nuttall, 1986; Murphy and Torrance, 1987; Wood, 1991; Gipps, 1994; Broadfoot, 1996; Goldstein and Lewis, 1996).

Central to David Hargreaves' argument is his call for a National Educational Forum. Not an instant remedy but something which would 'slowly change the culture of educational research to good effect and bring education into line with comparable professional fields such as medicine and engineering'. I have no objection to the setting up of such a forum; indeed the ESRC group of which I was a member suggested a similar strategy back in 1992. I do however see this sort of strategy as a very small cog in a very big wheel. I think that the experience in Scotland has demonstrated how difficult it is to get such a forum to operate all that effectively (Nisbet, 1995) – especially if it is trying to set an agenda for well over 3,000 educational researchers.

The other problems I have with the Hargreaves line of argument is that I do not agree that things are so much better in other professional areas. Certainly medical and engineering research have the advantage of vast resources, and one would hope that this vastly superior level of investment would produce some good outcomes. There is nevertheless plenty of really dreadful research going on, and in medicine for example the advances seen in education through the application of anthropological methods have barely had more than a very minor influence. Furthermore many of the hospital doctors and GPs I have had the chance to work with have never really had any serious training in research and have to rely a great deal on collaborators to help them with this aspect of their work. Meanwhile the debate about 'evidence-based medicine' is raging on – as illustrated for example by the tirade of letters from surgeons printed in *The Lancet* in May 1996. Reading those letters hardly leaves me with the type of Utopian vision set out by David Hargreaves in his Teacher Training Agency lecture (Hargreaves, 1996).

A more appropriate comparison can I think be made with nursing, where a drive to make nursing a 'research-led profession' (Briggs, 1972) some twenty-five years ago has in many ways foundered and failed. Many interpreted this as meaning that all nurses had to become researchers as well as practitioners, with fairly chaotic consequences. Now it is widely accepted that research in nursing requires highly specialised skills and that it is more realistic to assume that leading-edge nursing research will be done by a relatively small number of nursing researchers. If this research is done by, say, 1% of nurses, then a larger group of, say, 10% can be involved in research collaboration, and the rest of the nursing profession can learn from the outcomes (Murphy and Elwood, 1996). The recent RAE results again show how favourably educational research compares with nursing research at the current time.

The other interesting thing for me is the way in which nursing, midwifery, occupational therapy, social work, physiotherapy and so many other professional areas have looked to educational research in the UK as something they would like to aspire to in their own professional area. It has been interesting to notice how many people from such backgrounds have started to participate in BERA conferences and other activities, and the extent to which educational research is cited in their journals. The advances in theory and methodology which have been made in education have clearly had an impact well beyond the walls of conventional educational institutions. Indeed another weakness of the forum proposal is the extent to which it falls into the trap of assuming that educational research is synonymous with research into schools. Educational research in my terms is about research into lifelong learning, wherever it occurs, and I am delighted that BERA is increasingly able to encompass such a strong variety of research which spans so many educational settings, including but going well beyond the confines of schools.

I have far less problem with Michael Beveridge's chapter than with that of David Hargreaves, other than what I have already characterised as his unduly negative stance in terms of what educational research is achieving at present. I fully support his position over the advantages of a close continuing relationship between educational research and other types of social science research, as I hope I have already indicated. Together these chapters are helpful in the way that they have contributed to a critique of research in education. Like any good review process it is vital however to assess both the strengths and weaknesses of any system that is under review. I fear that Beveridge and Hargreaves have done educational research a disservice by failing to recognise its many strengths, in their desire to apply their critical minds to this review process.

REFERENCES

Atkinson, P. (1986) Research design in ethnography, *Open University Course DE304, Block 3B, Part 5.*

Ball, S. J. (1981) *Beechside Comprehensive*, Cambridge, Cambridge University Press.

Briggs, A. (1972) *Report of the Committee of Nursing*, London, HMSO.

Broadfoot, P. (1996) *Education, Assessment and Society*, Lewes, Falmer Press.

Gipps, C. (1994) *Beyond Testing: Towards a Theory of Educational Assessment*, London, Falmer Press.

Goldman, R. (1964) *Religious Thinking from Childhood to Adolescence*, London, Routledge & Kegan Paul.

Goldman, R. (1965) *Readiness for Religion*, London, Routledge & Kegan Paul.

Goldman, R. (1969) Dr Beeching I presume? *Religious Education*, Vol. 64, pp. 47–52.

Goldstein, H. and Lewis, T. (1996) *Assessment: Problems, Developments and Statistical Issues*, Chichester, Wiley.

Hargreaves, D. (1967) *Social Relations in a Secondary School*, London, Routledge & Kegan Paul.

Hargreaves, D. (1996) Teaching as a research-based profession: possibilities and prospects. Teacher Training Agency annual lecture 1996 .

Lacey, C. (1970) *Hightown Grammar*, Manchester, University of Manchester Press.

Murphy, R. (1996) Like a bridge over troubled water: realising the potential of educational research, *British Educational Research Journal*, Vol. 22, no. 1, pp. 3-16.

Murphy, R. J. L. and Broadfoot, P. (1995) *Effective Assessment and the Improvement of Education – A Tribute to Desmond Nuttall*, Lewes, Falmer Press.

Murphy, R. J. L. and Elwood, J. (1996) Back to the drawing board for ideas, *The Independent*, 1 August.

Murphy, R.J.L. and Torrance, H. (1987) *The Changing Face of Educational Assessment*, Buckingham, Open University Press.

Nisbet, J. D. (1995) *Pipers and Tunes: A Decade of Educational Research in Scotland*, Edinburgh, Scottish Council for Research in Education.

Nuttall, D. L. (1986) *Assessing Educational Achievement*, Lewes, Falmer Press.

Wood, R. (1991) *Assessment and Testing. A Survey of Research*, Cambridge, Cambridge University Press.

12

AN ECOLOGICAL PERSPECTIVE ON EDUCATIONAL RESEARCH

Peter Hannon

The problems of educational research in Britain today cannot be addressed solely in terms of what researchers do or fail to do – the issues they study, the methods they use, the quality of their work, how they disseminate findings and so on. These are obviously very important but they are not the whole picture. We also need to think about the wider system of which research is a part.

An ecological metaphor may give us a better grasp of the issues. Think of educational research as a living plant in interaction with its environment – constantly renewing itself, sometimes growing, sometimes declining. At present it could be healthier. That much at least is agreed by all contributors to this volume. Where we differ is in our estimation of the extent of ill-health and whether the causes are internal or environmental. We need to get the diagnosis right to foster healthy growth. A good gardener does not uproot or cut back a plant which fails to thrive if the real problem is choking weeds or lack of soil nutrients, pollination or sunlight.

The chapters by Michael Beveridge and David Hargreaves – to which I am invited to respond – are helpful in highlighting critical features of the ecological system. It is important at this stage of the debate to identify points of agreement within the research community so that future action can be based on maximum possible consensus. I do agree with much of what Michael and David have to say but, to get to those points, it is necessary to sift out others which I find somewhat exaggerated or inessential to main issues and to draw attention to what I regard as a serious omission in their analyses.

POINTS OF DISAGREEMENT

Exaggerating the weaknesses of educational research may be an effective way – perhaps the only way – of launching a debate about problems but taken too far it undermines our collective capacity to reach solutions. The picture painted by Michael and David is so overwhelmingly bleak as to be incredible. There is no sense of *any* educational research ever having been of *any* value. David's verdict, for example, that 'too little educational research is relevant and useful' and that 'researchers have become estranged from user communities' is not balanced by adequate recognition of research which is widely seen as relevant and useful and which has arisen through engagement with users. From that point of view it was interesting to read in 1996 in *Research Intelligence* (No. 57) summaries of research thought by some BERA members to have had an impact on classroom practice. Common features seemed to be sustained attention to a problem by a large number of researchers working closely with practitioners, some of whom were researchers too, over a long period of time. We can learn from these examples. I was sorry to see David dismissing them in the following issue of *Research Intelligence* merely as an attempt to reassure readers 'that all is well in the educational research community'. We have to move beyond 'all good' or 'all bad' judgements to more discernment if we are to make progress.

The comparison which David makes between engineering and education is a stimulus to fresh thinking but, like his earlier one with medicine, more useful for showing what may be, rather than what is, the case in another professional field. His conclusion that 'engineering user communities are more involved with research' is not based on evidence from users but on 'interviews with a number of professors of engineering'. I cannot imagine David being so trusting of the views of professors in education! I suspect closer inspection would reveal the situation in engineering to be more complicated than he implies. Perhaps the grass is greener there; perhaps not. Either way we are still left with problems in our own field which we have to address.

Both Michael and David acknowledge that research can have a 'diffuse' influence as well as a 'direct' influence but I think they are too dismissive of the former. Diffuse need not mean weak or unimportant. Atmospheric oxygen is diffuse but actually quite important. No one should expect single research studies to change classroom practice or policy. When research changes practice – as I have witnessed, for example, in the teaching of literacy – it is more often the cumulative effect of many researchers' work over many years. Such change is deep – at the level of teachers' thinking – as well as in the modification of specific techniques. Teachers do not use research as a cookbook but as a resource in constructing their view of what is worth aiming for and likely ways to get it.

On the question of priorities for future research, Michael and David have different approaches. Michael's identification of priorities (communication technology, policy research) and key developments outside educational research (cognitive science, neuroscience) is certainly interesting but I would prefer to consider them alongside suggestions from other colleagues (including respondents to the Leverhulme survey). Whilst it is worth trying to identify areas which are promising, neglected or urgent we need to be aware of at least three limitations. First, given the difficulties of avoiding either blandness or partiality, one should not expect to arrive at a perfect list. In fact we may not be able to improve much on the 11-point agenda put forward by the 1992 ESRC working group which at least had the merits of being clear, coherent and to some extent collective. Secondly, in so far as setting new priorities means treating the plant rather than changing the environment it can only be a partial solution to the problems of educational research. Thirdly, and most important, it is pointless for educational researchers to attempt to identify priorities in isolation from those whose decisions about funding and applying research will ultimately determine whether it is more than a paper exercise. The involvement of what David calls 'stakeholders' is essential. Therefore I favour his approach which is to refer the setting of strategic priorities to some kind of National Educational Research Forum.

A SERIOUS OMISSION

David lists six 'weaknesses' of educational research. Two could be considered symptoms (the low level of application of research and its non-cumulative character); the others are really hypotheses about causes (low stakeholder involvement, reliance on peer review, weak co-ordination among researchers and funders and the lack of large centres). I welcome the way in which his analysis shifts the search for remedies away from what researchers do to the wider system in which they operate – in my terms offering an ecological perspective.

There needs to be a seventh item on David's list – the weakened capacity of teachers to engage with research. This problem has not been given the attention it deserves in the debate so far – but it takes us to the heart of the education policy of both the current Labour government and the previous Conservative one.

Teachers need a certain amount of professional autonomy to engage with research. If they are not free to change what they do, why should they engage with research which might show them better ways of doing it? Teacher autonomy, however, has been severely reduced because a driving principle of government policy has been distrust of the profession. Teachers must still contend with a detailed prescriptive curriculum, exhausting bureaucratic demands and elaborate surveillance systems to ensure compliance. Where this fails to deliver desired results (in literacy and numeracy) government's response is even more specific central control. Top-down, supposedly teacher-proof programmes are *de rigueur*. As a result, professional development for teachers is too often reduced to training them to put other people's ideas into practice. Curricular and pedagogic initiatives at the level of the school or local area are suffocated. Gone are the days of local courses, teachers' centres, active professional organisations, support for masters' level study and the celebration of teacher researchers. Add to this worsened working conditions relating to class sizes and the physical deterioration of schools, and rising levels of stress, and one has to ask how much attention it is reasonable to expect teachers to give to educational research. For practitioners to be engaged *with* research some should ideally be engaged *in* it, and all must have the opportunity to read, reflect upon, discuss and act on research findings.

I hope this will not be misrepresented as an attempt to blame teachers for the problems of educational research. Rather it is to point to factors governing the application of research which are beyond researchers' control regardless of the relevance, quality and dissemination of their work. Michael rightly observes that 'there is little chance of relevant and important knowledge finding its way into education unless the outcomes are actively sought by practitioners'. I meet many practitioners who are interested in research, who would seek it out and often want to undertake it – if only they had better working conditions, less stress, more freedom to act and enough time to engage critically with it. It is in this area that comparisons with doctors and engineers are instructive – they do appear to have greater professional autonomy and opportunities for self-directed development.

The problem is two-way. For research to be any good, it needs to be challenged and shaped by a critical response from practitioners. If practitioners are denied opportunities for a dialogue with researchers, the eventual result will be low-quality research. Where is the reward or excitement for educational researchers if their only audience is other researchers? Again, an ecological perspective reveals how problems inside the educational research community are linked to those outside.

Putting this right will require radical action. The organisation best placed to do something is the Teacher Training Agency (TTA). In 1996 it published a policy statement, *Teaching as a Research-based Profession*, which, after rehearsing some criticisms of the quality of educational research, states that part of its role is 'helping teachers to play a more active role in conceiving, implementing, evaluating and disseminating research' (TTA, 1996, para. 7). This is very welcome.

I sincerely hope that the TTA is serious about this role but to make progress it has a lot to do. It has to overcome widespread cynicism as to its true motives. Is it not just another agency for tightening government control (and scapegoating professional groups)? This charge is not easily rebutted for, even if those associated with it gradually gain credibility, history shows they can easily be replaced by others keener to assist government aims. It will require a definite change in government policy towards teachers – of which there is little sign from the current government – for teachers and researchers to accept that the TTA means what it says. Another challenge facing the TTA is grasping the scale of the problem. What we are talking about is the use of teachers' time. I suggest that, at an absolute minimum, teachers need the equivalent of a day a year to engage with research. I cannot conceive of anyone reading or learning about a piece of non-trivial research, thinking about, discussing it, making it their own and acting on it in any less time. Probably it should be two or three days – much more if they are to do some research themselves. Where is this time to be found – from training days, release from classroom teaching, from the 1,265 directed hours or the teacher's own time? One day a year may not seem much but multiplied by the total number of teachers in the country it represents a huge redeployment of resources. Will it require extra funds? If so, how much and from what source? There is no sign yet that the TTA has begun to grapple with the issues. Indeed, by inflating the significance of its 1996–97 programme of twenty-seven teacher-researcher projects nationally, it unfortunately gives the impression of hoping to make an impact through gestures. More might be achieved by assisting teachers to take advantage of existing opportunities in universities. The TTA needs to be clearer about what it wishes to achieve and identify the resources required to make it happen.

POINTS OF AGREEMENT

I think David is correct in saying: 'While the research community will inevitably be divided on the nature and extent of weaknesses in the record of educational research, there may well be greater agreement on measures that might contribute to improvement.' For reasons of space, I will comment on just two points of agreement – the proposal for user involvement through a National Educational Research Forum and the need for centres of research.

First, a central point in David's argument is the necessity for greater user involvement. Whilst not a panacea (it is not sufficient for solving some problems and it will create new ones), it does seem to be a necessary condition for improving the impact of research. It is also seems fair that those who pay the piper, and who make up audiences, should choose some of the tunes. We have to accept that this means a shift in power.

We hardly need telling of the dangers. Research activity funded by the Higher Education Funding Councils is one of the few areas of education to have escaped close government control (and therefore one where government and its agencies can be challenged). Much control of education has been extended through a succession of agencies, *ad hoc* bodies and quangos, with those which have acted in a benign way often turning out to be Trojan horses for something more extreme (hence it is reasonable to view activities of the TTA, the latest to show interest in educational research, with suspicion). Would researchers sharing power in a National Educational Research Forum be putting their necks in a noose?

There are some difficult political judgements to be made. In an optimistic scenario, the forum could increase the flow of high-quality research feeding into practice and policy. Researchers could learn from practitioners and policy-makers. It might lead to teaching becoming a research-based profession. In a bleaker, Orwellian scenario, the forum might pave the way for some kind of 'National Educational Research Agency' responsible for all research funding, perhaps restricting it to approved, licensed researchers required to work to a government agenda. This could happen anyway, without educational researchers taking any initiative, in which case the advantage of having a forum could be in making the process explicit, visible and to that extent more challengeable. My own view is that the possible benefits of a forum, coupled with the unsatisfactoriness of the present situation, justify the risks of trying to establish it. Researchers should trade some – not all – of their autonomy for greater influence on education.

David's suggested functions for the forum are a good starting point. There needs to be an additional remit to review and extend teachers' opportunities to engage with, and act upon, research. This would mean that not just researchers but also, for example, the TTA, could be called to account.

On a second point, David tackles the related issues of the weak co-ordination and non-cumulative character of educational research and suggests that, in part, this could be remedied by concentrating research into fewer but larger centres across the country. I think he is right about both the problem and the solution but, of course, this point has been made before by others and has proved a most difficult nettle to grasp. Most members of the educational research community shrink from proposing a change in university funding which would deny colleagues in low-ranked institutions funded research time. Yet to carry on as now is to accept that few lines of research will ever be pursued intensively enough and long enough to achieve an impact. David's proposal to concentrate funding on as many as fourteen university centres may not be sufficiently radical. On the present distribution of researchers it would mean funding relatively unproductive researchers in generally strong departments and excluding some productive ones in apparently weaker departments. An alternative might be to concentrate funding at the level of research 'sub-areas' – investing in groups of named researchers over, say, five-year periods. Some departments might have several groups working at the highest level, others only one or two. I favour locating the majority of groups in universities so as to maximise researcher–practitioner dialogue in professional development courses (improving the quality of research by

requiring researchers to do some teaching is much more important than trying to improve university teaching by requiring lecturers to do research).

WHAT NEXT?

I feel that the key to progress is for the educational research community to
attempt, in partnership with others, to establish a National Educational
Research Forum. Such an attempt would in itself mean addressing other problems. If the idea of a forum is not pursued, it is not clear to me how we
deal with problems separately.

For effective action, two things are fairly clear. First, success will depend
on focusing steadily on areas of agreement (and exercising restraint in the
rhetoric of disagreement). Secondly, much could depend on whether the
British Educational Research Association can take on a leadership role. There
is no other organisation in a position to bring together and represent the
views of educational researchers in national debates. In the past, however,
the Association's limited resources have been focused mainly on promoting
internal dialogue between members – through conferences and publications
– rather than external dialogue. It remains to be seen whether BERA can
develop the capacity to shape the environment in which its members carry
out research and engage with the wider system of education.

13

A FORUM FOR RESEARCHERS AND USERS OF RESEARCH – SCOTTISH STYLE

Sally Brown and Wynne Harlen

THE RESEARCH CONTEXT IN THE NORTH

It is always flattering when the 'auld enemy' (England or David Hargreaves, whichever you please) cites an educational advantage to be found north of the border. In calling explicitly for a National Educational Research Forum (and implicitly a General Teaching Council – GTC) for England and Wales, David Hargreaves reminds other educational researchers that 'the Scots have . . . already created their own version of a forum, as they have of a GTC, and those south of the border should learn from the Scottish experience'. This exhortation is set within some trenchant criticism by Hargreaves of educational research in the UK. Our research colleagues in England and Wales are quite able to defend themselves against attack, but if we in Scotland are to be held up as an acceptable example (if not a paragon of virtue), then we have to make clear not only the extent to which our initiatives reflect Hargreaves' criteria but also the rather different circumstances in which they operate. Most of our contribution will be concerned with the idea of a National Research Forum and communication between researchers and users of research, but first we will briefly indicate what we see as the nature of the impact of educational research on users and mention some features of Scottish educational research which are relevant to the other proposal he has made for centres of excellence.

While we agree that ultimately the purpose of the major part of educational research must be 'the improvement of educational practice', we believe that much (though not all) of the influence which research will have on policy and practice will be indirect rather than direct. It will come from the greater understanding which research can generate, among policy-makers and practitioners, about how things are in education, why they are the way they are and how they might be different. This understanding is built up gradually through successive studies, each of which may not in itself appear conclusive but which together can combine to provide a firm basis for action. There are two important implications of this belief. First, Hargreaves is quite right to place so much importance on more effective ways of establishing communication between researchers and users of research. Publication of systematic reviews of research could and should play a more prominent part in this communication. Secondly, he is quite wrong to expect those users to answer positively when asked a stark question about the impact of research on their policy or practice. The development of understanding takes time to be internalised into users' thinking; it is often only when it becomes part of educational 'common sense' that it really has an impact and by that time no one remembers that the ideas came from research. Assessment of the impact of research on policy and practice, therefore, has to be much more sophisticated than Hargreaves' approach suggests and there is clearly development work to be done in this area.

The Scottish educational research scene differs in several important respects from that south of the border. Until the 1990s the association between preservice teacher education and research has been more tenuous. Most of the former was carried out in large colleges of education rather than the university departments of education (UDEs) which traditionally have been very small. Stirling University was the exception with a relatively small share of the market of secondary teacher training. The colleges did not have a tradition of most of their staff undertaking research. While this has been changing, that change is a relatively slow process. In each of the 1992 and 1996 Research Assessment Exercises, Scottish institutions received one 5 and two 4s in the 'older' universities of Aberdeen, Edinburgh and Stirling with the colleges or former colleges rated from 3a to 1. The high-ranking institutions have performed well in areas which are subject to peer review, but the sizes of their staffs are very modest indeed and it would be difficult for them to fulfil the ambitious requirements which Hargreaves lays down for large centres of research excellence. If the research resources were concentrated there, a substantial number of highly competent researchers in the colleges or former colleges would be neglected and, in our view, teacher education would suffer by its disconnection from research.

It is, however, the link between researchers and users (and in particular the idea of a forum for educational research), rather than notions of centres of excellence, with which this chapter is primarily concerned and it is to that we now turn. If we do not emphasise and implement communication between researchers and users, then our argument for a broad base for research is weakened.

THE EXPERIENCE OF THE FORUM ON EDUCATIONAL RESEARCH IN SCOTLAND

The Forum on Educational Research, which has existed in Scotland since 1986, has somewhat different aims than those of the National Educational Research Forum outlined by David Hargreaves. Indeed the Forum on Educational Research in Scotland does not exist as a 'body' with a defined membership as would the national forum being proposed, but rather as a set of functions which are promoted by the staff and Board of Directors of the Scottish Council for Research in Education (SCRE).

The original idea for the forum followed a review of SCRE by the Scottish Office which suggested that the Council should have a responsibility to identify national priorities for educational research. There was considerable opposition from the Scottish universities' education departments, through their organisation SUCSE (Scottish Universities Council for Studies in Education), to the idea of the board of SCRE deciding such priorities. Their main argument was that SCRE was an interested party, engaged in research and in competition for government research funding, and it was likely that any priority list would favour a programme fitting well with SCRE's own ambitions. This argument, together with concerns about whether a national list of priorities was a feasible aim (and if it were, whether the Scottish Office would pay attention to it), led SCRE to propose and introduce a national forum which would draw on a wide range of participants and expand the aims beyond a utilitarian list of priorities.

The main functions of the Scottish forum were identified by the SCRE chairman at the time as follows:

> In the first place, the Forum exists to affirm the importance of research in education . . .
>
> The second function of the Forum is to create a context for interaction between teachers, researchers and policy-makers.
>
> The third function that the Forum exists to perform is to create a context for the discussion of research priorities.
>
> (SCRE, 1986, pp. 3, 4)

There are clearly other functions, which David Hargreaves suggests for a national forum, that are not evident in this list. In the next section, however, we discuss the ways in which the Scottish forum has attempted to fulfil its original aims, the changes that have occurred and the reasons for them.

AFFIRMING THE IMPORTANCE OF RESEARCH IN EDUCATION

This phrase gives no hint that the quality of educational research might be a matter for debate. At its inception, the focus of the Scottish forum was not on the need to improve the quality of research but on the use of research to improve the quality of education. The point was made particularly in the context of pressures for change and on the grounds that 'those professionally involved in education have a commitment to monitor what they do and operate on the understanding that professional action is improvable' (SCRE, 1986, p. 3)

This could be taken as the kind of uncritical and smug comment that educational researchers *would* make about their role. The paper was written, however, by members of the board of SCRE including practitioners and other users of research.

At the inaugural meeting of the forum the comment was made that 'teachers have been known to criticise research for its irrelevance to the classroom', but there was also an acceptance that researchers in Scotland can be much closer to users, whether policy-makers or practitioners, than is possible in many other countries. Within the relatively small educational community, the opportunities are there to meet and develop good relationships, rather than to generate suspicion at a distance. This is set in the context of an education service which is relatively cohesive, and is more valued and trusted than in some parts of the UK. It is easier, therefore, both to avoid some of the pitfalls of poor communication which have been identified by Hargreaves and to find an audience ready to listen (albeit sceptically) and respond to affirmations of the importance of research.

CREATING A CONTEXT FOR INTERACTION BETWEEN TEACHERS, RESEARCHERS AND POLICY-MAKERS

The action taken to carry out this function has been to mount an annual meeting, taking place in different venues throughout the country, where researchers meet practitioners, policy-makers and, more recently, representatives of industry and of parents. The annual one-day meetings have generally attracted upwards of 150 participants, many being delegates of different organisations such as teachers' unions, local government, the Scottish Office, school boards and teacher educators. Participants at the 1996 meeting identified themselves as follows: 12% headteachers or teachers, 6% school board members, 20% researchers, 20% administrators, 16% lecturers, 12% advisers, 6% union representatives and 8% others.

The meetings have to cover themselves financially, and there continues to be an oversubscription for places. Readiness to pay and the positive evaluations from participants suggest that potential users of research find this event a worthwhile way to spend a day.

The current shape of the forum's main meeting is to identify a theme of concern in education and then to bring together researchers who have been working on relevant projects. The presenters may not all be from Scotland

and certainly not all from SCRE. The criteria for inviting contributions are that they are reporting research in one way or another, that is, they are not merely descriptive of policy or practice or stating opinions, that they are suitable for a mixed audience of researchers and practitioners and that the content is relevant to Scottish education.

The programmes of these meetings have included presentations by researchers and discussion in groups, and there has been some evolution of the format over the years. There is usually one plenary presentation and about twelve small group parallel presentations, repeated in the morning and afternoon so that participants can attend two groups. Whilst having the advantage of enabling small groups (usually of no more than sixteen delegates) to discuss each presentation, it has had the disadvantage of preventing group or plenary discussion of more general matters, and particularly of the priorities for research, which was initially an aim of the forum meeting.

It is relevant to note that there are other regular events where researchers, policy-makers and practitioners meet to discuss research in Scotland. For a start, the Scottish Educational Research Association (SERA) holds an annual conference and several seminars during the year. These are invariably attended not only by researchers but always also by staff of the Research and Intelligence Unit (RIU now named the Educational Research Unit – ERU) of the Scottish Office Education and Industry Department (SOEID) and members of HM Inspectorate. The SERA executive also has an annual meeting with RIU/ERU staff. Staff of SCRE hold annual meetings with representatives of the teachers' unions at which research findings are presented and discussed and teachers give their views on the areas of priority for future research. Similarly three or more times a year SCRE arranges seminars for HMI and other Scottish Office staff, often attended by the Senior Chief Inspector. Such seminars are also provided for policy-makers and practitioners by staff of university departments of education, and colleges.

These activities which fall outside the responsibility of the forum in Scotland have to be taken into account in discussing its function. If they did not already take place, then it might be necessary to create a body to ensure that they did happen. However, their existence is part of the context in which the forum operates and they influence decisions about the emphasis to be placed on different forum functions.

CREATE A CONTEXT FOR THE DISCUSSION OF RESEARCH PRIORITIES

At about the same time as the creation of the forum, the Scottish Office Education Department began to publish an annual statement of its priorities for research. For many years there had been a process of a trawl for ideas within the Scottish Office and the internal production of a priority list. In the mid-1980s, that trawl was opened up to input from relevant outside bodies and institutions. Thus the forum provided a route for the education professional to make an input into the decision-making on the areas of research to be funded by the Scottish Office through the RIU. At the same time the priorities identified through the forum could be communicated to other research funding bodies, including the charitable trusts and foundations.

Experience has shown that this function of the Scottish forum is far more difficult to carry out than is the provision for interaction between researchers and users about existing research. Using the discussions at the main meeting of the forum for this purpose, as originally attempted, was too dependent upon the particular participants and was not felt to be representative of all whose views should be included. An alternative that was tried was to write to organisations and groups concerned with education in Scotland and ask them to consider priorities for research. Those who responded were invited to a special meeting at which an attempt was made to draw together the views expressed and to ask others to comment on them. Inevitably there was a tremendous diversity in the types of research advocated (policy orientated, basic, and applied; short term and long term) as well as in the topics suggested. The report of the meeting, which identified 110 specific suggestions, commented:

> A basic dilemma remained: there can be no 'short-list' of research priorities which reflects the diverse views of all the educational community. If the procedures were to be sharpened up to reduce the flood of suggestions, the outcome would inevitably be biased towards the preferences of some groups and against those of others. There is, and can be, no consensus.
>
> (SCRE, 1988, p. 6)

For some years, this procedure was conducted only by correspondence, with SCRE writing to all the bodies whose work was of relevance to education, requesting their views, which were then put together in a report by SCRE. Inevitably each organisation consulted saw research needs from the point of view of its own constituency. This had to be accepted; the dilemma remained of how these could be combined, fairly and in a balanced way, in providing an input to those who distribute funds for research.

In an attempt to introduce some interaction and discussion among different interested bodies, in 1993 the forum function of determining research priorities was taken over by the Board of SCRE. This has members who are nominated by sixteen Scottish bodies, including organisations of parents, industry, teachers' unions, local authorities, higher education, further education, the GTC, the examination board and the curriculum council. Annually each member is asked to consult his or her nominating body about priorities for research and these are brought together for discussion. An emphasis on *areas* for research rather than on specific projects and a suggested limit to the number of proposals put forward have made the process rather more easy to handle since the procedure was introduced. This was, of course, exactly the course of action which was vigorously opposed in the mid-1980s by the university departments of education through SUCSE. The lack of opposition in the 1990s probably reflects four factors: SUCSE was disbanded with the reorganisation in higher education in 1992 and many people now working in the sector do not see involvement in the identification of areas of research priorities as a priority for them; the change to put the responsibility on the SCRE board had much less publicity than on the previous occasion, and so went unnoticed by researchers in other institutions; there is a large body of scepticism about whether such priority lists have any impact on the government's decisions about what research should be funded; and it is now open to anyone to submit suggestions for research to the Scottish Office. The research staff of SCRE submit their own suggestions, a step which goes some way to distancing SCRE as an interested body from the role of the board in representing other Scottish institutions.

There remain ambiguities in this process as to the purpose of the discussion, in particular as to whether priorities or preferences can or should be indicated. The list often includes areas where there is already research in progress of which the proposers are unaware. Yet the role of the Board, acting for the forum, is seen as one of collating rather than of editing. It does not match what is, for example, carried out by foresight panels, but such an extended process could hardly be conducted annually.

In relation to the kinds of functions which Hargreaves has laid out for a National Educational Research Forum, the Scottish forum, together with the other joint activities mentioned, goes some way to achieving the dialogue about educational research and networking among different stakeholders that he calls for. It does not, however, undertake the functions of regular *comprehensive* reviews of research. The way it is set up ensures that it provides information about, and perhaps reviews of, research activity in those specific areas which are chosen as its annual themes, and that choice offers the chance to move outside and beyond government priorities. In 1997, for example, the theme of 'Equity in Education', chosen during the period of a Conservative government, was not thought of as a central concept of that government's education policy.

It may be that the forum activities have a direct and recognised impact upon the thinking of those who participate; it would be surprising if they did not. To suggest, however, that this could bring 'education into line with comparable professional fields, such as medicine and engineering', as Hargreaves does, seems to us misguided. Those other fields are characterised by the major impact of research from the *natural* sciences on their technologies and practices. Impact on them from *social* sciences is much less clear. So, for example, while *technological* control of pollution is well within our capabilities, and the treatment of many illnesses through drugs and other medical techniques improves day by day, the impact of our research knowledge of *human* characteristics and responses to problems could be said to have had very little effect on the political and social behaviour towards pollution or the social-psychological treatment of those who are ill. In education, most of the research knowledge with a potential for impact is based on some aspect of social and human sciences.

The most ambitious aims for Hargreaves' forum are those of holding a research foresight exercise every four or five years and devising a national strategy for educational research. It is not clear to us what would count as a 'national strategy', but we take it that Hargreaves would look for something which

- identified themes closely related to policy and practice;
- emphasised partnership between researchers and users;
- provided a balance between short-term and long-term research goals; and
- included commissioned research, 'unconstrained inquiry' or 'pure research' and both 'decision-orientated' and 'conclusion-orientated' research.

Our experience does not suggest that a quinquennial foresight exercise could be used to identify themes, unless they were so broad as to be unhelpful. It is true that the identification of broad themes by the ESRC has encouraged researchers to be more creative in writing research proposals or applications for studentships in language which 'fits' one or more themes (this is very easily done). As part of a national strategy for educational research, however, our experience of i) the difficulties of establishing consensus on research priorities among the education community; and ii) the rapid shifts of general research focus as a result of political expediency, suggests that the usefulness of long-term themes is limited.

The partnership between researchers and users can be established without the foresight process, as we have shown. It is, nevertheless, a relatively loose partnership. The looseness discourages feelings of anyone being trapped in a centrally determined framework for research, and enables everyone to retain a sense of ownership of either the research they do or the use they make of research. The danger is that these relationships may also be fragile and at risk from other demands on people's time.

One thing which we cannot claim with confidence is that users have become convinced that research without immediate application is still of value. The pressure even after ten years of the Scottish forum is still for quick, direct, simple answers and shows remarkably little concern for the quality of research methods and validity (except for commonsense face validity) of claims made by research. The efforts of research in Scotland to focus on policy-related and practitioner-led questions have been at some element of cost to fundamental long-term research. We are unconvinced that a foresight strategy would resolve these issues.

Finally, we should comment on the collaboration among funding bodies. Despite this matter being one of the original concerns of the Scottish forum, there is little evidence of success in promoting it. There recently was, for example, a pair of co-existent research projects on provision for students with disabilities in higher education: one was undertaken by SCRE and is funded by the Scottish Office, the other by Stirling University and funded by the Scottish Higher Education Funding Council. These two projects were commissioned in isolation without any attempt to design them either to replicate or to complement each other. The resulting highly specified projects provided untidy and tiresome (for researchers and for those from whom data were collected) overlap and lack of clarity which had to be sorted out in the field. Other examples could be cited of concurrent, but unco-ordinated research on the same topic. Clearly funding bodies guard their autonomy and independence much more closely than researchers.

REFERENCES

SCRE (1986) *Forum on Educational Research in Scotland. Inaugural Meeting. Proceedings*, Edinburgh, SCRE.

SCRE (1988) *Forum on Educational Research in Scotland. Scottish Views for Educational Research Arising from the National Forum*, Edinburgh, SCRE.

Overviews

14

EDUCATIONAL RESEARCH PAST, PRESENT AND FUTURE: A FEMINIST SOCIAL SCIENCE PERSPECTIVE

Rosemary Deem

INTRODUCTION: EDUCATIONAL RESEARCH FROM A FEMINIST PERSPECTIVE

In writing this penultimate chapter and responding to the various contributors, I want to pay particular attention to feminist research on education and to the political and sociocultural significance of gender relations. My intention is to show how both of these have important implications for debates about the future of educational research. Feminist research, drawing on a variety of theoretical perspectives, sees women as an important and diverse social group whose many concerns need to be made central to social science investigations (Maynard and Purvis, 1994). Feminist approaches to research propose new, non-patriarchal approaches to methodology and epistemology, moving away from positivistic notions of science and social science and suggesting that women as knowers are different from men (Harding, 1987). Such approaches also emphasise the important links between personal experience, academic research and strategies for political change (Reinharz, 1992), connections often ignored or rejected by other social scientists. Informed knowledge of these important feminist debates is often missing from commentaries about the future of educational research, including the majority of contributions to this volume. This is a surprising omission since feminist researchers have tackled many concerns, such as the relationship of researchers to practitioners (Stanley and Wise, 1993; Weiner, 1994), which are of interest to educational researchers. Feminist educational researchers themselves have made a significant contribution to our understanding of methodological and epistemological issues (Lather, 1991; Weiner, 1994; Griffiths, 1995; Holland *et al.*, 1995).

Finally, feminist researchers in general have drawn attention to the importance of gender as a social division and to the significance of gender power relations between women and men in social, cultural, political and economic life (McDowell and Pringle, 1992; Cosslett *et al.*, 1996). Education is no more immune from the impact of gender relations than any other sphere of society, as is quickly evident whatever aspect of education we examine (Acker, 1994; Stone, 1994). Yet despite the concentration on the politics of educational research by two of the major contributors to this book (Hargreaves and Beveridge), little or no attempt is made to explore the gender power relations of such politics. This chapter seeks to remedy that omission.

It may be helpful to readers to explain how my particular contribution came about. At the time of the conference on which the book is based, my institution was in the throes of a serious financial crisis (Rowe, 1997) and as an academic manager involved in dealing with this, I was unable to attend. However, I did write to BERA's honorary secretary expressing concern that all the major speakers at the event were male. The response I got back was that this was simply a consequence of the fact that all the investigations and working groups being reported on happened to involve men as instigators or convenors. Yet if one examines the context in which the various debates and investigations reported in this volume took place, it can be seen that this male dominance of debates about educational research is no mere coincidence. Indeed, it does no more than reflect the extent to which men are generally the major movers in academic and research-related circles (Morley and Walsh, 1995; 1996), even though much of the housekeeping side of research is often done by female temporary contract researchers and secretaries. But if educational research is to move forward with confidence into the twenty-first century, it must surely challenge existing hierarchies and power structures, not just accept them as given. Rather than focus only on the impact of women academics working in the area of educational research, I also intend to examine the social and political consequences of feminist research and the connections between the gender of those doing research and those who might use it.

In common with all the other contributors to this volume, my ideas about educational research have in part been formed by my own biography, including the trajectory of my academic career and the different academic, social, political and cultural forces which have formed the contexts for my academic work. Being on the borders of several different academic areas (sociology, women's studies, leisure studies, education) has had a significant effect on my research and writing (Deem, 1996a), as well as shaping my views about the value, values and quality of the research of others.

I do not pretend that my stances on research in education are value neutral. My work in general, and this chapter in particular, are situated within an academic and political commitment to feminism and a heightened awareness of the importance of engendered cultures and structures, gender relations and gender identities to the study of education. Of course I am not unaware of the significance of other dimensions of social and cultural life. It would be difficult and indeed mistaken to deny the importance of social class, ethnicity, age and generation, sexual orientation and disability to the study of educational structures, processes and outcomes. Nor do my values prevent my work from being rigorous, although some commentators assume that good research is untouched by ideological and political concerns (Foster *et al.*, 1996). Indeed Hargreaves has himself a tendency to assume this. Yet there are no educational researchers (even those US policy analysts to whom Hargreaves refers so approvingly) whose work proceeds entirely without the intervention of values and beliefs. Indeed all academic researchers, in whatever field, approach their research from a value standpoint, even where this is not explicitly acknowledged. The notion of value freedom is and has always been a problematic concept, developed by those who wished to pretend that they were not affected by or part of, the very cultures and social life which make the human condition unique. Unlike many other researchers, feminists have not been afraid to examine the role of values in their research (Harding, 1987; Lather, 1991; Stanley and Wise, 1993).

Before going on to look at some of the research that feminists have carried out, examining the relationships between feminist researcher and potential research users, exploring debates between feminists about methodologies and epistemologies, and analysing how gender relations affect the politics of education, I want first to consider the nature of education as an academic subject.

EDUCATION: A UNIQUE DISCIPLINE IN ITS OWN RIGHT?

Unlike most other contributors to the book, except perhaps Beveridge, my academic identities are first and foremost related to and informed by the disciplines of the social sciences rather than by education itself. This does not mean that I have no commitment to educational research. Nevertheless, my social science orientation is important for two reasons. First, I spend a lot of time interacting with researchers across a broad range of disciplines from social policy to political science and management, researchers who are rarely, if ever, directly concerned with research on education. Secondly, I do not regard education as a discipline (Deem, 1996b). Instead, I see it as an arena in which different disciplines are brought to bear on theoretical, methodological, policy-related and practical aspects of education, or are used to shape and inform research taking place in educational settings and contexts.

There is also an important aspect of my auto/biography (Stanley and Morgan, 1993) so far unmentioned, which is relevant to the way in which I understand the social location and cultures of educational research. I have never been a schoolteacher, though I have had a wide and practical involvement with a number of levels of education throughout my adult life, as a governor (in primary, secondary, further and higher education), as a local politician sitting on an education committee responsible for educational service provision, and as a teacher and researcher in higher education. Though I accept the spirit of Hamilton's point (this volume) that much educational research is aligned to a particular occupation, I do not see this in quite the narrow sense that Hamilton implies. For one thing, the occupation in question is not simply schoolteaching but a broad range of related occupations including teaching and the work of trainers at all levels of the education system and in training organisations. I agree with Hamilton that this occupational link is different from the situation in some social science disciplines such as sociology, where there is no link to a specific occupation other than the practice of that discipline. But education differs not at all from social work, public policy or health research, key disciplinary and interdisciplinary areas in the social sciences which all have a strong link to a range of specialised occupations.

Though educational research draws on many disciplines, from natural sciences to history, the social sciences provide many of the methodological underpinnings of educational research and most, if not all, of the theoretical frameworks for the interpretation of research findings. That this is sometimes unacknowledged by educational researchers merely points to the particular nature of the academic experiences of many who conduct educational research.

Finally, but equally importantly, along with Murphy (this volume) I do not regard educational research as synonymous with the study of schooling and schools. Though this may sound obvious it is nevertheless an important issue. Many, though not all, of the contributors to this book have done the majority of their work within the confines of compulsory education. Murphy is one exception and Beveridge is also aware of the issues facing postcompulsory education. Hargreaves, on the other hand, despite his own recent research on medical education, talks as though educational research is, politicians apart, targeted only at schoolteachers and parents. Students, trainers and teachers outside school (including those of us in higher education) are ignored. But educational research involves much more than schools and embraces preschool education, postschool education, postschool training and informal as well as formal education. Nor is this just an impressionistic perception. In the 1996 UK Research Assessment Exercise, 62 units of assessment of the 104 submitted to the Education Panel had at least some of their research located in the area of postcompulsory education. This excludes a considerable number who also did research on preschool education.

Thus, to summarise: I regard education as an area of interdisciplinary research, not a discipline in its own right and also see close links between educational research in particular and social science research in general. I do not view education as being unique in having strong connections to a particular occupation and in any case that occupational category subsumes but is not exclusive to, schoolteaching. Finally, but importantly, educational research is not simply about schools but concerns the whole spectrum of educational and training activity, from early years to work-based learning.

FEMINIST RESEARCH ON EDUCATION

Educational research conducted by feminists, though forming a relatively small proportion of the total amount of UK educational research, and despite only very modest funding allocation, has nevertheless had an impact which is considerably greater than might be imagined. Feminist research on education is important to the generic debates about educational research because it has a number of noteworthy characteristics. It covers all sectors of education, it is often of high quality, it does not neglect the needs of 'users' and practitioners and it raises a topic which is of importance in educational systems throughout the world, not just in the UK or in Europe. Furthermore it is firmly grounded in social science and has paid considerable attention to dissemination to a wide range of audiences, including policy-makers, practitioners and students.

It is important, however, to distinguish between research which includes attention to gender, research which is gender-sensitive and research which is feminist. Research can mention gender as a variable (for example in examining reading performances or looking at the allocation of statements of special educational needs) without actually paying any attention to the social, cultural and political construction and significance of gender identities and gender relations. Gender-sensitive research goes beyond treating gender as a variable no more and no less important than height or eye colour and declares that gender is a social and cultural phenomenon whose influence deserves to be taken seriously in research. Though in the past most gender-sensitive research was done by women researchers, it is pleasing to note that a number of male researchers have now begun to undertake such research (Mac an Ghaill, 1994; Prichard, 1996).

Feminist research is also gender-sensitive but goes much further than this. It is based on feminist theories about the social, cultural and political world, about the nature of knowledge and knowers, about the status of science and social science and the place of non-patriarchal research methods within this (Fonow and Cook, 1991; Stanley and Wise, 1993; Maynard and Purvis, 1994; Blair *et al.*, 1995). It is concerned not just with conducting research and disseminating its findings but also with the politics of women's diverse situations in different cultures and countries and with applying the fruits of appropriate research to those many and varied contexts in which women live out their lives. However, it should not be thought that feminist research is conducted within the parameters of a single perspective, since those who declare themselves feminist do not regard themselves as having a monolithic theoretical stance (Weiner, 1994).

The importance of feminist research to debates about educational research is considerable and it is neither a very recent arrival on the scene nor does it deal only with the present day. As Purvis's work on the history of women's schooling indicates, women have long struggled over their access to and opportunities and experiences within education, whether at primary, secondary or postschool levels (Purvis, 1991).

Feminist research on educational themes has involved working with a broad range of practitioners and potential research users. As Weiner, Arnot and others make clear (Arnot, 1985; Weiner, 1985; 1994) such research is not simply conducted in a vacuum of interest only to researchers. A whole series of major concerns from gender and assessment in schools (Gipps and Murphy, 1994; Elwood, 1995a; 1995b) to equal opportunities, women academics and academic management in further and higher education (Farish *et al.*, 1995; Morley and Walsh, 1995; 1996; Deem and Ozga, 1997) have been addressed by feminist researchers. They have looked at both topical issues like the relationship between education reform and gender (Turner *et al.*, 1995; Arnot, *et al.*, 1996) and at the future by exploring engendered cyberspace and information structures. Thus, feminist and gender-sensitive research focuses on themes which are far from 'trivial pursuits' (Bassey, 1993). Indeed gender research is a theme which transnational as well as national political states and forums recognise as important. For example, both the European Union, for Europe and the British Council, for developing countries, are concerned about and have funded research and action programmes about girls' and women's access to and participation in education.

In the context of the UK itself, however, it is interesting to note that many male researchers have only become interested in gender issues as so-called 'male underachievement' has come to be regarded as a major problem in education (Wragg, 1997a; 1997b). Boys' and men's problems are suddenly a major political issue with school inspectors, headteachers and politicians – all highly agitated – but those problems relating only to girls and women are not and have historically never been imbued with the same significance and are now in danger of being ignored altogether (David and Weiner, 1997). Thus boys doing badly in exams has given rise to a serious moral panic but the sexual harassment of girls and women in educational settings (Halson, 1991; Larkin, 1994), which like boys' underachievement is not a new issue, has not. Here the interests of female students and practitioners have clearly been ignored whilst those of the dominant male group have not.

FEMINIST RESEARCHERS, PRACTITIONERS AND RESEARCH 'USERS'

Feminist researchers have made strenuous efforts to take into account research agenda and interests other than their own. Though indeed their research has often revealed more problems than were anticipated at the outset, feminist investigators have also been keen to suggest practical ways in which these might be solved, including collaboration with practitioners and the encouragement of action research (Griffiths and Davies, 1993). Both in this country and elsewhere, feminist researchers have joined forces with educational institutions and local and national policy-making bodies to formulate new ways of doing things (Arnot, 1985; Whyte *et al.*, 1985; Weiner, 1994). This wish to follow through research into the political arena is not unique to education as studies of the role of femocrats (feminists who enter senior levels of public sector bureaucracies) in countries like Australia show (Watson, 1992; Yeatman, 1990; 1995). The extent to which feminist researchers and feminists and others concerned with equal opportunities working in educational settings have combined their interests and concerns to mutual advantage has been very evident over the last three decades. There has rarely been a need for official national bodies to be set up to co-ordinate this, since it has often happened organically, as demonstrated in the recent ESRC-funded seminar series on gender and achievement organised by Debbie Epstein, Val Hey and Diana Leonard at the London Institute of Education (David and Weiner, 1997).

The collaboration of researchers with practitioners, and the dissemination of research findings direct to practitioners, as well as through scholarly publications, does not mean, of course, that feminist research findings have therefore been uncontroversial or that all have welcomed those findings. Indeed, as those involved with the pioneering research on women and science in the 1980s (Smail *et al.*, 1982; Whyte, 1986; Kelly, 1987) found, at first many science teachers and school heads were hostile to the messages of the research – namely, that school science ought to be concerned with making its various disciplines attractive to girls. When, after a period of time, the importance of ensuring that girls did not neglect science, and strategies to achieve this became widely accepted, it was then argued that this was the result of commonsense and not based on research at all. It may be that it is this process, whereby yesterday's social science research becomes today's commonsense, rather than the deficiencies of educational research, which explains why public and practitioner reactions to research sometimes emerge as hostile or as indifferent. When I was part of a research team investigating the impact of education reform on governing bodies, a project amongst other things which involved looking at the power relations of those bodies, including gender and ethnicity (Deem, 1995), we often found that governors were both receptive to and hostile towards different aspects of our findings. This never stopped us from disseminating the research to a range of audiences. Indeed we were asked to give oral evidence about school governance to the Nolan committee on standards in public life. This was not a 'use' or an audience we could have foreseen at the outset of the project. This raises the very controversial question of who are the users of research.

Some contributors to this volume assume that who the users of research are is self-evident. I do not accept this: first the concept of the research user has been subject to far too much government doctrine and research sponsor capture (Deem, 1996c). Exactly who is a research user and the conditions under which they will use the research remain a highly contested and complex matter, as shown by recent ESRC ventures into this area (Redclift and Shove, 1995; Shove, 1996). Feminist researchers may be more attuned than some to the likelihood that users comprise a wide and internally highly differentiated set of people, since recent debates in feminist theory have drawn attention to the extent to which differences between women are as significant as similarities between them. Not only are users different from each other but the contexts in which research is potentially useful also vary. Shove suggests too that relevance when applied to research is not a quality of research *per se* but rather 'a property of potential contexts of use' (Shove, 1996, p. 2). Feminist theorists have underlined the importance of situating knowledge about women in the contexts from which it is derived (McNay, 1992; Tong, 1992; James and Busia, 1993; Clough, 1994). Research users include those who produce research and those who interpret research for others, as well as those who consume it more directly. Feminists are well aware of this; in feminist research it is considered as important that research reaches other feminists as it is that it reaches practitioners in other fields (Deem, 1996c).

The concept of usefulness is also problematic in other ways, since the terms 'use' and 'relevance' are themselves social and cultural constructions. Thus in the 1970s and 1980s many male teachers and heads of institutions did not think that research on gender was 'useful'. Now that boys and young men are perceived to possess gender identities themselves and at a point where girls have begun to achieve academic if not labour market success, suddenly gender research is fashionable. It is rarely, if ever, possible to predict in advance whether any given research project will have utility to someone other than the researchers conducting it. It may not be until a long time afterwards, if ever, that recognition of the usefulness of a specific piece of research takes place. Feminists, unlike some educational researchers, have known this for a long time.

FEMINIST APPROACHES TO METHODOLOGY AND
EPISTEMOLOGY

Almost all the contributors to this book make some reference to research methodologies and one or two mention epistemology. However, with the possible exception of Hamilton, who has long been interested in methodology and epistemology, and Hargreaves' own early work on social relations in the secondary school, few of the contributors would regard methodology and epistemology as one of their major specialisms. Indeed some of those who have spent most time investigating questions of methodology and epistemology in the field of education have done relatively little empirical research themselves (Hammersley, 1990a; 1990b; 1992b), although there are notable exceptions to this (Burgess, 1984; 1988; 1990; Bryman and Burgess, 1993). Feminist researchers, however, see methodology and questions about the nature of knowledge and knowers as central to their research endeavours rather than as a separate furrow in a different field. Perhaps this in itself would make feminist researchers rather suspicious of the opaqueness, apparently limited sample and seemingly superficial data analysis involved in the investigation on educational research which Hargreaves and Beveridge carried out for the Leverhulme Trust and which is reported in this volume.

Feminists have had many lively debates about methodological approaches. During the early 1980s, feminist writers suggested a fit between particular (mainly qualitative) research techniques such as interviewing, and the aims and objectives of feminisms (Roberts, 1981; Bowles and Duelli Klein, 1984). Other techniques which are claimed to be well suited to feminist research include auto/biography, life histories (Middleton, 1993; Stanley, 1993; 1994) and ethnography (Skeggs, 1994a; 1997), all of which have been used successfully in educational settings. However, a number of writers have argued that quantitative methods are not incompatible with feminist purposes if sensitively used (Jayaratne, 1993; Dunne, 1996). The disadvantages of qualitative methods have also been noted, including the potential to exploit those being researched (Stacey, 1988). Maynard suggests that informative research on women must use a variety of methods (Maynard, 1990; Maynard and Purvis, 1994). This kind of debate is productive and contributors to it include both active researchers and practitioners in many fields. In educational research in general, however, there is still a latent positivism about the underlying assumptions of many researchers, such that it is still assumed by many that quantitative research and large-scale research are necessarily more rigorous than qualitative work. Yet many important topics in education can only be sensibly researched using qualitative methods in small-scale settings. Also, as Simons (1996) has pointed out, the study of single cases does not preclude and may indeed be significant in enabling the derivation of policy ideas from such research.

Other central concerns of feminist researchers include ideas about objectivity. This is an issue much discussed by educational and other social science researchers but often those debates lead to rather simplistic conclusions. Objectivity is often assumed to be a taken-for-granted idea of which we all 'know' the meaning. Feminists have approached objectivity in rather more sophisticated ways. Thus some feminists suggest that all knowledge is situated (Haraway, 1988), whilst others argue for 'strong objectivity', where conflicting standpoints provide a partial basis for assessing beliefs (Harding, 1987; 1991). Still others talk of 'minimal objectivity' where the existence of values is not seen to prevent practices about knowledge from maintaining their distance from those values (Longino, 1990). Some critics regard feminist research as highly problematic because of the combination of political commitment with academic research (Hammersley, 1992a; 1994). Yet as Morley (1996) notes, such criticisms could equally well be levied at every researcher since values often lead directly or indirectly to the choice of particular research themes.

The depth of the value commitments of feminist researchers to their research has been acclaimed as an important strength in feminist work (Ramazanoglu, 1992; Stanley and Wise, 1993). By contrast both Beveridge and Hargreaves see values as problematic in research. Of course it may be, as Beveridge argues, that 'government and policy-makers believe that all educational research is inherently politically biased'. Yet anyone who has researched processes of educational reform knows that governments are themselves powerfully driven by ideology; what is often meant by politically biased research is research that does not support a particular politician or political party's own ideas or policies. Feminist debates about objectivity allow us to examine questions about values, politics and the distancing or otherwise of researchers from the political consequences of their research in a refreshing and intellectually challenging way.

Feminist researchers have also examined how the gender of researchers affects both research processes and outcomes (Stanley and Wise, 1993). By implication, it also affects the contexts in which research may be likely to be used. A number of the contributors to this book say little or nothing about power and educational research, yet this is a fundamental issue particularly for those researchers whose research involves children or other less powerful groups. Questions about power have been considered in three ways by feminists: the relative status of feminist researchers *vis-à-vis* malestream researchers (Harding, 1987; 1991; Morley, 1996); consideration of the power relations involved in researching those who may become disempowered through the research process (Lennon and Whitford, 1994; Morley, 1996); and finally the problems of researching those who are themselves powerful (Deem, 1994; Gewirtz and Ozga, 1994). All these are crucial questions for educational researchers.

As consistent with research directed towards practical as well as theoretical purposes, feminists have also considered researcher reflexivity (Stanley and Wise, 1993; Morley, 1996), explored how to involve those researched in the research process (Griffiths and Davies, 1993; Griffiths, 1995) and examined the role played by experience in feminist research (Reinharz, 1992), including whether its importance is overemphasised (Lazreg, 1994). In addition, feminist researchers have also looked at the educational experiences of beginning researchers, including ethical problems likely to be encountered by postgraduate researchers especially when working with non-academic collaborating organisations (Lyon, 1995) and the ways in which beginning feminist researchers might be trained (Deem, 1995). Such questions have been addressed by BERA, most notably in the 1994 working party debates about quality in educational research but they have not necessarily had much influence on the contributions to this book. I am not suggesting that feminist research has all the answers to methodological and epistemological puzzles but rather that its practitioners are not afraid to ask difficult questions about objectivity, ethics, values, the connections between research and politics and the relative merits of qualitative versus quantitative methods, without worrying all the time that this will deter prospective 'users' of their research from taking it seriously. This is a principle which some educational researchers might wish to consider carefully in their anguished debates about the apparent need to do what practitioners or policy-makers want and expect, both in respect of methodology and in relation to content of the research. As Shove (1996) notes, most non-academic users of research make extensive use of non-academic criteria in their judgements about research and so may well find narrowly defined and unadventurous research more to their liking than more radical investigations. But surely we undervalue our own judgement and professional expertise if we continually yield to such pressures?

GENDER RELATIONS AND THE POLITICS OF EDUCATIONAL RESEARCH

In this final section I want to focus on the ways in which gender relations affect the politics of educational research – that is, the political processes which surround the emergence of topics and themes for research, the selection of some topics and themes for funding rather than others and attitudes about the value, quality and use of particular kinds of educational research. This is something scarcely considered by any of the contributors to the book. The nearest reference comes in Brown and Harlen's discussion of the Forum on Educational Research in Scotland, where they note that the particular mode of working adopted by that forum allows it to choose topics which are outside government priorities. They use as illustration the 1997 forum theme of 'Equity in education', though clearly such a theme goes well beyond gender. The way in which themes and foci for research emerge is directly or indirectly the focus of several contributors, though Hargreaves goes furthest in suggesting a way in which so-called stakeholders might become part of a National Educational Research Forum in which the agendas for future research would be hammered out. But any forum or organisation, actual or potential, is bound to be affected by gender relations, which are deeply embedded in the social systems of the four countries of the UK. This in turn will affect the kinds of research themes which emerge and the kinds of research which are awarded funding, accorded high prestige and regarded as high quality. All these political processes are underlain by social and cultural processes and ideologies which are themselves shot through with power plays and ideas related to gender.

A failure to be aware of the politics of gender relations and their connection to education may also be discerned in Hargreaves' attempt to compare teachers and their use of research with that prevalent in the medical profession. It is strange that Hargreaves chooses this particular comparator, since studies of teaching as a profession which women enter in large numbers at the lower levels, and as a form of caring and emotional work which is increasingly controlled by others, suggest that nursing or social work might be more appropriate comparators (Evetts, 1990; 1994; Glover, 1994; Acker, 1992a; 1992b; 1996).

If we look at who are likely to be key players in the politics of education, we need to have regard to the engendered structures of the major institutional players, namely schools, and institutions of further and higher education. These structures are, with the exception of early years education, populated by women only at the lower levels and are largely male dominated at the higher levels. This makes it likely that only rarely will women practitioners emerge as the definers and potential users of educational research, though as teachers and students they may often be the recipients of it. Whilst feminist researchers have taken steps to ensure that women do play a key role in shaping research, other educational researchers have not.

The effects of gender relations on who is likely to be identified as representing practitioner interests are mirrored by the situation found amongst researchers. Women academics in the UK higher education system continue to find it difficult to progress to senior positions; they are more numerous at lecturer, temporary teaching assistant and contract researcher levels, where they are often in part-time and relatively poorly remunerated jobs. So far as seniority in the academic world is concerned, in 1995–6 only 8% of all university professors in the UK were women, though it is not self-evident that this distribution accurately reflects the actual achievements and potential of women academics (Griffiths, 1997; Judd, 1997). It certainly contrasts with the other side of the higher education system in which half of all the undergraduate students are now female. Although there are more women professors in education (18.8%) than most other areas except librarianship (29.4%) and subjects allied to medicine (19.6%), this still means that senior women academics in education are heavily outnumbered by men. Nor are those women academics who have been promoted to the highest levels necessarily regarded by their institutions as equivalent to their male peers.

Given the male domination of senior and management posts at almost all levels of education, it is unlikely that those chosen to represent the world of research in national forums would contain significant numbers of women unless special steps were taken to ensure this, although women would certainly continue to be significant amongst the underlabourers of the research world. However, I do not simply wish to draw attention to the under-representation of women in the senior ranks of education departments and units. Like men, women who occupy senior positions in education come from a variety of backgrounds, do research on a wide range of topics and hold a range of political views, by no means all of which are sympathetic to feminisms of any kind. Although the argument about a critical mass of women being needed to change organisations has some merits, it does not in itself tell us anything about the political and academic views of the women concerned and it may be a necessary rather than a sufficient condition for change. However, as with women MPs, it is clear that the emergence of large numbers of women as senior players in the politics of educational research is unlikely without measures which facilitate this; processes of selection which omit this are likely to reproduce dominant patterns of male domination, just as they do in ordinary job recruitment practices (Collinson *et al.*, 1990).

If gender relations and gender ideologies affect who are defined as key players in the politics of education, they also affect the kinds of topics and themes that are chosen for research and research funding. Though Hargreaves suggests that peer review is problematic, he does not see gender politics as an important element of this; those who have had projects on women and education rejected by male referees on the basis that the themes are unimportant will not agree. The example I referred to earlier about the sudden popularity of the theme of gender and underachievement in relation to boys in school illustrates how the gender politics of educational research works. When gender was identified as a research theme about women and girls, it received relatively little funding. Now it is associated with boys and men, suddenly it is centre stage. This is also likely to affect judgements about the quality and value of the research produced, since the criteria used are neither purely rational nor detached from the interests and careers of those involved.

Unless ways are found of ensuring that patterns of male dominance and discrimination against women do not prevent women from becoming major players in the definition, funding and positive valuation of educational research, then these patterns will continue. Whilst the potential contexts of use of educational research reflect unequal gender power relations and prejudicial assumptions about women and girls, decisions about what research is funded, in which contexts it is useful and which research is considered of high quality, will continue to be regarded somewhat sceptically by feminist researchers.

CONCLUSION

I began by saying that I did not accept that education was either a discipline in its own right nor did I see it as being largely about schools and school-teachers. I then went on to look at the political as well as academic impact of some of the research carried out by feminists researching in the field of education. I see this as an arena of educational research which does not seem to suffer from some of the problems which a number of contributors to this book seem to feel are endemic to research on education. I then examined the necessity of not taking debates about users at face value (which Hargreaves seems to do) and suggested that feminist researchers are more aware than many of the complexities of these debates, and hence do not draw a clear distinction between research providers and research users. Next, some of the distinctive and important features of feminist research and feminist researchers were outlined. These included methodological pluralism but in the context of thorough and continuing debates, an honest and open recognition of the importance of values to all stages of research, an awareness of the significance of understanding knowledges and knowers and a particular sensitivity to encouraging researchers and practitioners to work together. Finally I analysed the extent to which the politics of educational research are suffused by gender relations. I argued that unless attention is paid to ensuring that gender relations and other power relations do not prevent certain kinds of research themes from surfacing, then merely organising new forums for the discussion of educational research will not achieve the kinds of far-sighted research horizons which Beveridge seems to want. Indeed we may be destined to years of researching boys' underachievement in school, FE and university.

I have not attempted to provide solutions to all the kinds of questions raised in the volume about educational research. However, I have tried to show that feminist researchers have engaged with many of the important questions and continue to do so, without feeling that controversy necessarily damages the value of their research. Furthermore, the extent to which feminist researchers on education are aware of the research of other feminists means that they are both unlikely to work in a theoretical, empirical or political vacuum and are also continually alert to new possibilities for interdisciplinary research. Finally, debates in feminist circles about the place of values and power in research and critiques of simplistic notions of objectivity mean that most feminist researchers are very aware that all of us, researchers, practitioners, politicians, work in ways which are very much affected by the sociocultural forces, power relations, and different and competing ideologies of our times. There is thus no special place for the free-floating intellectual or the guru who provides radical ideas but without exercising the kind of leadership which facilitates their implementation, the critic with no sense of democratic process or teamwork, the privileging of ungendered research users who seemingly have no class location, political allegiance or ethnicity either. Women (and of course men, as Marx noted a few decades earlier) make their own history but not in conditions of their own choosing. So too do educational researchers.

REFERENCES

Acker, S. (1992a) Gender, collegiality and teachers' workplace culture in Britain: in search of the women's culture. Paper presented to the American Educational Research Association conference, New Orleans.

Acker, S. (1992b) Creating careers: women teachers at work, *Curriculum Enquiry*, Vol. 22, no. 2, pp. 141–63.

Acker, S. (1994) *Gendered Education*, Buckingham, Open University Press.

Acker, S. (1996) Doing good and feeling bad: the work of women university teachers, *Cambridge Journal of Education*, Vol. 26, no. 3, p. 422.

Arnot, M. (1985) *Race and Gender; Equal Opportunities Policies in Education*, Oxford, Pergamon Press.

Arnot, M., David, M. and Weiner, G. (1996) *Educational Reforms and Gender Equality in Schools*, Manchester, Equal Opportunities Commission.

Bassey, M. (1993) Educational research in the universities and colleges of the United Kingdom: significant insights or trivial pursuits. Paper presented to conference on Evaluation, Social Science and Public Policy, Ottawa.

Blair, M., Holland, J. and Sheldon, S. (eds.) (1995) *Identity and Diversity: Gender and the Experience of Education*, Buckingham, Open University Press.

Bowles, G. and Duelli Klein, R. (1984) *Theories of Women's Studies*, London, Routledge.

Bryman, A. and Burgess, R. G. (eds.) (1993) *Analysing Qualitative Data*, London, Routledge.

Burgess, R. G. (ed.) (1984) *The Research Process in Educational Settings: Ten Case Studies*, Cambridge, Cambridge University Press.

Burgess, R. G. (ed.) (1988) *Studies in Qualitative Methodology: Conducting Qualitative Research*, London, JAI Press.

Burgess, R. G. (ed.) (1990) *Studies in Qualitative Methodology: Reflections on the Field Experience*, London, JAI Press.

Clough, P. (1994) *Feminist Thought*, Oxford, Blackwell.

Collinson, D., Collinson, C and Knights, D. (1990) *Managing to Discriminate*, London, Routledge.

Cosslett, T., Easton, A. and Somerfield, P. (eds.) (1996) *Women, Power and Resistance*, Buckingham, Open University Press.

David, M. and Weiner, G. (1997) Keeping balance on the gender agenda, *THES*, 23 May, p. 23.

Deem, R. (1994) Researching the locally powerful; a study of school governance, in G. Walford (ed.) *Researching The Powerful in Education*, London, UCL Press.

Deem, R. (1995) Do methodology and epistemology still matter to feminist educational researchers? Paper presented to European Conference of Educational Researchers, University of Bath.

Deem, R. (1996a) Border territories: a journey through sociology, education and women's studies, *British Journal of Sociology of Education*, Vol. 17, no. 1, pp. 5–19.

Deem, R. (1996b) Educational research in the context of the social sciences: a special case? *British Journal of Educational Studies*, Vol. XXXXIV, no. 2, pp. 141–58.

Deem, R. (1996c) Theory, user relevance and feminist research in education. Paper presented to British Educational Research Association Conference, Lancaster.

Deem, R., Brehony, K. J. and Heath, S. J. (1995) *Active Citizenship and the Governing of Schools*, Buckingham, Open University Press.

Deem, R. and Ozga, J. (1997) Women managing for diversity in a post modern world, in C. Marshall (ed.) *Feminist Critical Policy Analysis: A Perspective from Post Secondary Education*, London and New York, Falmer.

Dunne, M. (1996) The power of numbers: quantitative data and equal opportunities research, in L. Morley and V. Walsh (eds.) *Breaking Boundaries*, London, Taylor & Francis.

Elwood, J. (1995a) Gender differences in A Level examinations – the reinforcement of stereotypes. Paper presented to European Conference on Educational Research, University of Bath.

Elwood, J. (1995b) Undermining gender stereotypes: examination and coursework performance, *Assessment in Education*, Vol. 2, no. 3, pp. 283–303.

Evetts, J. (1990) *Women in Primary Teaching*, London, Unwin Hyman.

Evetts, J. (1994) *Becoming a Secondary Headteacher*, London, Cassell .

Farish, M., McPake, J., Powney, J. and Weiner, G. (1995) *Equal Opportunities in Colleges and Universities*, Buckingham, Open University Press.

Fonow, M. M. and Cook, J. A. (1991) *Beyond Methodology: Feminist Scholarship as Lived Research*, Bloomington Indiana, Indiana University Press.

Foster, P., Gomm, R. and Hammersley, M. (1996) *Constructing Educational Inequality: An Assessment of Research on School Processes*, London, Falmer.

Gewirtz, S. and Ozga, J. (1994) Interviewing the education policy elite, in G. Walford, (ed.) *Researching the Powerful in Education*, London, UCL Press.

Gipps, C. and Murphy, P. (1994) *A Fair Test*, Milton Keynes, Open University Press.

Glover, J. (1994) Women teachers and 'white collar' workers: domestic circumstances and paid work, *Work, Employment and Society*, Vol. 8, no. 1, pp. 87–100.

Griffiths, M. (1995) *Feminisms and the Self: The Web of Identity*, London, Routledge.

Griffiths, M. and Davies, C. (1993) Learning to learn: action research from an equal opportunities perspective in junior school, *British Educational Research Journal*, Vol. 19, no. 1, pp. 43–58.

Griffiths, S. (1997) The struggle for equality, *The Times Higher Educational Supplement*, 6 June.

Halson, J. (1991) Young women, sexual harassment and heterosexuality: violence, power relations and mixed-sex schooling, in P. Abbott and C. Wallace (eds.) *Gender, Power and Sexuality*, London, Macmillan.

Hammersley, M. (1990a) Classroom Ethnography, Milton Keynes, Open University Press.

Hammersley, M. (1990b) *Reading Ethnographic Research*, London, Longman.

Hammersley, M. (1992a) On feminist methodology, *Sociology*, Vol. 26, no. 2, pp. 187–206.

Hammersley, M. (1992b) *What's Wrong with Ethnography?* London, Routledge.

Hammersley, M. (1994) On feminist methodology: a response, *Sociology*, Vol. 28, no. 1, pp. 293–300.

Haraway, D. (1988) Situated knowledges: the science question in feminism and the privilege of partial perspectives, *Feminist Studies*, Vol. 14, no. 3, pp. 575–99.

Harding, S. (1987) *Feminism and Methodology*, Milton Keynes, Open University Press.

Harding, S. (1991) *Whose Science? Whose Knowledge?*, Milton Keynes, Open University Press.

Holland, J., Blair, M. and Sheldon, S. (eds.) (1995) *Debates and Issues in Feminist Research and Pedagogy*, Clevedon, Multilingual Matters.

James, S. M. and Busia, A.P.A. (eds.) (1993) *Theorizing Black Feminisms*, London, Routledge.

Jayaratne, T. (1993) The value of quantitative methodology for feminist research, in M. Hammersley (ed.) *Social Research; Philosophy, Policy and Practice*, London, Sage.

Judd, J. (1997) Bias that stops women academics reaching the top, *The Independent*, 7 June.

Kelly, A., (ed.) (1987) *Science for Girls*, Buckingham, Open University Press.

Larkin, J. (1994) Walking through walls: the sexual harassment of high school girls, *Gender and Education*, Vol. 6, no. 3, pp. 263–80.

Lather, P. (1991) *Getting Smart: Feminist Research and Pedagogy with/in the Post Modern*, London, Routledge.

Lazreg, M. (1994) Women's experience and feminist epistemology: a critical neo-rationalist approach, in: K. Lennon and M. Whitford. (eds.) *Knowing the Difference*, London, Routledge.

Lennon, K. and Whitford, M. (eds.) (1994) *Knowing the Difference: Feminist Perspectives in Epistemology*, London, Routledge.

Longino, H. (1990) *Science as Social Knowledge: Values and Objectivity in Scientific Enquiry*, Princeton, NJ, Princeton University Press.

Lyon, E. S. (1995) Dilemmas of power in postgraduate practice: a comment on research training, *Sociology*, Vol. 29, no. 3. pp. 531–40.

Mac an Ghaill, M. (1994) *The Making of Men*, Buckingham, Open University Press.

Maynard, M. (1990) The reshaping of sociology? Trends in the study of gender, *Sociology*, Vol. 24, no. 2, pp. 269–90.

Maynard, M. and Purvis, J. (eds.) (1994) *Researching Women's Lives from a Feminist Perspective*, London, Taylor & Francis.

McDowell, L. and Pringle, R. (eds.) (1992) *Defining Women: Social Institutions and Gender Divisions*, Cambridge, Polity Press.

McNay, L. (1992) *Foucault and Feminism*, Cambridge, Polity Press.

Middleton, S. (1993) *Educating Feminists: Life Histories and Pedagogies*, New York, Teachers College Press.

Morley, L. (1996) Interrogating patriarchy; the challenges of feminist research.

Morley, L. and Walsh, V. (eds.) (1995) *Feminist Academics: Creative Agents for Change*, London, Taylor & Francis.

Morley, L. and Walsh, V. (eds.) (1996) *Breaking Boundaries: Women in Higher Education*, London, Taylor & Francis.

Prichard, C. (1996) University management: is it men's work? in D. Collinson and J. Hearn (eds.) *Men as Managers: Managers as Men: Critical Perspectives on Men,*

Masculinities and Managements, London, Sage.

Purvis, J. (1991) *A History of Women's Education in England*, Milton Keynes, Open University Press.

Ramazanoglu, C. (1992) On feminist methodology, *Sociology*, Vol. 26, no. 2, pp. 207–12.

Redclift, M. and Shove, E. (1995) *Engaging with Users: A Review of Economic and Social Research Council Research Support Teams' Engagement with Users and Beneficiaries in Programme Development*, Swindon, Economic and Social Research Council.

Reinharz, S. (1992) *Feminist Methods in Social Research*, Oxford, Oxford University Press.

Roberts, H. (ed.) (1981) *Doing Feminist Research*, London, Routledge.

Rowe, P. (ed.) (1997) *Review of Institutional Lessons to be Learned 1994 to 1996*, Lancaster, Lancaster University.

Shove, E. (1996) *Researchers, Users and Window Frames*, Swindon, Economic and Social Research Council.

Simons, H. (1996) The paradox of case study, *Cambridge Journal of Education*, Vol. 26, no. 2, pp. 225–40.

Skeggs, B. (1994) Situating the production of feminist ethnography, in M. Maynard and J. Purvis, (eds.) *Researching Women's Lives*, London, Taylor & Francis.

Skeggs, B. (1997) *Becoming Respectable: An Ethnography of White Working Class Women*, Cambridge, Polity Press.

Smail, B., Whyte, J. and Kelly, A. (1982) Girls into science and technology: the first two years, *School Science Review*, Vol. 64, pp. 620–30.

Stacey, J. (1988) Can there be a feminist ethnography? *Women's Studies International Forum*, Vol. 11, no. 1, pp. 21–7.

Stanley, L. (1993) On auto/biography in sociology, *Sociology*, Vol. 27, no. 1, pp. 41–52.

Stanley, L. (1994) The knowing because experiencing subject: narratives, lives and autobiography, in K. Lennon and M. Whitford, (eds.) *Knowing the Difference*, London, Routledge.

Stanley, L. and Morgan, D. (1993) Special issue: auto/biography in sociology, *Sociology*, Vol. 27, no. 1, pp. 1–178.

Stanley, L. and Wise, S. (1993) *Breaking out Again*, London, Routledge.

Stone, L. (ed.) (1994) *The Education Feminism Reader*, London and New York, Routledge.

Tong, R. (1992) *Feminist Thought: A Comprehensive Introduction*, London, Routledge.

Turner, E., Riddell, S. and Brown, S. (1995) *Gender Equality in Scottish Schools: The Impact of Recent Educational Reforms*, Manchester, Equal Opportunities Commission.

Watson, S. (1992) Femocratic feminisms, in M. Savage and A. Witz, (eds.) *Gender and Bureaucracy*, Oxford, Blackwell.

Weiner, G., (ed.) (1985) *Just a Bunch of Girls*, Milton Keynes, Open University Press.

Weiner, G. (1994) *Feminisms in Education*, Milton Keynes, Open University Press.

Whyte, J. (1986) *Girls into Science and Technology*, London, Routledge.

Whyte, J., Deem, R., Kant, L. and Cruickshank, M. (1985) *Girl Friendly Schooling*, London, Methuen.

Wragg, T. (1997a) Oh Boy! *Times Educational Supplement*, pp. 4–5, 16 May.

Wragg, T. (1997b) Support for boys need not harm girls, *The Times Educational Supplement*, 30 May.

Yeatman, A. (1990) *Bureaucrats, Technocrats, Femocrats*, Sydney, Allen & Unwin.

Yeatman, A. (1995) The gendered management of equity-oriented change in higher education, in J. Smyth (ed.) *Academic Work*, Buckingham, Open University Press.

15

THE USEFULNESS OF EDUCATIONAL RESEARCH: AN AGENDA FOR CONSIDERATION AND ACTION

Donald McIntyre

INTRODUCTION

The history of educational research in the UK should teach us that we can and should use the debate in which the contributors to this book have engaged in order to enhance the quality and usefulness of educational research. For example, a quarter of a century ago, BERA was formed in a context of vigorous and often angry debate about what could count as valid educational research. That vigorous debate was very productive: as Jean Rudduck noted in her introduction, much fuller, richer and more diverse patterns of educational research thinking and practice have since developed, growing out of these early debates. We must ensure that the present debate is similarly productive.

My primary aim in this concluding chapter must therefore be to highlight some of the useful questions that have been raised and to suggest how these questions may offer us an agenda for moving constructively forward.

Aggressive debate is not however necessarily or uniformly beneficial. Its value stems from the way it can force one to take account of perspectives very different from one's own, and so to rethink one's position. That is a very academic type of value. Its dangers are that the forcefulness of the rhetoric may lead opinions to be shaped and decisions to be made on the basis of pleasing images or gross caricatures rather than on the merits of informed and analytic argument. And while we as educational researchers no doubt maintain our morale by cultivating pleasing images of our activities and our usefulness, the more important issue may be about the merit of the overall picture of educational research that has been projected to others, and especially to those who have the power to allocate and distribute resources for educational research. We should first, then, look at that overall picture.

THE OVERALL PICTURE OF EDUCATIONAL RESEARCH

Many educational researchers have been shocked at what they have seen as sweeping, simplistic and unjustified public attacks on educational research as a whole, attacks which seem quite deliberately designed to reduce the already very limited resources available for educational research by trained professional researchers. In particular, David Hargreaves in his Teacher Training Agency (TTA) annual lecture (1996) made such global judgements as 'educational research is not in a healthy state; it is not having adequate influence on the improvement of practice; it is not good value for money'. Although he made it clear that these were his subjective judgements, not claims which could be substantiated on the basis of evidence, many educational researchers would argue that it was irresponsible for such an authoritative figure to express such negative subjective views of educational research so publicly in such a setting at a time when major public bodies were reviewing the use of their research budgets. Especially irresponsible, some would suggest, was the specific suggestion *(ibid.)* that 'a substantial proportion of the research budget can be prised out of the academic community, who currently distribute it as they think fit, and over several years transferred in phases to agencies committed to evidence-based research and to full partnership with teachers in the interests of improving practice'.

There would, of course, be nothing at all irresponsible about this suggestion if a well argued case were made for the dire state that British educational research was claimed to be in, and if in addition an equally strong case were made both for 'evidence-based research' and for the clear superiority of 'agencies' other than 'the academic community' for conducting such research. In this volume, David Hargreaves and others have provided more detailed and analytic critiques of what they see as the weaknesses of educational research in the UK. Other educational researchers have offered a stout defence of the quality of educational research as a whole in this country. Roger Murphy for example has argued that David Hargreaves' claims about the lack of impact of educational research are unjustified and ill-informed, and his comparisons with research in other professional areas ill-judged; and Peter Hannon has suggested that a greater impact of research on teachers would depend, perhaps primarily, on teachers being given more opportunity to take advantage of what research can offer. Readers must judge for themselves the relative merits of the opposing claims about the overall health of educational research. My own view is that, while many important specific problems require urgent attention, global judgements in either direction are unhelpful, and any sweeping reforms should be based on more detailed analysis of the specific problems than we have yet had. Similarly, I do not see that anything is to be gained from attempts to make overall comparisons or contrasts with other professions, although there may be much to be learned from specific ideas or arrangements they have used (e.g. evidence-based medicine).

IDENTIFYING PRIORITIES FOR EDUCATIONAL RESEARCH

A pervading concern in this book has been the question of identifying priorities for educational research. For some purposes this is a very necessary exercise. Government departments need to decide on their research priorities as part of the process of policy planning: what are their policy priorities and in which of these policy areas are they in most need of information, understanding and useful ideas? Many other funding bodies have good reasons for identifying priorities, both to reflect the values underlying their establishment and to avoid the danger of spreading their efforts so thinly that they would not make a significant impact anywhere. Similarly, university departments and individual researchers need to decide what they can best do in the light of their expertise, interests and opportunities. On the other hand, it is difficult to understand why it might be necessary or how it might be possible to establish overarching priorities which should shape the total research agenda of a large country like the UK. I find it difficult to identify *any* aspect of education which could not benefit greatly from sustained high-quality research attention; and this is I believe a widely shared view.

When the ESRC working party chaired by John Gray were asked to identify priorities for educational research, they found it predictably difficult even to establish quite a long list of priorities. Although many of us thought that they identified an excellent set of possible areas for special ESRC initiatives, their own aspirations were more ambitious, since they took the view that there was a need for national priorities to 'inject a measure of coherence' into educational research in the country as a whole. David Hargreaves has developed this theme, arguing that there is a need for 'a national strategy for educational research', based on conclusions about 'the most desirable research (the priorities especially of users) and the most practicable research (based especially on researchers' knowledge, skills and experience)'.

Contributors to this book seem to differ quite widely in their views on the identification of priorities. While there is considerable support for David Hargreaves' views, those expressing that support do not tend to explain their reasons. In contrast, others argue against policies framed in terms of such national priorities or against the feasibility of establishing such priorities, or else demonstrate, in arguing for their own priorities, how difficult it would be to establish any measure of consensus.

David Bridges 'would like to see a more positive commitment to the *func-*

tional desirability of the principle of decentralised, multisite, unco-ordinated research – to the principle of anarchy in the research community and to a structure for research which, like the Internet, inherently eludes attempts at its control' and 'to reaffirm the crucial role of the education research community in sustaining an informed, independent voice (or, more accurately, a variety of voices)'. Sally Brown and Wynne Harlen quote the Scottish Council for Research in Education (SCRE) report of a systematic attempt to identify the research priorities of educational groups in Scotland, an exercise which generated 110 different suggestions:

> A basic dilemma remained: there can be no 'short-list' of research priorities which reflects the diverse views of all the educational community. If the procedures were to be sharpened up to reduce the flood of suggestions, the outcome would inevitably be biased towards the preferences of some groups and against those of others. There is, and can be, no consensus.

Michael Bassey reminds us of the highly value-laden nature of any educational research agenda, and demonstrates the political difficulty of achieving consensus, by asserting his own firm commitment to priorities stemming from an environmentalist stance. Rosemary Deem does the same by pointing to a feminist agenda. Stewart Ranson argues persuasively that our existing thinking about priorities tends to be too narrow, thus making the choice of priorities even more difficult. David Hamilton, perceiving the ESRC working group's agenda as reflecting 'the shadowy yet persistent empiricist and positivist inheritance of British educational research', emphasises the dependence of priorities on different epistemological stances.

A national strategy based on an agreed set of all-purpose educational research priorities would clearly be difficult to achieve; but if there were good reasons for having such a strategy, we ought not to be put off by the difficulties. Are such all-purpose priorities important, or is it more useful – as well as much easier – to develop priorities for more specific purposes and in specific contexts, in different ways and by different groups? The benefits as well as the inevitability of pluralism lead me to suspect that this is so, and that we should conclude that the case for a national strategy based on a single set of priorities is as yet unproven; but there is clearly a need for further debate on this issue.

THE NEGLECT OF RESEARCH ON 'WHAT WORKS'

An alternative to the strategy of attempting to establish priorities is to try to establish a framework which helps one to identify what is being neglected. Thus the ESRC's *Thematic Priorities Framework* is useful primarily not at all because it establishes priorities for social science research but rather because it excludes very little that social science researchers and users are interested in, and so provides a framework for monitoring what issues are or are not receiving research attention. Perhaps we need an equivalent framework for looking nationally at what is and is not being neglected in educational research.

Stewart Ranson is clearly using an implicit framework of this kind when he concludes, not that there is too much research on schooling, but that research on education in other contexts is neglected. He also identifies *learning* and the facilitation of learning as matters which should be at the centre of an educational research agenda, but as not being given the attention they deserve. What I believe to be David Hargreaves' most fundamental complaint about the present state of educational research in this country is also of this kind: it is that 'relatively little educational research leads to [directly] applied outcomes in either the policy or practice in education'. What he is especially concerned about, and what he sees to be seriously lacking in comparison to such other professions as medicine and engineering, is the kind of research that could contribute to 'evidence-based teaching', to teachers' decision-making about how they can best – for different pupils, content and contexts – facilitate learning. It seems to me abundantly clear that he is right at least in his description of the situation: very little of our research is of that kind.

Can we as educational researchers defend ourselves against this complaint? We should certainly ask whether the kind of research that is sought carries a particular view of teaching, perhaps a fairly simple one of teachers implementing wholesale 'approved' teaching methods; but I think that we have no reason to believe that there is such an implication, and indeed we have received repeated assurances that none is intended (Hargreaves, 1996; 1997). Thus while there is certainly room for much more debate about how any prescriptive implications of research can most appropriately be integrated into teachers' professional repertoires, I do not believe that anyone involved in this debate disagrees with Peter Hannon when he suggests that teachers do not, and should not be asked to, 'use research as a cookbook but as a resource in constructing their views of what is worth aiming for and likely ways to get there'.

The contributors to this book have not discussed this particular suggested weakness very fully, no doubt because it was not here but in his TTA lecture (1996) that David Hargreaves emphasised it most strongly. It has, however, been addressed very fully in an excellent paper by Martyn Hammersley (1997), who offers what I believe to be the correct explanation for the neglect of this kind of research. Those of us who in the 1970s were doing such research – seeking systematic patterns of association between what teachers did and pupils' successful learning – encountered at least six major kinds of problem:

1) We became aware, through helpful critiques from qualitative researchers, of questionable assumptions we were making in our descriptions of classroom activity.

2) We became aware, with the help of critical reviews by leading exponents of this kind of research (e.g. Rosenshine and Furst, 1973; Dunkin and Biddle, 1974), of the atheoretical and ungrounded nature of our selection of variables for study.
3) We found it difficult to design research which took account, as we increasingly recognised we needed to, of the thinking of teachers which informed their actions and of the thinking of pupils which underlay their successful learning.
4) We encountered in practice difficulties of validly translating the complex realities of school life into measurable variables (e.g. McIntyre and Brown, 1978).
5) Since problems concerning ethics, power and external validity led us not to conduct controlled experiments, we were dependent on correlational studies the results of which were necessarily ambiguous in relation to questions of 'What caused (or facilitated) what?'
6) With Cronbach (1975), we were aware that whatever truths we might uncover would be culturally and historically bounded; and our confidence in the cumulative usefulness of our work was shaken.

These then are some of the good reasons, I still believe, that led fastidious educational researchers to abandon research on 'What works in classroom teaching?' in the 1980s, at least temporarily. Basically, doing such research well seemed too difficult; and understanding classroom teaching and learning better seemed in any case to be a desirable next step before returning to that question.

I do not however think that such an explanation is an adequate defence against the complaint that educational research in the UK currently neglects questions of effective teaching and learning, in classrooms and in other contexts. Nor do I agree with Martyn Hammersley's conclusion that for politicians and practitioners to seek guidance from research and researchers on such matters is to ask too much of them. He may be right, but I think that that would at this stage be a premature conclusion. The need now is for imaginative fresh thinking about research strategies which can throw useful light on effective teaching and learning. Perhaps we were too fastidious in the past. In any case, we are much better placed now to think of these matters, drawing as we can on the understandings generated by qualitative research over the last twenty years. I believe that useful quantitative, qualitative and action research strategies can be developed for this purpose. It will not be easy, and it will depend on considerable research expertise; but unless we make real efforts to generate and implement such strategies, complaints of this kind will continue and will be justified.

HOW SHOULD THE IMPACT OF EDUCATIONAL RESEARCH BE EVALUATED?

Perhaps the most heated element of this debate has been the controversy over the impact of educational research on policy and practice. I suspect that this is because educational researchers are in general exceptionally concerned about the impact of their work. For many years, it has been a source of concern and often of embarrassment that teachers do not seem to take much notice of research findings (cf. Cane and Schroeder, 1970). Especially in recent decades, furthermore, policy-makers' lack of attention to research has been a frequent source of irritation. So David Hargreaves has attacked us in a particularly vulnerable area when he suggests not only that the impact of educational research in this country is slight but also that the responsibility for this is unambiguously that of researchers themselves.

The debate seems to be about three main issues. First, what kinds of impact should we expect from educational research? Secondly, where does the responsibility for ensuring that research has an impact lie? And thirdly, how substantial has the impact of educational research actually been?

In relation to the first of these questions, it is surely more obvious than the debate has sometimes suggested that different kinds of educational research may be expected to have, and are indeed designed to have, different kinds of impact. At least five different kinds can be distinguished:

1) Research and development work, in which the research is explicitly designed, and has often been commissioned, to inform the development of new policy and practice in a specific area; the research flows into, and its impact should be directly evident in, the development.

2) Evaluation and critique, in which the focus is on particular policies, institutions, programmes or practices, and where the intended impact is to inform and enlighten the subsequent thinking, debates, planning and practice of the various stakeholders in these.

3) Action research, aimed directly at achieving educational improvement in a particular context and also at generating understanding to inform ongoing action to achieve such improvement in that and similar contexts.

4) Research aimed at generating and/or testing new knowledge and understanding of aspects of education; the impact is likely to be diffuse, unpredictable and long term, but may be profound.

5) Research aimed at identifying practices which are distinctively effective for the realisation of specified educational values or the achievement of specified types of educational goal; the intended impact is that these identified practices should be more widely facilitated and adopted.

The debate has been partly about whether there has been enough research of the fifth kind; and, as explained in the previous section, I am in considerable sympathy with David Hargreaves on that point. There are however other elements. One of these is David's apparent reluctance to accept the nature, or perhaps the value, of research of the fourth kind, despite the many examples, mentioned for example by Caroline Gipps and by Roger Murphy, of valuable work of this kind, and despite the fact that his own work has included some seminally important examples of such research (e.g. Hargreaves, 1967; Hargreaves *et al.*, 1975). There are also questions, as Michael Beveridge most explicitly recognises, concerning the far from straightforward use of research results even of the fifth kind. That leads to the issue of responsibility for ensuring that research has an impact.

It is, I believe, very important to resist the suggestion that researchers should accept responsibility for the impact their research has on policy or practice. To take a simple personal example, I have been doing research on initial teacher education for several decades, and I am struck by the very limited impact my research seems to have had on the practice of teacher educators in the UK. Now I have no doubt that I might have made more or better efforts to enhance its impact. Even so, it would be outrageously presumptuous of me to accept responsibility for the thinking and practice of my fellow British teacher educators, or therefore for the impact of my research on them; and the same surely applies to the work of all educational researchers.

That does not mean that researchers have no responsibilities for the usefulness of their research. On the contrary, researchers must accept responsibility for, among other things, the usefulness of their research questions, the validity of their conclusions, the care they take in considering the implications of these conclusions, and the clarity, appropriateness and thoroughness with which they communicate about these. As an educational research community, we have not in my view fulfilled these responsibilities as well as we might; but it is our frequent overconcern with the immediate impact of our research that concerns some of us, such as Stewart Ranson and myself. The history of educational research shows that the results of any one investigation, and even more the interpretations put on these results by any one researcher, are frequently shown on subsequent examination to be invalid, or are not replicated, or can later be seen to reflect the researcher's own ideology more than they reflect the reality studied. That is not surprising, nor a reason for complaint; but it is a reason for extreme caution in seeking an impact on policy or practice on the basis of a single research project.

It is therefore important, as several of the protagonists in this debate have emphasised, that it is the cumulative understandings from research that should be highlighted when we seek to have an impact. That is the case both for the fourth and for the fifth of the types of research outlined above. As Sally Brown and Wynne Harlen say, 'understanding is built up gradually through successive studies, each of which may not in itself appear conclusive but which together can combine to provide a firm basis for action'. They therefore, like several other contributors to this book, including John Gray's

ESRC working party, conclude that publication of systematic reviews of research could and should play a more prominent part in the communication of research findings. Such reviews need to be critical and scholarly, and they need to examine very carefully the implications of bodies of research for policy and for practice; it is when and only when that has been done that priority should be given to dissemination and seeking to have an impact. This task of critically reviewing and synthesising research so that it can authoritatively inform policy and practice is one which the research community itself should be encouraging its members to treat as of equal importance and prestige to doing and publishing research. BERA, for example, should encourage and facilitate the publication of such reviews; and an explicit emphasis on these by the Research Assessment Exercise (RAE) Education Panel would exemplify responsible use of the power of peer review.

Does educational research have an impact on policy and practice commensurate with the money spent on it? It is easier to judge this with regard to policy than with regard to practice. It is also clearer that the former depends primarily not on researchers but on the policy-makers themselves. Thus while researchers had little influence on policy in the 1980s, there has clearly been much more enthusiasm among policy-makers in the last few years to make use of research, in some areas at least. With regard to practitioners, Rosemary Deem among other contributors points out that it is only when research-based insights become part of educational commonsense that they really have an impact, and that by then nobody remembers that research was the source of these insights. Michael Beveridge asks 'Would it be possible to develop research impact indices?' Whether or not it is possible, it is certainly necessary if the debate on this point is to get beyond an exchange of highly subjective views.

WHO SHOULD DO THE EDUCATIONAL RESEARCH?

A great deal of the debate in this book has been concerned with the people who do and should do research, and with the institutional contexts in which research can best be done. There are questions here of the numbers of researchers needed, of the expertise needed to do good educational research and of the conditions likely to facilitate good research.

Michael Beveridge has been one of the few contributors to the book who has emphasised the issue of expertise. There is perhaps a danger that, in our awareness of all the different political, epistemological, practical and methodological concerns that shape research practices and products, we may neglect the basic truth that research will be useless unless those doing it have the necessary expertise. We should take very seriously, then, Michael's concern, based on his survey of researcher views, about the 'considerable differences among educational researchers as to what they believe represents quality work', and his emphasis on the need for a 'higher standard of technical understanding'. I have emphasised in a previous section what I believe to be the severe difficulties of doing good research on effective teaching; but educational research generally is difficult and distinctive professional work, which needs a lot of learning. It is also work which draws on a number of different disciplines, so the diversity of standards that Michael Beveridge notes is not surprising although it is certainly not satisfactory. Many of the problems of educational research stem from the lack of sufficient people with adequately developed expertise.

One has to be cautious here however when discussing the range and depth of expertise needed by educational researchers, because for very good reasons there is a widely held view within the educational research community that defining 'educational researchers' in an exclusive way would be unhelpful. In particular, to adopt highly demanding standards in relation to the distinctive professional expertise required of educational researchers might be seen as inimical to the 'teachers as researchers' movement. I have argued elsewhere (McIntyre, 1997) that, while there is no merit in exclusive definitions of educational research or researchers, high standards of expertise should be demanded from *professional* educational researchers – people specifically employed to do research. While many schoolteachers will certainly attain these levels of research expertise as well as having acquired the very different kind of expertise needed for teaching, I follow Lawrence Stenhouse in believing that the kind of research in which it is important for teachers to engage does not necessarily require the same flexible expertise, the same explicit reporting or the same public scrutiny as is needed for professional educational research.

This point needs to be stressed because some very simplistic ideas have been promoted in the last few years, mainly by the Teacher Training Agency (TTA), which has seemed to suggest that weaknesses in educational research might be overcome by encouraging teachers to do more research. As Peter Hannon comments, giving teachers the time, the support and the encouragement 'to play an active role in conceiving, implementing, evaluating and disseminating research' would be very widely welcomed, although it would be a much more expensive undertaking than the TTA has yet seemed to envisage. But for the TTA to give teachers tiny amounts of money and time to research serious professional problems showed a contempt as much for teachers and teaching as it did for researchers and research. Most educational researchers have been schoolteachers, and for many research projects, although not by any means all, this experience is helpful in doing the research; for some projects, it is helpful or even necessary to be a practising teacher, although there are usually also disadvantages; but in no case does past or present experience as a teacher compensate for lack of professional expertise as a researcher.

A recurrent theme in this book has been the need for educational research to be able to draw more fully on theoretical ideas and methodological advances in the different social science disciplines. The strengths in educational research applications to the ESRC, John Gray's working party noted, tend to be in their practical significance; but there was a need to develop methodology and theory, and especially to keep abreast of methodological and theoretical developments in the other social sciences. Stewart Ranson expresses similar concerns, as does David Hargreaves; and no dissent is expressed by any contributor. David Bridges judges, rather harshly perhaps, that 'in my observation the theory that comes out of empirical research in education rarely represents much of an advance of the theory that went into it', and accordingly stresses the importance of drawing on 'the richest and most radical seams of current and historical intellectual life'.

Working in collaboration with social scientists from other disciplines is a theme considered at some length and very thoughtfully by Michael Beveridge. He is firm in his view that educational research needs new interdisciplinary approaches, indicating for example the important contributions that could come from economics, cognitive science and neuroscience. He also, however, highlights some of the significant problems involved: the danger of inappropriate crude *application* of theories from the social and behavioural sciences; institutional problems of the effective transfer of information between disciplinary fields; and the danger that interdisciplinary work often lacks rigour, especially in applied social science. The need to adapt is not, he emphasises, all on the education side: 'Cognitive science is now addressing issues which are important to education . . . However, closing the gap between cognitive science and education will also require that some cognitive scientists change their approach to investigating learning and teaching.' For example, he suggests, cognitive scientists would need to consider learning over more extended periods and in more varied contexts than they are accustomed to doing in their laboratory studies. The striking contrast between the almost obsessive concern of educational researchers with the real world and with immediate implications for policy and practice, and the concern of most psychologists and cognitive scientists only for the development and testing of their laboratory-relevant theories, does seem a major barrier to effective collaboration.

Most educational research is of course done in university departments of education (UDEs). It is the value of much of this research done in UDEs that is most under attack, and especially the very large element of the total educational research budget which is distributed by the Higher Education Funding Councils to UDEs according to their RAE ratings. As noted earlier, David Hargreaves suggests that 'a substantial proportion' of this money should be redistributed to other agencies. Seamus Hegarty agrees.

Whether or not this would be a sensible course of action is not obvious. The RAE is itself a mechanism for concentrating research funds in those centres where the best research is being done; and it is that criterion which should surely be given the highest priority, in education as in other areas.

Three questions seem important in thinking about the place that UDEs should have in the work of educational research.

How much educational research expertise do we need?

The 'value for money' question is relatively easily answered if the country needs relatively little educational research, with that research concentrated in a few demonstrable centres of excellence, and most of the money spent on other things. With David Hargreaves as virtually the sole exception, however, there is general agreement in pointing out how little this country spends on educational research, in comparison to other comparably rich countries; and there are certainly many questions about educational policy and practice, in the short and long term, which could very usefully receive more attention than they are being given. I have no doubt at all that among our priority needs is, as Michael Beveridge suggests, 'the training of a larger cadre of research workers' in education, and of course making use of their expertise. If this conclusion were accepted, then it is in UDEs that there are already a large number of posts requiring such research expertise, although as a consequence of their history many of the incumbents of these posts are not currently trained or experienced educational researchers. The other primary task of these people is to work on the initial and continuing professional education of teachers in order to develop 'teaching as a research-based profession', a task for which they clearly need research expertise. The obvious and urgent need, one might conclude, is for the development of the research expertise of the incumbents of these posts.

Where can educational research which draws strongly on the wider social science field best be developed?

The answer to this question which has received most support in this book is that a number of high-quality multidisciplinary educational research centres could usefully be developed. This seems unexceptionable, but one then has to ask where such centres might be. Most UDEs do have at least sociologists and psychologists on their staff, but none the less do not have a good record of interdisciplinary research. Michael Beveridge comments on the lack of crossdisciplinary work, and on his 'strong impression of individualism, of researchers working in isolation from each other, dabbling in a rather amateurish way at issues which are too big to be tackled by lone researchers'. That is not of course the whole truth, and I believe it is much less true than even a few years ago, but there is certainly sufficient truth in it to hurt. None the less, given the serious difficulties highlighted by Michael Beveridge of establishing effective crossdisciplinary work, and given the generally inward-looking cultures of other social science disciplines, the possibilities of reforming UDEs so that they can be the sites of good interdisciplinary educational research seem to me stronger than any other large-scale means of achieving that end.

Where can scholarly educational research be most easily and closely linked to the main educational research user communities?

Because of their work in the initial and continuing education of teachers, and especially because of the partnership mode in which that work is now conducted, the staff of UDEs are in constant dialogue with schoolteachers and managers and with LEA officers and inspectors. Through their courses and their developmental and advisory work, they are also in close contact with a wide range of educational policy-makers and of other practitioners. Whatever their other weaknesses, UDEs in general cannot reasonably be criticised for being out of touch with the users and potential users of educational research. It is difficult to think of other actual or potential educational research institutions as well placed as UDEs in this respect.

A strong case can thus be made for continuing the research funding of UDEs through the RAE mechanism. The case for continued research funding for UDEs is not however either exclusive or unqualified. The Scottish Council for Research in Education (SCRE) and the National Foundation for Educational Research (NFER) are two non-university institutions with extremely impressive research records; and both of them would benefit from being less completely dependent on specific research contracts, especially in that they would thus be allowed to maintain more easily long-term sustained research agendas, and so to develop both increased research expertise and cumulative research findings in a number of areas. There may be a case too for a small number of other non-university bodies to be funded for educational research, especially if these are of a distinctively interdisciplinary nature.

The case for sustained funding of UDEs, approximately at present levels, must be dependent on their internal reform: present levels of funding cannot be justified while large numbers of UDE staff are so clearly lacking in research training, experience and therefore expertise, and while staff, especially those employed as specialists in social science disciplines, pursue individual furrows rather than contributing to interdisciplinary teams. John Gray's ESRC working party made valuable suggestions about building and sustaining departmental research programmes, creating conditions for establishing and creating research teams, and securing continuity in research careers. Some considerable progress has, I believe, been made in recent years, but UDEs need to accelerate such reforms, in order to become effective research organisations; and both pressure and support will be necessary for this to happen.

HOW COULD FUNDERS, USERS AND PRACTITIONERS OF EDUCATIONAL RESEARCH WORK TOGETHER MORE EFFECTIVELY?

One recurrent theme in this book is about the lack of coherence in the funding of educational research in the UK. John Gray and his colleagues noted in 1992 the absence of any joint planning by funding bodies and the consequent incoherence of the national educational research effort. Michael Beveridge judges that it remains true that 'the national research effort is incoherent and unplanned'. David Hargreaves concludes that 'there is weak co-ordination among funders and among researchers, and between funders and researchers'. Sally Brown and Wynne Harlen complain about the funding 'of concurrent, but unco-ordinated research on the same topic' even within the relatively closely knit Scottish system, and conclude pessimistically that 'funding bodies guard their autonomy and independence much more closely than researchers'. However, none of the contributors to the book discusses this problem of incoherence among funders at any length. It is relationships between researchers and 'users' of research that attracts much more attention.

David Hargreaves sees lack of user involvement as a primary weakness in educational research. Citing in this book engineering as a field which education should emulate, he emphasises the close interaction between industrial practice and academic research in engineering. Educational researchers may reasonably claim that some aspects of what he describes are equally true of education: 'The university-based engineers usually have substantial industrial experience and are convinced that it is essential to maintain their connection with the industrial base. Some successful universities have established centres in which industrialists and academic researchers work together. Many research ideas originate in the industrial context.' Other aspects of what he describes, however, are clearly very different: 'The engineering community is research-led ... Engineers take a positive attitude towards putting research into practice and industrial enthusiasm is a major force in their research culture.'

This account, and similar comparisons with medicine, are not of course accepted by everyone as accurate. Roger Murphy, for example, is not impressed with the comparison: 'I do not agree that things are so much better in other professional areas. Certainly medical and enginering research have the advantage of vast resources, and one would hope that this vastly superior level of investment would produce some good outcomes.' Any such comparative judgements are difficult and inevitably very subjective. However the purpose of the comparison is to suggest that the quality and usefulness of educational research could be significantly improved if users were more consistently involved 'at all stages of the research process', in decision-making at both local and national levels. The lack of such user involvement is claimed to be a 'main weakness' of educational research; and 'creating a new partnership between researchers and user communities should be at the heart of any reform, in part because success here will help to solve so many other problems'.

In some ways this seems a surprising and even implausible complaint, because it is clear that most members of the UK educational research community – especially as reflected in BERA membership and concerns – identify very closely indeed with the most obvious population of potential 'users', schoolteachers. Greater involvement of teachers is certainly an uncontentious aspiration, when expressed in general terms: several contributors to this book have enthusiastically agreed with it, and none have dissented. Furthermore, educational researchers are very widely agreed in their eagerness for teachers to value and make use of their research and, as already noted, in their readiness to disseminate their research conclusions. And, as also noted, researchers show no lack of concern to relate their research closely to the decisions being made by those other users, policy-makers.

There are also a number of questions raised by contributors about the terms in which these issues should be discussed. Most fundamentally, perhaps, David Hamilton suggests that educational researchers and in particular UDEs need to see research as being concerned with the refinement of educational practice *rather than* with the extension of knowledge; in which case educational research would be meaningless except in terms of 'user involvement'. Seamus Hegarty and Rosemary Deem both point out that the concept of 'users', and the groups to whom it should be applied, are far from straightforward. Seamus Hegarty also raises questions about the realism of the suggestion that all the diverse groups of users should be significantly involved in *all* stages of the research process. Thus there are clearly contentious issues here. But although the involvement of users in the practice of educational research has been a recurring issue in this book, no clear or sustained critique of this aspect of the day-to-day work of research, and no clear alternatives to current practice, have been offered. It is at the national level that both clear critique and proposals have been put forward.

The core of the critique is the suggestion that research users have too little *power* over the educational research agenda, and that too much power is contentrated in the hands of researchers themselves: there are no good reasons why researchers' perceptions of what is needed, or their ideological commitments (such as those expressed by Michael Bassey and by Rosemary Deem) should be given greater importance than those of people whose work ought to be informed by the research. The lack of power of potential users of research is difficult to deny, so long at least as a clear distinction is made between users and funders. If that distinction *is* made, it is clear that policy-making bodies, as both funders and users of research, exert a very powerful influence on research. Other funders who are not users, notably ESRC and the Higher Education Funding Council for England (HEFCE), and the peer reviewers to whom they delegate part of their decision-making, also exercise a powerful influence. Other potential users who are not funders, notably teachers, learners and parents, are the people who lack power.

For David Hargreaves, the central problem is this lack of user power over educational research, and what he sees as the complementary 'excessive reliance' on a peer review system. The inadequate usefulness of educational research is unlikely, he believes, to be set right by researchers themselves or therefore by the peer review system; what is needed is that potential users of research should be in a position to apply their very different perspectives in deciding what kinds of research are worth funding. Rosemary Deem, on the other hand, very plausibly suggests that non-academic users are likely to want relatively 'narrowly defined and unadventurous research', applying criteria of usefulness relevant to their own immediate needs rather than to the longer-term improvement of education. It seems clear too that users are unlikely to be have the necessary expertise to be able to judge the methodological quality of research plans or reports. There is clearly a need for a system with checks and balances.

In considering what that system might be, we need to be alert to the extreme dangers of treating educational research as uniquely different from other fields of academic scholarship in the mechanisms by which it is controlled. We need to learn from such fields as medicine and engineering that the necessary trust, respect and resources for a profession's work stem primarily from public recognition that that work is underpinned by academic scholarship validated by the university system. Thus the aspiration that teaching should be recognised as a research-based profession is something that neither the TTA nor the profession itself can on their own deliver, not even with the help of independent educational research centres: it is the university system that gives credibility to claims of research-based knowledge. The question is therefore one of how the crucial university-based peer review systems employed by HEFCE and ESRC can be complemented by other mechanisms to overcome the limitations of these systems.

The additional mechanism that has been suggested, both to enhance user power at the national level and also to achieve greater coherence in the funding of research, is a National Educational Research Forum. The idea was proposed by John Gray and his ESRC working party colleagues, is developed quite fully in David Hargreaves' contribution to this book and receives the support of several other contributors. There has also been some scepticism about what could be achieved by such a forum. Most authoritatively, Sally Brown and Wynne Harlen use their experience of a similar national forum in Scotland to examine the functions that it could realistically be expected to fulfil. They point out that an explicit and useful purpose towards which the Scottish forum is effectively directed is 'to affirm the importance of research in education', surely a purpose that an English or UK national forum ought to share. There are too important similarities and differences between the other things that they have found a national forum can do and the purposes proposed by David Hargreaves.

The important common ground is that such a forum can and should 'provide [an] arena in which all kinds of stakeholder could talk to one another in [a] necessarily broad and open conversation about matters of educational interest'. The ways in which this has been achieved in Scotland could provide one useful starting point in the consideration of how it can be effectively achieved in England and Wales also. With regard to a further common purpose, however, that of creating a context for the discussion of research priorities, 'experience has shown that this function of the Scottish forum is far more difficult to carry out than is the provision for interaction between researchers and users about existing research'; as noted earlier, the priorities of different groups have been highly diverse and have seemed non-negotiable. Furthermore, political expediency leads to 'rapid shifts' in the research priorities of policy-making bodies. On the basis of their experience, then, these successive organisers of the Scottish forum are sceptical of the Hargreaves proposal that 'the forum would, on a regular basis (say every four to five years), conduct or commission a review of current achievements, omissions and problems in educational research, leading to a research foresight exercise, involving researcher, user and lay communities, and the establishment thereafter of a *national research strategy*'.

It may be necessary, therefore, and also desirable, to aim for a more open and pluralist approach than is implied by a 'national research strategy'. I have already suggested that something equivalent to the kind of balanced, inclusive framework offered by the ESRC for the social sciences generally, in its misleadingly titled *Research Priorities Framework*, could be very useful for education specifically. The generation of such a framework would be a highly appropriate task for a national forum, since it would not require the achievement of consensus about relative priorities. If the suggested national research strategy were to be replaced by such a *Framework of Useful Educational Research*, then in my view all of David Hargreaves' other important suggestions for the tasks of a National Educational Research Forum and its staff appear realistic and valuable. In particular, the gathering and dissemination of regular information from and to funding bodies and individual researchers, about neglected areas and about potential unproductive overlaps, could do much to reduce the current incoherence in research funding and practice. It would also be of the greatest importance that the HEFCE Education Panel for the Research Assessment Exercise should, as a major part of their evaluation of UDE strategies and performance, examine the effectiveness with which UDEs were taking account of the framework and related information.

CONCLUSION

The debate about how educational research is useful, how useful it is and about how it can be made more useful, is far from over. It will be clear to readers that there is no suggestion that any of the major questions have been resolved: countless differences remain about what is the case, about what changes are desirable and about the likely consequences of suggested innovations. As Jean Rudduck explained in her introductory chapter, 'this book is an attempt to record, disseminate and extend the debate'. And as Jean also made very clear, although the debate as conducted in this book is clearly focused on British policies, practices and institutions, and although there are certainly parochial British elements to it, the concerns which it reflects are international in nature.

None the less, the issues under debate are practical and pressing. Decisions are needed about practical measures to optimise the quality and usefulness of educational research. It is clear too that decisions will shortly be made. After years of apparent governmental indifference to educational research, there has been a notable change in the last few years. This change in attitude has accelerated greatly since the general election of May 1997: the new government, its Department for Education and Employment (DfEE), and especially its Standards and Effectiveness Unit, clearly want useful educational research to help in the attainment of new educational standards, and in the resolution of old and new educational problems. Accordingly, a review is being commissioned by the DfEE into the state of educational research and into any reforms that are necessary. BERA will wish to contribute fully to that review. As part of that contribution, we hope that this book will be viewed as evidence of the concerns, understandings and aspirations of a cross-section of experiencd British educational researchers.

REFERENCES

Cane, B. and Schroeder, C. (1970) *The Teacher and Research*, Slough, National Foundation for Educational Research.

Cronbach, L. (1975) Beyond the two disciplines of scientific psychology, *American Psychologist*, Vol. 30, pp. 116–27.

Dunkin, M. J. and Biddle, B. J. (1974) *The Study of Teaching*, New York, Holt, Rinehart & Winston.

Hammersley, M. (1997) Educational research and teaching: a response to David Hargreaves' TTA lecture, *British Educational Research Journal*, Vol. 23, pp. 141–61.

Hargreaves, D. H. (1967) *Social Relations in a Secondary School*, London, Routledge & Kegan Paul.

Hargreaves, D. H. (1996) Teaching as a research-based profession: possibilities and prospects. Teacher Training Agency annual lecture 1996.

Hargreaves, D. H. (1997) In defence of research for evidence-based teaching: a rejoinder to Martyn Hammersley, *British Educational Research Journal*, Vol. 23, pp. 405–20.

Hargreaves, D. H., Hester, S. and Mellor, F. (1975) *Deviance in Classrooms*, London, Routledge & Kegan Paul.

McIntyre, D. (1997) The profession of educational research, *British Educational Research Journal*, Vol. 23, pp. 127–40.

McIntyre, D. and Brown, S. (1978) The conceptualisation of attainment, *British Educational Research Journal*, Vol. 4, pp. 41–50.

Rosenshine, B. and Furst, N. (1973) The use of direct observation to study teaching' in R. M. W. Travers (ed.) *Second Handbook of Research on Teaching*, Chicago, IL, Rand McNally.

INDEX